Private Medicine and Public Health

Private Medicine and Public Health

Profit, Politics, and Prejudice in the
American Health Care Enterprise

Lawrence D. Weiss

 WestviewPress

A Division of HarperCollins*Publishers*

Copyright © 1997 by Westview Press, A Division of HarperCollins Publishers, Inc.

Published in 1997 in the United States of America by Westview Press, 5500 Central
Avenue, Boulder, Colorado 80301-2877, and in the United Kingdom by Westview
Press, 12 Hid's Copse Road, Cumnor Hill, Oxford OX2 9JJ

Library of Congress Cataloging-in-Publication Data
Weiss, Lawrence David.
    Private medicine and public health: profit, politics, and
prejudice in the American health care enterprise/ Lawrence D.
Weiss.
        p. cm.
    Includes bibliographical references and index.
    ISBN 0-8133-3350-4 (hc.)—ISBN 0-8133-3351-2 (pbk.)
    1. Medical policy—United States.   2. Medical economics—United
States.   I. Title.
RA395.A3W445   1997
362.1'0973—dc21   96-40916
                                                                       CIP

The paper used in this publication meets the requirements of the American National
Standard for Permanence of Paper for Printed Library Materials Z39.48-1984.

10   9   8   7   6   5   4   3   2   1

To those who have suffered or died as
victims of a health care system dedicated to
maximum profit rather than universal access

Contents

Acronyms

AALL	American Association for Labour Legislation
AAMC	Association of American Medical Colleges
AARP	American Association of Retired Persons
ABMS	American Boards of Medical Specialities
ACGME	Accreditation Council for Graduate Medical Education
AFDC	Aid to Families with Dependent Children
AFL-CIO	American Federation of Labor—Congress of Industrial Organizations
AHA	American Hospital Association
AIDS	Acquired immunodeficiency syndrome
AMA	American Medical Association
AMPAC	American Medical Association Political Action Committee
ANA	American Nursing Association
APA	American Pharmaceutical Association
APHA	American Public Health Association
CAT	Computerized axial tomography
CERCLA	Comprehensive Environmental Response, Compensation, and Liability Act
CHAMPUS	Civilian Health and Medical Program of the Uniformed Services
CLIA '88	Clinical Laboratory Improvement Amendments of 1988
CME	Continuing medical education
COLA	Commission on Office Laboratory Accreditation
CON	Certificate of need
CPI	Consumer Price Index
DEA	Drug Enforcement Agency
DoD	Department of Defense
DRG	Diagnostic related group
EPA	Environmental Protection Agency
ER	Emergency room
ESRD	End stage renal disease

FDA	Food and Drug Administration
FIFRA	Federal Insecticide, Fungicide, and Rodenticide Act
FY	Fiscal year
GAO	General Accounting Office
GDP	Gross domestic product
GE	General Electric
GHCPS	Group Health Cooperative of Puget Sound
HCA	Hospital Corporation of America
HCFA	Health Care Financing Administration
HHS	Department of Health and Human Services
HIMA	Health Industry Manufacturers Association
HIV	Human immunodeficiency virus
HMO	Health maintenance organization
IHS	Indian Health Service
IPA	Independent Practice Association
IRS	Internal Revenue Service
JCAHO	Joint Commission on Accreditation of Health Care Organizations
KNA	Kentucky Nursing Association
LPN	Licensed practical nurse
MCHR	Medical Committee for Human Rights
MCO	Managed care organization
MHSS	Military Health Services System
MNN	Medical News Network
MRI	Magnetic resonance imaging
MSHA	Mine Safety and Health Administration
NAACP	National Association for the Advancement of Colored People
NACGN	National Association of Colored Graduate Nurses
NARD	National Association of Retail Druggists
NCI	National Cancer Institute
NIH	National Institutes of Health
NIOSH	National Institute of Occupational Safety and Health
NLRB	National Labor Relations Board
NMA	National Medical Association
NMC	National Medical Care
NP	Nurse practitioner
NPL	National Priorities List
NWDA	National Wholesale Druggist Association
OEO	Office of Economic Opportunity
OMB	Office of Management and Budget

OSHA	Occupational Safety and Health Administration
OTA	Office of Technology Assessment
OTC	Over-the-counter
PA	Physician assistant
PAA	Proprietary Association of America
PAC	Political action committee
PCCM	Primary care case management
PET	Positron emission tomography
PHS	Public Health Service
PMA	Pharmaceutical Manufacturers Association
PMPRB	Patented Medicine Prices Review Board (Canadian)
PNHP	Physicians for a National Health Program
POL	Physician office laboratory
POS	Point of service
PPO	Preferred provider organization
RCT	Registered care technologist
RDA	Recommended daily allowance
RN	Registered nurse
RWDSU	Retail, Wholesale, and Department Store Union
SEIU	Service Employees International Union
SSI	Supplemental Security Income
UFCW	United Food and Commercial Workers
VA	Veterans Affairs
WHP	Wellhead protection

Preface

During the twentieth century the issue of health care burst out of the private confines of the physician's office to become a monumental, contentious social issue. Giant multinational corporations scooped up proprietary hospitals and nursing homes and assembled them into vast chains crisscrossing America. The private health insurance industry exploded into a business worth hundreds of billions of dollars and wielding massive political power while controlling the life chances of scores of millions of citizens. The incomes of entrepreneurial fee-for-service physicians grew several times faster than the rate of inflation year after year, while the cost of health care grew to consume 14 percent of the gross domestic product, and it continues to climb. The government gingerly applied various cost-containment strategies, while hospitals expanded capacity with abandon and filled multiple "profit centers" with expensive high-tech equipment. Health care administration emerged as the fastest growing segment of all health-related occupations.

Growth of the "medical-industrial complex," to use the term coined by Arnold Relman, the then-editor of the conservative *New England Journal of Medicine*, is uncontrolled (Relman 1980). Meanwhile, nearly 40 million Americans have no health insurance, and an additional 60 million have inadequate coverage. The numbers grow larger each year. Infant mortality in the United States grows increasingly excessive compared with other industrialized countries, and the gulf of health status disparities between white Americans and minorities does not diminish. Tens of thousands of Americans each year die from complications due to unnecessary but profitable surgeries, while millions suffer from medical neglect because they cannot pay for health care. The cost of malpractice insurance skyrockets, driving health care out of rural and underserved regions across America, while physicians inadequately discipline one another for medical negligence.

Every social institution involved with health care in the United States is in crisis: hospitals, private insurance, public insurance, community clinics, public health, private practice, HMOs, self-insured businesses, and others. The health care crisis is a large-scale problem, and the social devastation in its wake is a tragedy of national scope. Existing assumptions, power structures, political and economic interests, and social organizations have contributed to the crisis. Their roles must be critically examined and analyzed in the search for solutions. It cannot be assumed that the roles they have played in the past will be the same roles they play in the future. In some cases it cannot be assumed that they will have any role at all in the future.

The Perspective

Private Medicine and Public Health surveys the broad expanse of health and health care institutions in America from a critical, macro, political-economic, and social problems–oriented perspective. Moreover, the issue of racism emerges repeatedly as central to the analysis.

The Critical Stance

A critical perspective does not blithely accept the common or official explanation of why things are the way they are. A critical analysis may start with a thorough description of a social institution or process, but it goes beyond that. It tries to dig under assumptions and peer around ideologies that are used to justify vested interests but that may play fast and loose with facts. A critical analysis exposes the relationship between ideologies and objective interests, particularly financial interests. A critical analysis of the tobacco industry, for example, would note that the industry repeatedly testifies at hearings across the country that there is no definitive proof that smoking tobacco causes cancer. While a few well-paid scientists parrot this distortion of scientific method, the rest of the scientific world understands that the correlation between smoking and various cancers is strong enough to assume a causal relationship and to develop public policy based on that assumption. The ideological stance of the tobacco industry has little to do with an honest debate about the scientific determination of a causal relationship, but it has everything to do with avoiding lawsuits, blunting antismoking campaigns, and maximizing profits.

Macro Unit of Analysis

Private Medicine and Public Health has a macro focus. Macro units of analysis include social institutions, corporations, government programs, political coalitions, and social processes. Health care in the United States is increasingly organized in for-profit corporations, such as health maintenance organizations, hospitals, and nursing homes. Moreover, hospitals and nursing homes, for example, are increasingly organized into huge corporate regional and national chains. These corporate behemoths not only represent the current face of medicine in America, but they are determining its future as well.

The Political-Economic Context

Private Medicine and Public Health strives to make a political-economic analysis. Political-economy concerns the relationships between politics and economics, for example, between state or federal governments and the pharmaceutical industry or the American Medical Association. A political-economic analysis, however, is not simply a formal description of laws affecting industry; rather, it is a deeper analysis of the political influences exercised by industry to extract laws and favors from well-lobbied politicians plied with ample contributions.

Social Problems Orientation

Finally, *Private Medicine and Public Health* has a social problems orientation. Modern medicine and public health in America are awash in problems and crises. Access, racism, sexism, cost, and quality of care are problems for wage-earners, for the retired, and for the unemployed who need health care. Cost containment, government regulation, consumer advocacy groups, uncompensated care, and empty beds are problems for corporate health care providers and manufacturers of drugs and medical equipment. The problems in health care and public health have become so overwhelming that the impetus for significant change, perhaps dramatic change, is everywhere being studied, discussed, negotiated, or implemented. The principal issues in American health care today are its problems. It seems appropriate to focus on the nature of these problems in health care, on their origins, and on their proposed solutions.

Race

As a result of the historical and current social impacts of the concepts of "race" and "racism" in America, these concepts are central to any serious discussion of health care in America. Conditions of poverty known to have a major impact on health status vary by race. Health status, even when poverty is taken into account, varies by race. Access to health care providers varies by race. Coverage by health insurance varies by race. Health care outcomes vary by race. Environmental pollution varies by the racial composition of communities. Even the health care professions themselves are highly stratified by race. All of this, however, begs the question "What is race?"

Racial classification systems based on skin color, hair qualities, skull measurements, or even the more modern analysis of blood are simply arbitrary classifications that may tell us far more about the researcher's agenda than about those who are being researched. So, too, may comparisons based on race. For example, those who claim that some races are smarter than others as determined by IQ tests stand on highly unstable intellectual quicksand. There is overwhelming evidence that environmental factors such as class, language, and other social variables are far more influential in predicting IQ test outcomes than is race. Moreover, there is virtually no consensus over the concept of "intelligence" or how it can be adequately measured. Ultimately "race" is not a scientific concept but, rather, a social invention.

So it is with caveat upon caveat that I use the terms "race" and "racism" in this book. Occasionally I may use the phrase "people of color," a popular term that is not rooted in the flawed concept of "race" and that seems to have historical face validity. So much of the American experience with racism has been boiled down to the pragmatic distinction of skin color that this single factor appears to have more social consequence than other imputed features of "race." Finally, I would like to mention the distinction between "African-American" and "black." Many contemporary leaders of American descendants of African slaves currently use and prefer the term "African-American" to describe people with that common heritage. I respect the logic behind the use of the phrase and use it as appropriate. Throughout this book, however, the term "black" is often used, possibly appearing to be a synonym for "African-American." I often use the term "black" because that is the category used by much of the research referred to in this book and because a significant number of dark-skinned people of African heritage in the United States are not "Americans"; that is, they are resident foreign nationals. Often these residents are found working in the health professions as well as being treated as patients by the health care system. The more generic term "blacks" seems to capture both "African-Americans" and Africans who are resident in the United States but are not citizens.

Organization of the Text

Private Medicine and Public Health is organized around principal medical and public health social institutions such as governments, corporations, hospitals, and various health care financing and delivery programs. Within these various institutions, the roles of key groups of players such as physicians and other health care providers, patients, and management are discussed. Selected aspects of health care institutions are critically analyzed in detail from a social problems perspective. The strength of this approach is that the health care system as a whole is described and the relationships of the parts are discussed at length, with the focus on problem areas. The weakness of any comprehensive approach is that important detail has to be left out because of limitations of space and theoretical focus. *Private Medi-*

cine and Public Health is a broad-brush description and analysis of the social institutions of medicine and public health in the United States

Chapter 1 provides a historical overview of the development of key components of the health care system and makes an initial foray into problem areas such as cost, quality of care, and political influence. Chapter 2 focuses on the critical issue of access to health care, with special attention paid to minorities, the uninsured, and low-income families. Chapter 3 discusses the historical political-economic role of the American Medical Association and focuses on key problems created when physicians mix the practice of medicine with entrepreneurship. Chapter 4 discusses the historical development of nursing, particularly in relationship to the historical drive of physicians for professional dominance. Changes in the nursing work environment are discussed, including issues such as minority participation, sexism, nurse-entrepreneurs, and labor struggles. Chapter 5 explores one of the key institutions in America's health care system: hospitals. The historical development of the modern hospital is discussed, as well as current trends in corporate chain ownership and resulting social consequences. Chapter 6 explores the complicated but crucial issue of managed care. The chapter discusses why managed care has boomed recently, its relationship to the health insurance industry, and actual and potential negative social consequences that this industry has spawned across the United States. Chapter 7 surveys the alternative health care industry, looking at the historical struggle between alternative practitioners and "regular" physicians. Special attention is given to areas such as chiropractic, homeopathy, food supplements, fraud, and cancer quackery. Chapter 8 conducts an in-depth analysis of the powerful prescription drug industry, paying particular attention to political influence of the industry, marketing, and the use of ideology. Chapter 9 reviews a number of major medical services industries, including the dialysis industry, medical laboratories, and diagnostic imaging equipment. Selected social and political-economic problems relevant to each industry are analyzed and discussed. Chapter 10 provides an overview of the massive federal health care and public health establishment. Federal involvement in health care and public health delivery, financing, regulation, and research is explored. Some of the institutions reviewed include military medicine, Medicare, the Food and Drug Administration, and the National Institutes of Health. Chapter 11 looks at health care institutions primarily housed in state and local jurisdictions. At the state level Medicaid, is by far the largest single health care program. It is beset with an array of major problems that merit special review. Finally, Chapter 12 sums up the previous chapters and looks at health reform issues ranging from proposals to take the Canadian health care system as a potential model for the United States to the political actors and struggles involved in these difficult issues.

Acknowledgments

Many people have helped me conceptualize, research, and finally publish this book. Thanks to all of you who have made this possible. Profound apologies to those of you who have worked with me at some point during the last few years but whose names have inadvertently been omitted.

Editors Alan McClare, Dean Birkenkamp, and Jill Rothenberg have all played a major role in shepherding me through the process of writing this book and moving it toward publication. Innumerable discussions of concepts, facts, and resources with Dr. Frank Goldsmith and Dr. John Booker had a profound influence in shaping this work (but, of course, I take all responsibility for its final form). Many thanks to the extraordinarily knowledgeable and helpful staff at the University of Alaska Anchorage Consortium Library who helped me find everything. A tip of the hat to former Dean Wayne Miller for providing some important extra resources to allow me the time to work on key sections of the book. Thanks to my colleagues on the faculty research committee who awarded me a grant to pay for duplication costs and to buy the services of student researchers. I have an eternal debt of gratitude to my two ace researchers—Heidi Waldern and Michele Williams. Finally, a big hug and a kiss for my wife, Christy Smith, who graciously put up with years of me being preoccupied, occupied, or simply gone. Researching and writing a book can be tough on a relationship. Thanks to her understanding, we survived.

References

Relman, Arnold S. 1980. "The New Medical-Industrial Complex." *The New England Journal of Medicine* 303:963–70.

1

The Big Picture

The history of health care and public health in the United States is every bit as interesting and is certainly more revealing than would be a mere snapshot of current struggles and social dynamics. After all, the social institutions and processes that currently constitute the mammoth edifice we call health care have their origins in America's tumultuous history. In the course of the development of our democratic capitalist economy, the institutions of health care have been radically transformed by revolutionary social processes. Today's health care institutions are built on these historical processes. In fact, one could easily demonstrate that today's health care struggles emerge from social forces unleashed by the Civil War over 130 years ago. An understanding of the social dynamics of health care in the United States today is impossible without an awareness of how these dynamics burst forth from the past and of how they took their present form. This chapter provides a brief overview of the historical emergence of both medicine and public health in the United States. From that foundation the narrative proceeds through an initial discussion of three fundamental issues: health status, the cost of health care, and the politics of health care.

The Development of Health Care in an Emerging Capitalist System

Until approximately the last decade of the 1800s, women in the household ministered to most of the births and other health and medical needs of their families. In this system of domestic health care, they were typically not paid for their services. They performed these services strictly for their "use value," that is, principally because all concerned believed that the health care provided was beneficial. They received most of their information from older women who were living repositories of medical folklore. During most of the 1800s the oral tradition of folk medicine was largely supplemented by a variety of health care manuals. Natural herbs and substances with alleged medicinal powers were usually available in nearby forests and streams or grown in home gardens. Before the 1860s most of the curative elixirs and potions were prepared in the home. After the Civil War, however, the commercial patent medicine industry boomed, increasingly displacing homemade medicines with commercially sold concoctions but not displacing the providers of domestic health care: the women who purchased the patent medicines. Throughout the 1800s the patent medicine industry ranked first in terms of total advertising expenditures. By 1905 the patent medicine industry was immense by the business standards of the period, with annual revenues exceeding $100 million. Individual patent medicines had yearly advertising budgets of as much as $400,000 (Caplan 1989, 1139–41).

The Displacement of Domestic Health Care

The patent medicine industry was not developing in a vacuum. The 1800s was also a period of explosive growth of capitalism both in North America and worldwide. Capitalist relations of production challenged and displaced the former relations of production everywhere: Clothing and farming implements once made by the family for use by the family were replaced by manufactured commodities made commercially by wage laborers and sold by capitalists in order to amass cash and reinvest it. Crops and agricultural products once produced by the family for use by the family were sold as commodities for cash in the market to merchants and capitalists, who resold in larger markets to ever more distant strangers. In this historical context, and as families were ripped away from their rural environs and dropped into the middle of urban areas as landless wage laborers, forever separated from their rural sources of herbs and folk medicines, the medical potions once produced by the family for family consumption were displaced by store-bought patent medicines.

Domestic health care had been successfully tapped for massive profits by the patent medicine industry. However, other capitalists and investors, particularly in the latter half of the 1800s, found that the connection between domestic health care and the patent medicine industry cramped their aspirations. For example, the American Medical Association (AMA) waged war against domestic health care and the patent medicine industry well into the twentieth century. Every domestically treated illness and every bottle of patent medicine sold represented a lost visit to the physician and that much less physician revenue. In the nineteenth century physicians had neither great status nor significant income. The average physician practiced on a fee-for-service basis but was often paid in services or agricultural products (rather than cash), a form of payment that typified the physician delivery of health care to the poor or simply cash-poor during the period dominated by domestic health care (Fichtenbaum 1982–83, 33).

The American Pharmaceutical Association (APA) and the National Association of Retail Druggists (NARD) were allied with the AMA in their financial links to prescription medicines and their hatred of domestic health care and the associated patent medicine industry. Pharmacists, like physicians, had a relatively lowly status at the time. They made their largest profits from compounding and selling prescription medicines and, to a lesser extent, medicines for domestic health care. The patent medicine industry simply bypassed the pharmacist, edging him or her out of the business of compounding both prescription and over-the-counter medicines. By 1905 these three organizations had formed a coalition to fight the patent medicine industry. They were joined by a fourth organization—hospital administrators.

Financing Hospital Care

During most of the nineteenth century hospitals were generally places where the wretched and the destitute went to die. Hospitals were largely financed through private donations, with some assistance from local government. However, by the beginning of the twentieth century a decade-long economic downturn had pushed many hospitals to the edge of solvency. The need for services by the impoverished escalated dramatically while private and public support dwindled:

> In response to these deficits, a group of hospital administrators founded in 1899 the Association of Hospital Superintendents, later renamed the American Hospital Association (AHA). According to this group, the principal cause of the "deficit dilemma" was the extremely low demand for hospital care by people able to pay for it. The association devised a two-pronged solution. To decrease costs, the amount of free or charity care had to be drastically reduced. On the revenue side, the number of "pay patients" had to be significantly increased. The AHA sought to turn charity hospitals into sound businesses with costs to minimize and a product to sell.
>
> . . . As part of this realignment, the AHA strongly condemned the public's dependence on [domestic health care] techniques. It also denounced the patent medicine industry for its encouragement of self-medication and home care. According to the AHA, the patent medicine industry was diametrically opposed to the aims and ideals of the hospital administrator, and for this reason alone the industry "should be killed [and] not injured." (Caplan 1989, 1141)

Hospital administrators began to spruce up their hospitals, to fill them with the latest pieces of medical equipment, and to otherwise do all they could to woo the American middle class away from domestic home care and into the hospital. This was capitalism's frontal assault on the provision of health care as a use value and the first significant effort to convert health care into a commodity bought and sold to make a profit. However, in the earlier period, the people who streamed into hospitals to purchase health care often could not pay for it. Consequently, "before health care could be fully transformed into a capitalist commodity, an elaborate system of financing had to be set up" (Fichtenbaum 1982–83, 36).

Battle for Hearts and Minds—and Wallets

Meanwhile the AHA, the AMA, NARD, and the APA made up a formidable coalition of emerging capitalist interests against domestic health care and the patent medicine industry. However, the merchants of nostrums had their impressive bloc of capitalist allies as well. The Proprietary Association of America (PAA), the trade association for producers of patent medicines, was the cornerstone of the opposition. Joining them were most popular newspapers, magazines, and journals. Most of the nation's periodicals carried an impressive array of patent medicine advertisements, and these periodicals usually depended heavily on revenues from this advertising. Patent medicines accounted for well over half of the wholesale drug trade and for over half of the nation's total drug sales by the early 1900s.

An ideological battle for the hearts and minds of domestic home care adherents followed. In arguments foreshadowing the modern rallying cry of food supplement manufacturers, the patent medicine industry and its allies argued that people had an inherent, natural right to purchase medicine and treat themselves in their own homes. Furthermore, they argued that whereas the AMA was a powerful and dangerous organization with its own agenda, the patent medicine manufacturers were on the side of the people. The AMA and its allies, for their part, published endless stories in selected popular women's magazines about the horrors of poorly manufactured, useless, or dangerous patent medicines. The AMA and the druggists set up councils that developed rules for endorsement of approved medicines, which excluded all patent medicines. The AMA also fought for and often won the establishment of federal and state regulatory bodies to effectively curtail the sale of patent medicines. By the early 1920s the strategy used by the AMA and its allies was clearly winning. Sales of patent medicines were on the decline. Many of the patent medicine manufacturers had gone belly up or had merged. Meanwhile physicians, hospitals, and pharmacists were all sweeping in more cash from a public who had formerly made their own medicines and cared for one another but who now increasingly purchased health care and medicine as a commodity from health care entrepreneurs and corporations.

By 1920 the AMA, which since its founding had been controlled primarily by academic physicians, had come to be dominated by the emerging physician-as-entrepreneur, and by the end of the 1920s the effective defeat of domestic health care was complete. Between 1929 and 1960 the average number of physicians doubled, and medical care costs rose from 3.7 percent to 6 percent of every dollar spent on consumer items. Real (i.e., taking into account inflation) annual per capita expenditures for medical care during this period more than doubled, rising from $32 to more than $70. During the same period the sales of prescription drugs increased explosively, by 1,000 percent, exceeding $2 billion in annual revenue. Even the hardiest former patent medicine manufacturers were falling, often to be purchased by their archenemies, the victorious pharmaceutical industry (Caplan 1989, 1144; Fichtenbaum 1982–83, 36).

To address the problem of the deplorable abilities of many practicing physicians in the United States, in 1910 the AMA, in conjunction with the Carnegie Foundation, conducted a nationwide investigation of the quality of medical students and medical schools. The two influential bodies managed to close 46 of the worst medical schools by 1920, leaving a total of 131 medical schools in the United States. This upgraded the training of physicians and at the same time conveniently limited their production, giving existing physicians less competition and a tighter grip on the market. In addition:

> By 1920, the character of the medical care system changed due to the development of medical science and technology. Significant developments included the discovery and use of X-rays for diagnostic purposes (1895), the electrocardiograph (1903), the electroencephalograph (1929), the development of endocrinology and the discovery of insulin (1921), the use of chemotherapy . . . and the widespread use of rubber gloves, surgical caps, and masks. The introduction of these new scientific discoveries, along with advances in technology, created a situation where the practitioner, in order to compete with other health care providers, had to receive systematic training, and had to use more equipment than he could handle in his black bag. This necessitated his transition to a small businessman, employing a small number of workers. He needed at least a receptionist, a bookkeeper, and a nurse, and as the cost of setting up a private practice began to grow, doctors began to form partnerships to share the expenses of maintaining an office. This enabled them to take advantage of the benefits of social production on a small scale while maintaining their independence as entrepreneurs. (Fichtenbaum 1982–83, 35)

The depression of the 1930s threatened the march toward making health care a profitable commodity for physician-entrepreneurs and for the emerging cash-on-the-barrelhead hospitals. By 1933, for example, income for nonsalaried physicians had fallen to less than 60 percent of what it had been just four or five years earlier. The hospitals saw a prepaid health plan as the answer. Blue Cross was started and was controlled entirely by the AHA to guarantee cash flow and income, finally adding the missing financing piece to complete the conversion of health care into a commodity. The AMA followed suit shortly thereafter with Blue Shield, fashioned in the same mold as Blue Cross, to guarantee physicians' fees (Fichtenbaum 1982–83, 37).

From Craft to Assembly Line

The pattern with any industry as it develops under capitalism is for work to be increasingly broken into simple, finite tasks so that the least expensive worker possible may be hired to accomplish them. At the same time, the gathering of more and more expensive technology under one corporate roof requires the increasing division of labor into specialties. One hundred years ago, just prior to the development of corporate medicine, the medical occupations were physician, nurse, midwife, and pharmacist. Now there are hundreds of health care occupations in corporate settings with multiple hierarchies of providers, aides, interns, residents, assistants, and so on. In 1950 only about 30 percent of practicing physicians in the United States were specialists, but now the proportion is more than twice that (Fichtenbaum 1982–83, 38). As the market for health care grew and as expensive technology proliferated, physicians were able to specialize and keep their income high and rising because of the restriction of competition by the limited number of medical schools and because of the payment of larger reimbursements for specialists by insurers. However, currently, as they increasingly become salaried workers for large corporations such as hospitals and health maintenance organizations (HMOs), physicians are losing control over income.

Sidelining Public Health

Brief History

Periodic epidemics of cholera and yellow fever, and fears about the larger health consequences of filthy low-income neighborhoods and shantytowns during the first half of the 1800s led to the development of sometimes ephemeral citizens' hygiene associations to tidy up the cities. It was generally thought at the time that dirt and squalor had some relationship to these and other diseases, but there was little unanimity about exactly what the nature of the relationship was. After the Civil War, beginning in the late 1860s, some states established state boards of health, and New York City founded the Metropolitan Board of Health. After a series of cholera and yellow fever outbreaks in the 1870s, Congress established a National Board of Health. A few years later, however, the board was terminated by Congress at the request of a bureaucratically threatened surgeon general, thereafter relegating the organized pursuit of public health to states and cities (Starr 1982, 184–85).

Physicians, pharmacists, and drug manufacturers viewed public health predominantly through entrepreneurial eyes even during the early days of the development of public health institutions and activities. They supported public health as long as it funneled patients and customers into their offices, but the moment they saw public health as competition, they turned their backs. In the 1890s, for example, the New York City Health Department was a leader in the development of public health diagnostic bacteriological laboratories. The department pioneered a way to manufacture inexpensive diphtheria serum, distributed free diphtheria testing kits to physicians, manufactured and sold diphtheria and other serums to physicians through drug stores, and gave serum away free for use by low-income patients. Fatalities from diphtheria declined dramatically, but that was not the issue. Local pharmaceutical manufacturers and physicians feared competition and demanded a halt to "municipal socialism." A petition signed by more than a thousand physicians and druggists demanded a halt to the dreaded manufacturing and distribution of vaccines, which resulted in the implementation of a far less effective program (Starr 1982, 185–87).

Public health began to change qualitatively about the second decade of the twentieth century. The bacterial origin of many diseases was now well known. Physicians were more effectively able to prevent, treat, or cure many of the infectious diseases that had been the largely exclusive bailiwick of environmentally oriented public health practitioners. Classic public health approaches such as cleaning up neighborhoods, improving poor housing, and building treatment facilities to ensure clean water receded behind the personal hygiene message: Wash your hands and see the physician regularly for checkups. Politically this message was far more appealing to both legislators and voters since it was much cheaper than undertaking public works for a clean environment. Unfortunately, many of those involved with public health also bought the faulty argument that personal hygiene was sufficient protection against public health problems, undermining the principals of public health and yielding to the leadership of physicians and the medical establishment:

> The emphasis on personal hygiene and medical examinations was not, in fact, always a logical response to bacteriological discoveries. The campaign against tuberculosis provides a case in point. The use of the tuberculin test, introduced around 1890 and refined in 1907, disclosed that latent tuberculosis infection was widespread in the population. The discovery of large numbers of people who were infected without being ill indicated that in combating the disease, strengthening resistance—for example, by improving nutrition, housing, and working conditions—might be as valuable as preventing infection.
>
> So, in the case of tuberculosis, bacteriological findings might logically have led to an interest in social reforms of the type [that some people] in public health were repudiating as irrelevant to their professional tasks. But instead, the antituberculosis movement of the early 1900s sought primarily to change individual health habits. (Starr 1982, 191)

Coincident with the new idea that public health centered on personal hygiene and individual medical care, hundreds of baby clinics and tuberculosis clinics sprouted up across the country in the second decade of the century. In most of them public health workers provided health education and conducted medical exams but found it politically expedient to refer patients to the private for-profit sector for treatment. A venereal disease clinic in Chicago, for example, bucked the tide by providing treatment to low-income patients at a fraction of the cost for which the treatment was offered in the offices of private physicians. Mentioning something about unethical practice and unfair competition, the Chicago Medical Society expelled the clinic's staff physicians. By the 1930s public health had become permanently exiled to a position behind medical care.

Beginning late in the nineteenth century in the United States, instruction in "hygiene," an early name for some public health–type activities, was linked to instruction in bacteriology in medical schools. As early as the 1930s medical schools began establishing "departments of preventive medicine" that dealt primarily with environmental health issues like sewage, food, and communicable diseases. Courses taught by departments of preventive medicine were typically very unpopular with medical students. How could sewage compete with the latest advances in surgery? After World War II departments of "community medicine" or "community health" sprang up in medical schools, reflecting a trend toward discussing community health issues by starting with clinically appropriate cases. For example, examining a patient with syphilis would lead to a discussion of community control of sexually transmitted diseases. Despite the new name and the new approach, most medical students felt that public health was boring compared to the wonders of medical technology and emerging new antibiotics (Roemer 1986, 23).

The first graduate school of public health to open in the United States was the Johns Hopkins School of Hygiene and Public Health founded in 1916, but for at least another three decades this school of public health and others opened during the period would admit only physicians. After World War II U.S. schools of public health began to admit students from a wide variety of backgrounds, such as social science, nursing, laboratory technology, and humanities. Today there are twenty-three schools of public health. About three-quarters of the graduates get masters-level degrees, and the remaining students receive doctor of public health (Dr.P.H.) degrees (Roemer 1986, 23).

Current Public Health Practice

While there is no one definition of public health accepted by all public health professionals today, perhaps the most often quoted is that offered by C. E. A. Winslow:

Public health is the science and the art of (1) preventing disease, (2) prolonging life, and (3) promoting physical health and efficiency through organized community efforts for (a) the sanitation of the environment, (b) the control of communicable infections, (c) the education of the individual in personal hygiene, (d) the organization of medical and nursing services for the early diagnosis and preventive treatment of disease, and (e) the development of the social machinery to ensure everyone a standard of living adequate for the maintenance of health, so organizing the benefits as to enable every citizen to realize his birthright of health and longevity. (Hanlon 1969, 4, quoted in Stivers 1991, 357)

Clearly, this is a very broad definition of public health. It could easily include the organization of medical care, advocacy for good jobs and benefits for all, a critique of military policies and actions, national and local housing improvements, and advocacy of occupational and environmental health, not to mention passive restraint regulations for cars and bicycle helmet laws for kids. In fact, public health as commonly institutionalized at the local and state level, even at the national level, is a wan actor in the shadow of an imposing role. The practice of medicine, once significantly guided by the leadership of public health, has come to totally dominate the field of health care, overwhelming an emaciated public health sector.

Historically, the focus of the public health system in the United States has been at the state level. Given that, however, there is still tremendous variation among state health departments in terms of what they actually do. About a third of all the state health departments act as the primary environmental agency, a third have primary responsibility for mental health, and a third are the main Medicaid agency for the state. Some health departments have more than one of these responsibilities, and some have none of them:

Nearly all states collect and analyze vital statistics, do epidemiological studies and laboratory analyses, screen the population for various diseases, and do some health-related research. Nearly all engage in some type of health education activity. Most state health departments engage in inspection and quality assurance activities such as food and milk control, health facility licensing, and environmental protection, particularly with respect to public and individual water supplies and sewage disposal systems. Nearly all are involved in maternal and child health, prenatal and family planning services, immunizations, chronic diseases and dental services. Nevertheless, although it is possible to list functions performed by "nearly all" or "most" state health departments, few generalizations can be made about how deeply or in what manner (e.g., data collection, research, policy planning, or direct service provision) these agencies are involved in any particular activity, or which health problems they address. (Stivers 1991, 358)

Local county or municipal health departments vary even more widely than do state health departments. Small towns or rural areas may have a visiting nurse occasionally but no permanent public health facility. Larger towns may have a rudimentary public health facility with two or three staff members.

Large cities will have much larger and more comprehensive public health capabilities. Most local health departments do some health education, environmental inspections, and control of some infectious diseases, but unlike state health departments many local departments provide personal health services to individuals, particularly low-income persons. This latter activity increasingly diverts public health departments from focusing resources on the heart of public health activities: community-based services.

Problems with Current Public Health Practice

Fragmentation of public health functions is a serious problem with the organization of public health in the United States. At the federal level, for example, basic public health functions are scattered throughout the bureaucracy. Occupational health and safety programs are in the Department of Labor. The Department of Health and Human Services houses the Public Health Service, but it also houses programs unrelated to public health such as Medicare and Medicaid, which provide funds for medical services to individuals. Environmental health programs are in the Environmental Protection Agency, a semiautonomous agency that does not come under any of the executive departments. Public health functions are similarly scattered throughout state and local government bureaucracies as well. The dismembering of public health programs in the twentieth century has led to the inefficient duplication of some services and, simultaneously, to gaps in other public health functions; to the inability to plan comprehensive public health programs; to confusion on the part of legislators, policymakers, and the public in terms of what public health actually is; and perhaps most importantly, to the diffusion of public health advocacy among professionals and the public, blunting the political influence needed to address most of the other problems. Camilla Stivers offers an interesting additional explanation for the lack of a widespread constituency for public health:

> Not being able to promise to save individuals, only the community-at-large, the professional practice of public health became separated from people, and public health activity, when viewed in contrast to the "miracles" performed by the medical profession, acquired an anonymity that precluded the kind of support that grateful clients can afford professionals who provide personal care. Faced with a *de facto* interprofessional rivalry over the terrain of health knowledge and practice, public health found itself at a disadvantage, lacking the natural practice links with individual clients which supported the status claims of physicians. (Stivers 1991, 367)

Other problems with contemporary public health practice include widespread obsolete public health laws that hamper the abilities of public health officials. In recent years public health programs nationwide have had increasing workloads and responsibilities due to emerging challenges such as AIDS and a burgeoning indigent population. Simultaneously, however, federal funds for public health–related block grants have been cut year after year, and state spending on public health has only just kept up with inflation (Stivers 1991, 359–60).

AIDS cases have grown from 15,000 or 20,000 cases in 1985 to nearly a quarter million cases by 1992, and up to 1.5 million Americans may be infected with the HIV virus that triggers AIDS. Hepatitis B is a disease, usually sexually transmitted, that affects the livers of 300,000 people annually. The number of cases doubled between 1985 and 1990 to 1.2 million people. While an effective vaccine has existed since the early 1980s, only 1 percent of the 28 million young people at risk have had this protection administered. The incidence of syphilis has doubled from 70,000 cases per year in 1985 to nearly 140,000 cases per year in 1990, with young black men and women particularly at risk. Moreover, people with syphilis are at higher risk for contracting and transmitting HIV. Widespread immunization programs in the early 1980s lowered the incidence of measles among children to just a few thousand cases per year. Cutbacks in these programs in the late 1980s had provoked a resurgence of the disease by 1990 to 600–700 percent of its earlier incidence (Freundlich, Kelly, and Carey 1992). Tuberculosis was declining in the early 1980s, but the trend has since reversed, with the result that 10–15 million persons are infected. Moreover, a drug-resistant variety of tuberculosis is spreading rapidly in urban areas, particularly among those who are HIV-positive (McKenzie 1994, 266).

The Politics of Public Health

Although the AMA and its state affiliates are extremely political organizations, the day-to-day delivery of private medical care takes place essentially outside the political arena. In other words, private practitioners have considerable latitude over location, type, size, and other details of a practice they may want to establish. There is very little public accountability for the practice of private medicine. In contrast, public health agencies are located in government bureaucracies directly in the middle of the public sector and therefore have the potential to be highly politicized entities. Beyond that, the actual community-based work done under the auspices of public health evokes a political response that treating individuals in a medical setting does not. Providing free or discounted health care services, even to low-income families who could not afford them from the private sector, can provoke the political wrath of a local medical society in the 1990s just as it did in the 1890s. A visit by an inspector from the Occupational Safety and Health Administration (OSHA) easily results in irate calls to the employer's legislators and adds fuel to the fire of a longer-term commitment by industry to weaken

OSHA in every way possible. Environmental inspectors intent on minimizing harmful pollution of the environment evoke similar responses from industry. Public health is an innately political pursuit.

Curiously, public health professionals, who typically find themselves enmeshed in political struggles for scarce resources coveted by other government agencies and who often tread lightly for fear of waking a private-sector political giant by an enforcement procedure, are not usually taught government agency street fighting in schools of public health. Too often the hope of public health professionals is that the scientific merit of their case combined with the humanitarian virtues of good health for all will win the day with miserly, balky legislators prone to sink the money into capital projects rather than public health.

Some public health officials do not want to aggressively enforce their own regulations even if they are wise to the ways of internal political wrangling. This results from the so-called revolving door phenomenon: The door revolves both ways. On the one hand, enforcement officers or their superiors may be told, or may come to believe based on their observations, that weak enforcement of occupational health and safety regulations or environmental regulations in the case of certain large employers may later result in a very lucrative private-sector job offer. On the other hand, big wheels from the private sector often do a stint in the public sector to round out their careers. There is no telling what might happen to the enthusiastic compliance officer who levies big fines on his or her new supervisor's colleagues in the private sector. Quite apart from the revolving door, the enthusiastic compliance officer who naively slaps a hefty fine on the politically well-connected employer just might find him- or herself in deep trouble. Active political struggle is central to the success of public health, but the fear of retribution and the hope of a high-flying job in the private sector tend to mute the effectiveness of too many players in public health.

Summary and Discussion

From about the 1870s through the 1930s the development of capitalism in health care radically and permanently altered the social institution. The earlier dominant mode of health care, often referred to as "domestic health care," was characterized by women in the household making their own medical preparations and providing health care to their own families. The rise of a for-profit patent medicine industry in the latter half of the 1800s drew domestic health care partly into the capitalist orbit by replacing homemade medicines with commercially prepared purchased medicines. By the beginning of the twentieth century patent medicines had become a major industry in the United States and at the same time a major obstacle to the development of other entrepreneurial activities in health care by physicians, hospital administrators, and manufacturers and distributors of prescription medicines. These entrepreneurs' combined assault on the patent medicine industry and domestic health care succeeded, fully converting health care from a social institution characterized by production and distribution of medical services within the family to production and distribution of medical commodities over ever wider markets.

During roughly the same period, former charity hospitals transformed themselves into profit-making, or surplus-generating (among the nonprofit institutions), businesses, increasingly dependent on cash-paying customers and third-party payers (for example, insurers). Their development of prepaid hospital plans such as Blue Cross provided the needed steady inflow of cash to complete the transition. The AMA, representing the emerging class of physician-entrepreneurs, systematically knocked out competing providers of health care while positioning themselves as the exclusive providers or gatekeepers to health care as a commodity. As the institution of medicine became increasingly capital-intensive and technologically oriented, individual physicians lost out to group practices, hospitals, HMOs, and other corporate forms of medicine. In addition, the emerging plethora of allied health workers had the contradictory consequences of both increasing the profits of physician-entrepreneurs and at the same time threatening the central importance of physicians in medical institutions.

Public health, central to the struggle for health care outside the physician's office—for example in the community and among specific populations—rose in importance during the early and mid-1800s in response to epidemics of infectious diseases. As a result of the critical efforts of public health officials working separately from the medical care establishment, Congress established a National Board of Health in the 1870s. This was a threat, however, to the emerging medical establishment, and the board was eliminated as a result of pressure from the surgeon general. It was the last time in the United States that public health held a central position of relative equality with private medicine. From that day to this, public health institutions and activities have been politically feasible primarily in health niches deemed irrelevant to private medicine or considered contributory to the profitability of private medicine. The inferior position of public health compared to private medicine has kept public health in a condition of anarchy—balkanized among the states and scattered about a number of federal agencies. Today the nation's public health apparatus is barely able to respond to the epidemics of the late twentieth century such as tuberculosis, AIDS, and measles, much less play a leadership role in health care planning and reform.

References

Caplan, Ronald L. 1989. "The Commodification of American Health Care." *Social Science and Medicine* 28(11):1139–48.

Fichtenbaum, Rudy. 1982–83. "Health Care as a Commodity and the Current Crisis in U.S. Medicine." *The Forum for Social Economics* (Fall-Winter):31–46.

Freundlich, Naomi, Gwendolyn Kelly, and John Carey. 1992. "Public Health Is in a Bad Way." *Business Week* (August 17):102–4.

Hanlon, John J. 1969. *Principles of Public Health Administration.* St. Louis: Mosby.

McKenzie, Nancy F. 1994. "The Real Health Care Crisis." *The Nation* (February 28):266–68.

Roemer, Milton I. 1986. "The Need for Professional Doctors of Public Health." *Public Health Reports* 101(1):21–29.

Starr, Paul. 1982. *The Social Transformation of American Medicine.* New York: Basic Books.

Stivers, Camilla. 1991. "The Politics of Public Health: The Dilemma of a Public Profession." In Theodore J. Litman and Leonard S. Robins, eds., *Health Politics and Policy,* 356–69. Albany, N.Y.: Delmar Publishers.

2

Access to Health Care

There are two ways to look at the issue of access to health care. The first is legal and theoretical. For example, say a federal or state law mandates that any family whose income is within 150 percent of the federal poverty level qualifies for a particular public health insurance program. Having accomplished this, legislators claim that they have provided access to health care for all these low-income people. The problem is resolved. The legislators feel good, knowing that they have pushed through important legislation. Most of the tax-paying public feels good, knowing that a portion of their taxes is being spent for a legitimate humanitarian purpose, to help those not in a position to help themselves. Low-income families that can take full advantage of the public health insurance feel good because they have access to health care that otherwise would have been prohibitively expensive.

The second way to analyze the issue of access is to look past image, myth, and ideology—to look beyond abstract laws and regulations that address access. While the importance of these government programs cannot be denied, the mere fact of their existence does not guarantee that the target population will have access to health care and certainly does not guarantee access to health care for those in need but outside the target population. The reality of access to health care is that it is influenced not only by government programs but also by a wide range of political, economic, cultural, and other social factors. For example, how many legally qualified applicants for a public health insurance program cannot complete the initial application and interview process because they are illiterate or have a poor grasp of the English language because it is not their native tongue? How many cannot go to the office for the required interview because they lack money for transportation, because they lack day care for their children, or because they cannot take time off from their job for fear of losing it? Once enrolled in the public health insurance program, how many families cannot use the benefits because they cannot afford required deductibles and copayments? How many are forced to use emergency rooms because physicians will not give appointments to patients enrolled in the public program? How many receive sub-standard care or no care at all due to racism or sexism? All these social factors are obstacles to access. Moreover, they are not minor obstacles—they are fundamental barriers to access.

Health Status in the United States

The United States has an unhealthy population compared to many other in-dustrialized nations. Worldwide, the United States is ranked twenty-fourth in infant mortality, a ranking that has dropped from twentieth since 1980. At 18.6 deaths per 1,000 live births, the infant mortality rate among blacks is 230 percent greater than among whites (Byrd 1992). "A child in Chile or Malaysia is more likely to celebrate his first birthday than a black baby born in the Mississippi Delta" (McKenzie 1994, 266). Death rates from homi-cides and other violence in males age twenty-five to thirty-four in the United was nearly 30 per 100,000 in 1989. This rate is at least two and one-half times the rate of any Western European nation and about eight times that of Japan.

At every age up to sixty-five, the risk of dying is higher in the United States than in a number of European countries, Japan, and Canada. The death rate for males aged twenty-five to forty-four in the United States is 250 per 100,000, but it drops to about 150 or 160 per 100,000 in Canada, Germany, and Sweden. If the United States had Canada's superior age-specific mortality rates, there would be roughly 200,000 fewer deaths per year (Office of Technology Assessment 1993). (Nor can these excess Ameri-can deaths be blamed on smoking: Americans smoke less than the citizens of most of these other countries.)

The high U.S. mortality rates are not distributed evenly among all Ameri-cans. According to the Office of Technology Assessment (1993), low-in-come persons and minorities are more likely to have higher infant mortality rates and higher mortality rates at most ages and are more likely to die younger than their white and more affluent counterparts. "Black men in central Harlem are less likely to reach age 65 than men in Bangladesh" (McKenzie 1994, 266). To cite more statistics:

> African-Americans aged 1–14 are 60 percent more likely to die overall than white Americans, and five times as likely to die of homicides than white Ameri-can children. Hispanic children are twice as likely as non-Hispanic white Ameri-cans to die as a result of homicide.
>
> African-Americans aged 15–24 years are more than 7 times more likely than white Americans to die of homicide, and 50 percent more likely to die of all causes. Hispanics in the same age group are 3.5 times as likely to die of homi-cide than white, non-Hispanic children in the same age range.

African-Americans aged 45–64 are 70 percent more likely to die of all causes than whites in the same age brackets. Middle-aged African-Americans are also 70 percent more likely to die of injuries, and diseases of the heart, 40 percent more likely to die from malignant neoplasms (cancers), and three times as likely to die from cerebrovascular disease (strokes). (Lillie-Blanton et al. 1993, 566)

Minorities and Access to Health Care

A variety of factors apart from overt racism contribute to the reduced access to health care experienced by many ethnic minorities compared to whites. Poverty is a major factor. Fewer than 9 percent of all non-Hispanic whites live in poverty, but nearly a third of all African-Americans and over 28 percent of all Hispanics live in poverty. African-Americans are nearly twice as likely as non-Hispanic whites to lack health insurance, and Hispanics are nearly two and one-half times as likely not to have health insurance (Short, Monheit, and Beauregard 1989). Moreover, these minorities are losing their health insurance coverage at a faster rate than non-Hispanic whites. Despite the fact that African-Americans and Hispanics together account for a bit more than 20 percent of the total population, between 1977 and 1987 these minorities accounted for over half the increase in the number of uninsured Americans. In the ten-year period beginning 1977, the percent of uninsured whites climbed from 12 percent to 15 percent, but the percent of uninsured African-Americans grew from 18 percent to 25 percent, and of Hispanics from 20 percent to a shocking 35 percent. A national survey found that 86 percent of those in fair or poor health who were covered by health insurance saw a physician in a one-year period, whereas only 63 percent of those not insured but in fair or poor health saw a physician. The uninsured have significantly less access, and minorities are much more likely to be uninsured (Cornelius 1993, 16, 18, 22, 24).

When seeking health care, Hispanics are more than twice as likely as non-Hispanic whites to use hospital outpatient clinics or emergency rooms, and African-Americans are more than three times as likely. As these minorities progressively lose health insurance coverage, they often have nowhere else to turn but the emergency room for health care. Although their acute care needs may be more or less met in this manner, emergency rooms and clinics cannot provide the continuity of care necessary for adequate, comprehensive health care, particularly for the chronically ill.

On average, fewer than 10 percent of non-Hispanic whites wait more than an hour to be seen by a health care provider, but as many as 20 percent of Hispanics and African-Americans wait at least one hour. Long waits act as a deterrent to seeking needed care and put these patients at higher risk for leaving the health care facility before receiving care. Long waits may also be one of the factors that have contributed to a serious decline in recent years of physician visits by African-Americans.

In 1982, 80 percent of all African-Americans saw a physician at least once during the year. By 1987 only 63 percent had seen a physician during that year. Even after waiting for long periods of time, language barriers may put Hispanics and other minorities who may speak little or no English at a serious disadvantage in the physician's office. A study of Medicaid sites in seven states that represent nearly 85 percent of the Hispanic population in the United States found that a third of these sites had no special services to help monolingual (that is, non-English-speaking) Hispanic patients (Cornelius 1993, 16, 20).

Commenting on differences in mammography use according to income and education, Lawrence Bergner of the National Cancer Institute has expressed concern that simply expanding mammography programs (and by implication any health care service) without specifically targeting the underserved populations simply results in larger gaps based on income and education. In addition he critiques the pejorative "blame the victim" implication made by some health planners and educators who fail to reach their target populations. He notes that despite the expected expansion of mammography programs nationwide,

> it is not unlikely that the differences between groups will persist. Women in the medical care mainstream—those who have an ongoing relationship with a health care professional, who are native English speakers, who have no significant cultural taboos or skepticism about medical care, and who are able to deal with copayments or other marginal costs—will have gotten the message and obtained the service. Women who are disadvantaged in these and other characteristics will be reported to have "failed" to obtain mammography. They will probably be referred to as "hard to reach." Would "underserved" be more accurate? (Bergner 1993, 940)

Historical Obstacles to Health Care Access in African-American Communities

Until the 1960s there was overt discrimination against African-American physicians and patients by white-dominated hospitals and associated white physicians. While discrimination was most extreme in the southern and border states, there was significant discrimination in health care institutions across the nation. African-American physicians could not admit their patients to segregated white hospitals, and they could not gain hospital privileges in those hospitals. As a result they were effectively barred from the practice of medicine in white hospitals. In addition, white hospitals for the most part simply abandoned African-American communities by locating elsewhere. Under these adverse conditions, African-Americans and some white entrepreneurs founded at least two hundred black hospitals since the 1800s; these hospitals featured African-American physicians and support personnel and served African-American patients in their own communities. The historical importance of these institutions can hardly be overstated. They provided health care for African-Americans, who could get it nowhere else. They provided training grounds and facilities in which to practice medicine for African-American physicians, who could not practice elsewhere. They trained and gave experience to many African-American workers, professionals, and entrepreneurs, who would not have found comparable employment elsewhere (Taravella 1990).

Ironically, as a result of civil rights victories that eliminated overt discrimination in many health care facilities in the 1960s, formerly black hospitals faced an extremely difficult situation. In effect, one of the main historical reasons for their existence appeared to have evaporated. Black hospitals lost the struggle for black physicians and patients, who streamed to the better-appointed formerly all-white hospitals. In addition the black hospitals were increasingly financially squeezed by the growing poverty of the inner-city patients they served. In 1944 there were at least 124 black hospitals, but only 8 remained by the end of 1989. All the rest had been closed or had merged with formerly all-white institutions (McBride 1993).

From the mid-1940s to the mid-1960s, federal Hill-Burton grants disbursed about $2 billion to help establish a network of acute-care hospitals across America. While the federal program prohibited discrimination on the basis of "race, creed, or color" in facilities funded by Hill-Burton, there was a widely used provision that allowed for the construction of separate health care facilities for African-Americans if such facilities were "of like quality." In reality, however, facilities for African-Americans were often separate but were rarely equal to those of whites. By the end of 1962, eighty-nine "racially exclusive" facilities in fourteen southern and border states had received $37 million in Hill-Burton funds for construction or remodeling. In North Carolina, for example, in the mid-1960s Hill-Burton funds had constructed twenty-seven hospitals exclusively for whites and only four for blacks (Smith 1990).

Segregation of hospitals and nursing homes was extensive in the North as well. A mid-1950s study of hospital segregation in Chicago found that over half of all patients in the county public hospital were black but that fewer than 1 percent of the patients in area private hospitals were black, despite the fact that nearly half of the city's black population had hospital insurance. A mid-1960s study of hospitals in Buffalo also found rampant discrimination (New York State Advisory Committee 1964, 10, quoted in Smith 1990, 594).

The Civil Rights Struggle for Access

David B. Smith (1990, 567) identifies five social processes that he considers primarily responsible for largely eliminating segregation in health care facilities by the end of the 1960s:

1. World War II, which weakened Jim Crow ideology in the United States because it was similar to Nazi ideology of racial superiority;
2. The Cold War with the Soviet Union, which heightened the international awareness of racist discrimination in the United States, embarrassing the federal government;
3. The civil rights movement;
4. The expansion of health care programs at the federal level after World War II; and
5. The strong growth of the national economy in the 1950s and 1960s.

Of all these factors, the civil rights movement was the only one that specifically mobilized organizations and large groups of people to fight racism and discrimination in medical facilities. One of the key organizations in this struggle was the National Medical Association (NMA), founded just before the turn of the century when Jim Crow racism had reached its peak in the South. The NMA was composed of about sixty medical societies scattered across the nation. These societies were started by African-American physicians who had been excluded from the white-dominated state medical societies that made up the national constituency of the AMA. During the 1930s and 1940s the NMA's struggle against discrimination focused on the racist exclusion of African-Americans from AMA-affiliated state medical societies and from most segregated hospitals:

> The medical-staff by-laws of most hospitals stipulated that appointments would be made only from members in good standing with the local medical society. Exclusion from these local medical societies blocked any chance of gaining staff privileges at white hospitals. Black physicians were thus far more likely than black patients to face restrictions in access to hospitals. As the practice of medicine became increasingly hospital dependent, access to hospitals became an increasingly critical problem. (Smith 1990, 568–69)

The NMA Good Will Committee was formed in 1938 to try to fight racism in the AMA and its constituent state societies by friendly persuasion. The committee's first significant victory came a couple of years later when it convinced the AMA to leave off the special notation "(Col.)" after every "colored" physician in the AMA directory. A decade later the committee influenced the AMA to pass a weak resolution requesting AMA-affiliated state medical societies to "study" the question of racist exclusionary practices.

This watered-down concession was probably a political move to try to wean the NMA away from supporting the Truman administration's proposal for a national health insurance program, which was adamantly opposed by the AMA. During the late 1940s the NMA urged the Association of American Medical Colleges (AAMC) to adopt a resolution against racist discrimination in medical school admissions. In its annual meetings, the AAMC repeatedly refused to do so; however, about this same time the Legal Defense Fund of the National Association for the Advancement of Colored People (NAACP) took a couple of cases to the Supreme Court, which resulted in the admission of African-Americans into medical schools in Arkansas and Texas.

In 1953 the NMA and the NAACP formally joined forces to establish the NAACP National Health Program. The program's strategy had two components: The first was to try to convince hospitals to voluntarily eliminate segregation and the exclusion of African-American physicians, and the second was to build legal cases against those hospitals that refused. A series of annual national conferences beginning in the late 1950s jointly held by the NMA and the NAACP focused on the issue of ending segregation in medical care facilities. These goals were eventually adopted by the Kennedy and Johnson administrations, "due in part to the strong support that the NMA, in contrast to the AMA, had provided in the early 1960s to pending Medicare legislation" (Smith 1990, 573). A series of suits brought by the NAACP and the NMA in the late 1950s and early 1960s against hospitals made the case that since the hospitals had accepted Hill-Burton funds, they could not discriminate under the "due-process, equal-protection provisions of the U.S. Constitution." A 1963 victory in the U.S. Court of Appeals for one of these cases resulted in the issuance of new, more stringent antidiscrimination language by the surgeon general for health care facilities receiving Hill-Burton funds. A year later the historic Civil Rights Act was passed; the act prohibited discrimination based on "race" for any entity receiving federal financial assistance—which included most hospitals in the United States. In 1964 the Johnson administration held a widely attended conference to encourage the private health care facilities to desegregate according to the law. The following year Medicare and Medicaid legislation passed, which required any facility accepting money from either program to comply with civil rights legislation prohibiting discrimination based on "race." This tied both physician and hospital revenue to the elimination of discriminatory practices—an important carrot to accompany the punitive legal stick.

By the end of 1966 the staff of the Office of Equal Health Opportunity in the Public Health Service had grown to six hundred persons. Thousands of hospitals had been reviewed for compliance with the Medicare antidiscrimination provisions. A couple of years later, the acting director of the Office for Civil Rights reported that 97 percent of all hospitals in the United States were committed to providing nondiscriminatory services. Civil rights groups argued that the federal government was glossing over its duty to enforce the law and should withhold funds from many hospitals that had been certified as complying with the civil rights provisions. However, on the whole, most hospitals eliminated overt discriminatory practices to comply with federal regulations.

On another front, discriminatory practices in nursing homes were barely affected by the civil rights advances of the 1960s (Smith 1990, 581). In the mid-1980s an elderly white person was 1.36 times more likely than an elderly African-American to be a resident of a nursing home. Over half of all nursing home payments came from Medicaid. African-Americans accounted for 31 percent of all Medicaid recipients but for only 8 percent of the recipients of Medicaid in skilled nursing homes. Moreover, across the nation there is a biased geographic pattern of the distribution of long-term care facilities. States and counties with higher proportions of white residents have higher proportions of nursing home beds. Various studies tend to point to discrimination as the principal cause of these gross discrepancies:

> The effect of these patterns of discrimination in geographic access and the economic barriers that help create them, while exacerbating their consequences, is racial discrimination in access. As a result, a large proportion of the Medicaid dollars for nursing-home care, intended to provide access to the poor without regard to race, actually provides a catastrophic long-term-care insurance benefit to the white middle class. (Smith 1990, 586)

During the latter half of the 1960s and through the 1970s, the NMA became extremely active as a lobbying organization for civil rights legislation and for progressive health care reforms, often at odds with the AMA. After the murder of three civil rights workers in 1964, the NMA provided dozens of medical workers to serve in the South with civil rights organizations. Many of these medical professionals joined the Medical Committee for Human Rights (MCHR), which by 1966 had various health workers established in branches in thirty northern and southern cities. In the late 1960s the MCHR expanded its mission to include exposing discrimination in health care facilities in northern cities as well as in the South. By the early 1970s the MCHR had ceased to have much of a national political presence, but in its heyday it "managed significant initiatives in the North that included establishing child health programs for ghetto neighborhoods, protest marches against discrimination in local hospitals, and support for recruiting black and Hispanic youth into medical work fields" (McBride 1993, 323). On another front, in the late 1960s African-American physicians of the NMA, in conjunction with progressive whites, used funds from the Office of Economic Opportunity (OEO) to establish over one hundred neighborhood comprehensive health centers targeting public health and individual medical needs of low-income minority communities.

Despite some successes in the areas of civil rights and health care and despite the delivery of better health care services in some minority communities, the health of African-Americans as a group entered a critical stage. As a result, in 1976 Atlanta University convened the W.E.B. DuBois Conference, a national meeting of scholars from a variety of fields, to address the serious and growing problem of the health status of African-Americans and the lack of adequate health care facilities in their communities. NMA physicians warned against health care reform in the shape of a monolithic health insurance bureaucracy, arguing that such a system would not serve the needs of the poor and the inner-city ghettos. Instead, NMA members argued for an expansion of Medicaid, which, they noted, was more directly pertinent to low-income communities. In the 1980s, under the conservative Reagan administration, free-market health care emerged as the ideology buttressing the medical-industrial complex. NMA African-American physicians and other progressive health care activists argued that market medicine responds to well-insured individuals rather than to groups of people (such as African-Americans) with shorter life spans, higher rates of chronic diseases and incapacitating disabilities, and minimal protection from infectious diseases.

In 1984 the NMA published a series of studies documenting serious problems with the health care system as a whole and specific health problems among African-Americans. It focused on "the wide disparity in the health of black and white Americans: black Americans show higher maternal and infant mortality rates, lower life expectancy, and higher death rates linked to cardiovascular disease and cancer" (quoted in McBride 1993, 330). The following year the Department of Health and Human Services released a report compiled by a task force of high-ranking federal health officials. The *Report of the Secretary's Task Force on Black and Minority Health* documented the failure of the health care system to eliminate differences in mortality and illness based on skin color and ethnicity. The report noted specifically that African-Americans were experiencing nearly 60,000 preventable deaths annually compared to the white population, due in large part to "cancer, cardiovascular disease and stroke, substance abuse, diabetes, homicides and accidents, and infant mortality" (quoted in McBride 1993, 331). A couple of years later the AIDS epidemic hit African-American communities with a vengeance. A massively inadequate health care system was entirely unprepared for yet another health care crisis in minority communities. Dr. Louis W. Sullivan, secretary of Health and Human Services in the Bush administration, summarized the situation in a brief article published in the *Journal of the American Medical Association:* "I contend that there is clear, demonstrable, undeniable evidence of discrimination and racism in our health care system. For example, each year since 1984, while the health status of the general population has increased, black health status has actually declined. This decline is not in one or two health categories; it is across the board" (Sullivan 1991, 2574).

Even the conservative AMA admits that racism continues to play a significant role in explaining persistent differences between whites and minorities in health care access and treatment. According to a report published by the AMA's Council on Ethical and Judicial Affairs: "Disparities in treatment decisions may reflect the existence of subconscious bias. This is a serious and troubling problem. Despite the progress of the past 25 years, racial prejudice has not been entirely eliminated in this country. The health care system, like all other elements of society, has not fully eradicated this prejudice" (Council on Ethical and Judicial Affairs, AMA 1990, 2346).

Hispanic Access to Health Care

Socioeconomic factors play a major role in limiting Hispanic access to health care; however, there are important differences among various Hispanic peoples. Mexicans comprise about 62 percent of the roughly 20 million Hispanics in the United States. Puerto Ricans make up 13 percent, Cubans 5 percent, Central and South Americans 12 percent, and other Hispanics 8 percent. As a group, Hispanics are overrepresented in low-income inner-city urban areas. All Hispanic groups have lower average levels of education compared to non-Hispanic whites. For example, 15.4 percent of Mexican-Americans over twenty-five years of age and 10.3 percent of Puerto Ricans over twenty-five have had fewer than five years of schooling; only 2 percent of non-Hispanic whites in that age group have had fewer than five years of schooling. All Hispanic groups except for Cubans are significantly underrepresented among the higher-paying occupational groups such as managerial/professional and technical/sales. Mexicans are particularly disadvantaged because 9 percent are employed in the seasonal, low-income, hazardous farming sector. In the late 1980s the median Hispanic family income was 36 percent less than the median income of non-Hispanic whites, and Hispanics were two and one-half times as likely as non-Hispanic whites to lack either private or public health insurance (Ginzberg 1991, 238–39).

The underrepresentation of Hispanic health care providers is a contributing obstacle to health care access. Although Hispanics make up about 10 percent of the total population, only between 2.2 percent and 3.0 percent of dentists, registered nurses, therapists, and pharmacists are of Hispanic origin. Interestingly, about 5.4 percent of all physicians are Hispanics, but many of these trained outside the United States and subsequently immigrated. Hispanic students, particularly Mexican students, are still very underrepresented in American medical schools (Ginzberg 1991, 240).

Mexicans are not only the most numerous of the Hispanics, but they also encounter some of the most onerous access difficulties. A significant number of Mexicans live along the U.S.-Mexican border. There they suffer disproportionally from hazardous waste contamination, air pollution, and water pollution, as well as a serious paucity of available and affordable health care facilities. Over 110,000 Mexicans live in *colonias* in Texas, unincorporated areas lacking basic sanitation facilities and running water. California has legislated particularly draconian measures limiting access to need-based medical services, such as Medicaid, for Mexican immigrants (Ginzberg 1991, 239–40).

Access to Health Care for the Uninsured

There is no legal or de facto right to health care for U.S. citizens or residents. Rather, access to health care in the United States is principally determined by private insurers seeking to maximize profits by excluding coverage of "high risk" unhealthy populations and insuring healthy "low risk" populations who need a minimum of health care. The process of selecting which groups will be most profitable to insure and which groups will be least profitable is called "underwriting."

The related underwriting processes of "rejecting insurance risks" and charging "the proper premium" for those not rejected maximize profitability for the insurer while simultaneously instigating massive adverse consequences in the larger society. The underwriting principle of private insurance may be "equitable" for the insurer, but it is not equitable for tens of millions of people denied health care by the use of a principle intended to maximize profit rather than access. Nationwide reliance on the underwriting principle has created a vast army of uninsured.

The lack of health insurance has very real consequences concerning access to health care, quality of life, and the very question of life itself. Hundreds of thousands of critically ill uninsured persons are denied treatment every year at emergency rooms across the nation. Some have serious complications as a result of being dumped from an emergency room, and some die needlessly (Ansberry 1988). Even if admitted for hospital care, the uninsured are far less likely to receive standard medical diagnosis or treatment than are those with adequate insurance. One study of more than one hundred hospitals found that privately insured patients with cardiac problems were 80 percent more likely to receive a standard test for clogged arteries than were the uninsured, 40 percent more likely to have coronary bypass surgery, and 28 percent more likely to have a specific procedure to enlarge diseased arteries (Angier 1990). Poverty and lack of health insurance combine to give the United States an extremely high infant mortality rate compared to other industrialized nations. In some low-income areas of the United States, the infant mortality rate is actually rising (Nazario 1988).

On the other hand, fewer than 1 percent of the elderly, those aged sixty-five years old or more, lack health insurance (*Health Insurance Coverage in the U.S.* 1989). Rich or poor, white or people of color, they have public health insurance. Medicare automatically covers nearly all persons sixty-five years of age or older. Despite the shortcomings of Medicare, there is no private health insurance, no insurance profits, no excessive overhead costs, no medical underwriting, and no denial of coverage.

Who Are the Uninsured?

A study by the Census Bureau found that 63 million Americans lacked health insurance coverage for at least one month during a twenty-eight-month period beginning in 1985. This was approximately a quarter of the nation's population during that period of time. Half of all young Americans between the ages of eighteen and twenty-four were not covered at some point during the twenty-eight-month period ("Census Heightens National Health Insurance Issue" 1991). At any given time there are about 37 million uninsured, approximately 15 percent of the U.S. population. The uninsured are not a random selection of citizens. On the contrary, they are concentrated in certain age, ethnic, and other social categories. These groups of people have been hurt the most by a health care system dominated by private health insurance.

The 1987 National Medical Expenditure Survey is the most recent comprehensive national survey profiling groups of Americans without health insurance (Short, Monheit, and Beauregard 1989). Approximately 75 percent of all persons in families with a working adult had employment-related insurance. The major proximate factor determining the total number of uninsured persons was whether or not they were insured at the workplace: "Generally, those who were most likely to lack employment-related insurance included the self-employed and their families, part-time employees, persons employed in small establishments or drawing low wages, and those employed in industries characterized by seasonal or temporary employment" (Short, Monheit, and Beauregard 1989, 10).

In 1987 nearly 29 percent of all uninsured persons were in families without a working adult. However, approximately 40 percent of all low-income employees earning $10,000 per year or less were uninsured by either private or public sources. This group was hit particularly hard because public assistance programs like Medicaid do not cover most of the working poor. Industries with especially high rates of uninsured (about double the national average) included agriculture, construction, personal services, and entertainment.

Uninsured Young Adults and Minorities

The 1987 survey indicated that over 30 percent of all young adults between the ages of nineteen and twenty-four were uninsured by public or private sources, the largest percentage of any age group. Separated and single persons were more than twice as likely to be uninsured than married persons, and divorced persons were nearly twice as likely to be uninsured than married persons. People living in the South and West were about 1.7 times more likely to be uninsured than persons living in the Northeast or Midwest because employers in these areas were more likely to provide employment-related health insurance. Largely because they tended to be employed in jobs with fewer fringe benefits than whites, blacks were nearly twice as likely and Hispanics were nearly 2.5 times as likely to be uninsured as whites.

The AMA's Council on Ethical and Judicial Affairs released a report reviewing a number of studies indicating that the health care of African-Americans and other minorities is inferior to that of whites. Minorities get less-frequent and less-aggressive treatment than whites. Their infant mortality rate is higher and their lives are shorter. A major contributing factor is that minorities are disproportionally uninsured ("Report Cites Racial Discrepancies in Medical Care" 1990).

Children, Race, and Income

Family income is a major factor in determining whether children are insured. In 1986 almost a third of the children who lived in families with incomes below the federal poverty level were completely uninsured, and 28.7 percent of the children living in families with incomes between 100 percent and 200 percent of the federal poverty level were uninsured. An extraordinary 42 percent of children in poor working families were uninsured in 1986 because of declining availability of work-related health insurance and strict Medicaid eligibility provisions. Compare these percentages of uninsured children with the aggregate figure of 18 percent of children in families of all income levels who were uninsured in 1986. Nearly all the growth of the uninsured during the 1980s has been the result of shrinking coverage of dependents by employer-based insurance.

Race is also an important determinant of uninsured children. At every income level African-American children are more likely to be entirely uninsured than white children. In 1986 three of every ten African-American children in families with at least one employed adult were uninsured. In addition, income and race are principal determinants of the insurance coverage of women of childbearing age. In 1985, 17 percent of all women ages fifteen to forty-four, a total of about 9.5 million women, had no health in-

surance of any kind. Another 4.5 million women had health insurance policies that did not cover maternity care. As a result, fully one in every four
women of childbearing age had no maternity care coverage. Unemployed
women and those working in low-paying jobs were most likely to be uninsured. Overall, African-American women were more likely to be uninsured
than white women. Low-income women lacking health insurance were twice
as likely as insured women to receive late or no prenatal care, which is associated with much higher infant mortality rates.

Finally, even those covered by health insurance may find themselves in a
situation similar to those with no health insurance: Depending on the provisions of the insurance policy, insured persons may be required to spend large
sums of money out-of-pocket or forego medical treatment altogether. A
1984 study by the Department of Health and Human Services, for example,
found that approximately 60 million persons under age sixty-five with (obviously inadequate) private health insurance would have had the burden of unlimited medical expenses if they had experienced a major accident or illness.
The study also found that in excess of 2 million families annually are forced
to pay at least $3,000 in medical bills not covered by health insurance (U.S.
Congress, Joint Economic Committee 1989).

Unique Obstacles to Access with Long-Term-Care Insurance

Long-term-care insurance theoretically provides medical and support services to people who cannot live and function independently because of a
chronic illness or other conditions. Prior to the mid-1980s very few people
carried this kind of coverage; however, by the beginning of 1992 nearly two
and one-half million policies had been sold by more than 130 companies.
This type of insurance policy has been plagued by high-pressure sales tactics,
misrepresentation, and outright fraud. Obviously, all these problems act as
obstacles to access to long-term care. In addition, a study by the U.S. General Accounting Office (GAO) found that nearly 15 percent of all long-term
policyholders let the policy lapse after the first year without having received
any benefit but having spent $1,100 to $3,000 in annual premiums. Insurance companies estimate that about half of all long-term-care policyholders
will have let their policies lapse without having used them after five years,
and up to 85 percent will let them lapse after ten years: "As of June 1990,
the average purchase age of persons buying individual long-term-care insurance policies was 72. . . . The average age of persons admitted to a nursing
home was 76 years. Therefore, if 50 percent of policyholders allow their
policies to lapse over a 5-year period as the insurers in our review estimated,
many policyholders may not receive benefits when they need them" (U.S.
General Accounting Office 1993, 8).

Long-term-care policyholders let their policies lapse for a variety of reasons. Many policyholders simply cannot keep up the payments. Others may cancel a policy in the first month after they have studied the provisions; some die; and many upgrade to a newer policy. In a marketing scam called "churning," insurance agents sell new policies to replace or add to older but perfectly good ones because the agents' commissions are several hundred percent higher on the first year's premiums than on subsequent years' premiums.

Women and Access

Women, particularly low-income and minority women, have special obstacles accessing health care. Looking at women of all colors and ethnicities, in 1988 one in four women with incomes under $10,000 reported that they were in fair or poor health, whereas only one of every twenty-five women with incomes over $35,000 responded that they were in fair or poor health. At the same time, among all women, those with incomes in the $10,000 to $19,999 range were least likely to have visited a physician in the last year, and those earning less were only slightly more likely to have visited a physician.

Physician contacts per person per year and short-stay hospital discharges per 100 persons per year among all women vary inversely by income. In other words, low-income women who do see a physician tend to see the physician more often each year than do high-income women, presumably because they are more ill, as they have self-reported. In addition, low-income women are more likely to land in the hospital than high-income women, again presumably because of poorer health status (Lillie-Blanton et al. 1993, 576–77).

Barriers to Prenatal Care

Despite the fact that prenatal care is typically associated with better birth outcomes, one-quarter to one-third of all pregnant women in the United States do not or cannot obtain adequate prenatal care. Those at highest risk for inadequate prenatal care are minorities, those on Medicaid, and the uninsured. Part of the problem arises from the declining number of physicians practicing obstetrics—about one in eight have stopped practicing obstetrics in recent years. Another problem involves the increasing number of physicians who limit or refuse to take low-income patients on Medicaid, a federal and state health insurance program for low-income persons that typically reimburses health care services at rates below those charged private insurers.

Pregnant teenagers face all the obstacles to adequate prenatal care that adult women do, plus more. A national study completed in the mid-1980s found that 5 percent of pregnant teens received no prenatal care whatsoever and that fully one-half of all pregnant teens received prenatal care only after the first trimester (Cartwright et al. 1993, 737). Cartwright and colleagues were interested in finding out what pregnant teens perceived as obstacles to prenatal care as a first step to attempting toward improving their access. The researchers summarized several unpublished studies that had investigated similar concerns:

> Review of these reports reveals that in communities where prenatal care was not free, teenagers said that lack of money was the main barrier to their obtaining prenatal care. Other commonly cited reasons for delayed entry into prenatal care were denial and/or shame that they were pregnant, fear of telling their parents, fear of physicians and obstetric procedures, and problems getting transportation to and from clinics. In communities where the health care system was overburdened and understaffed, having to wait long periods for an appointment also delayed their entry into prenatal care. (Cartwright et al. 1993, 737)

A History of Racist Population Control

A particularly pernicious obstacle to access to reproductive counseling and services involves the class bias and racism that have permeated the history of birth control in the United States. Initially the birth control movement was promoted by progressive advocates who wanted women to have more control over their lives. By the 1930s, however, the movement for birth control had been subverted to become a program for population control:

> More and more, it was assumed within birth control circles that poor women, black and immigrant alike, have a "moral obligation to restrict the size of their families." What was demanded as a "right" for the privileged came to be interpreted as a "duty" for the poor.
>
> This "duty" of the poor to have fewer children who might possibly need welfare and other government services has become an underlying theme of many federally funded programs. One of the most blatant expressions of the population control theses is the involuntary sterilization of women of color. (Nsiah-Jefferson 1993, 120–21)

Some of the examples given include the facts that one in four women giving birth at an Indian Health Service (IHS) hospital in Oklahoma was subsequently sterilized and that over a third of all women of childbearing age in Puerto Rico have been sterilized. Similar abuses have been documented for other Hispanic women and African-American teenagers. Nsiah-Jefferson notes that "the reproductive technologies may be perceived by poor women and women of color within this tradition of eugenics and population control. The meanings and values associated with having children and abortion are often played out between a white, educated genetics counselor and a low-income black or Hispanic client against a historical background of distrust, control and unequal power" (Nsiah-Jefferson 1993, 121).

Breast Cancer and Uninsured Women

Breast cancer "causes the loss of more years of potential life among women under 65 years of age than any other nontraumatic condition in the United States, yet it is curable if detected early" (Ayanian et al. 1993, 326). Ayanian and colleagues note that prior research indicates that uninsured women are less likely to receive cancer-screening services than are women with private insurance, that they are less likely to have their breast cancer adequately evaluated, and that they are less likely to have the cancer aggressively treated. In light of these facts, the researchers wanted to know if women who have breast cancer and are uninsured or who are covered by Medicaid are found to have a more advanced cancer than the privately insured. In addition, the researchers wanted to know if these uninsured and publicly insured women die sooner than the privately insured.

They found that uninsured women and those insured by Medicaid did have significantly more-advanced breast cancer at first diagnosis compared to those who were privately insured. They found, for example, that 7.3 percent of privately insured women had the most advanced stage of breast cancer, whereas 12.3 percent of the uninsured and 17.4 percent of those covered by Medicaid had the most advanced stage of cancer at initial diagnosis. The relationship was nearly as strong even when controlling for age. The investigators also found that uninsured women and those covered by Medicaid were significantly less likely than the privately insured to survive the period fifty-four to eighty-nine months after initial diagnosis for all stages of the disease except the most severe. After adjusting for age, race, stage at diagnosis, and household income, the researchers found that uninsured women and those on Medicare were between 40 and 89 percent more likely to die in the 7.5 years after initial diagnosis than those privately insured.

The authors suggest that reduced access to health care may explain why uninsured and publicly insured women are initially diagnosed with more serious breast cancers than the privately insured. They also note that inadequate evaluation of the cancers may lead to inadequate therapy, and differences in treatment may account for the differences in survival rates. Importantly, the authors note that "the comparable outcomes of uninsured patients and patients covered by Medicaid suggest that Medicaid coverage alone—without efforts to enhance primary care and screening—may be insufficient to improve outcomes for poor women with breast cancer" (Ayanian et al. 1993, 330).

Summary and Discussion

Real access to quality health care goes far beyond the mere passage of a law establishing, for example, a funding mechanism for qualified applicants. Those who are most in need of access to health care are frequently those who have a whole series of hurdles to clear before access can actually be attained. African-Americans have a long, well-documented history of overt discrimination blocking access to quality health care facilities. African-American health care providers were refused entrance to medical schools, membership in local medical societies, and privileges at hospitals. The legal basis for this kind of overt discrimination was largely defeated in the civil rights struggles of the 1960s. Nevertheless, there is a wealth of evidence indicating or implying that there is still massive discrimination against African-Americans in terms of access to any health care and in terms of access to the same quality of health care received by whites. Hispanics appear to suffer many of the same obstacles to access to quality health care as do African-Americans. Low-income Hispanics, and migrant agricultural workers in particular, are plagued by the double impact of extremely hazardous working and living conditions combined with severely limited access to health care.

The private health insurance industry in the United States produces tens of millions of uninsured children and adults. They are deprived of private health insurance for a wide variety of reasons—most relating to how the industry maximizes profits and minimizes financial risks. The high cost of private insurance precludes many smaller businesses from offering any health insurance whatsoever to employees, and those that do may charge the employee so much that her or she cannot take advantage of it. Larger businesses have the option of self-insuring, but without state regulation their health insurance plans may be substandard and inadequate. Those who apply for individual health insurance policies face extremely high premiums if accepted; however, those most in need of health care are weeded out by insurers by the process of "medical underwriting." Nationwide institutional discrimination by the health insurance industry is evidenced by much lower levels of coverage of minorities and single female heads of households. Long-term-care insurance is too expensive for most of those who may need it and has a unique history of blocking access to long-term-care facilities by misrepresentation and outright fraud.

Systematic discrimination against minority women seeking or attaining access to health care has been amply documented. The barriers range from cost and transportation problems to cultural insensitivity and inferior health care. Distrust by young minority women is heightened by a history of racist population control policies influencing family planning services.

References

Angier, Natalie. 1990. "Study Finds Uninsured Receive Less Hospital Care." *New York Times* (September 12):A1, A28.

Ansberry, Clare. 1988. "Dumping the Poor." *Wall Street Journal* (November 29):A1, A11.

Ayanian, John Z., Betsy A. Kohler, Toshi Abe, and Arnold M. Epstein. 1993. "The Relation Between Health Insurance Coverage and Clinical Outcomes Among Women with Breast Cancer." *The New England Journal of Medicine* 329(5):326–31.

Bergner, Lawrence. 1993 "Race, Health, and Health Services." *American Journal of Public Health* 83(7):939–41.

Byrd, Robert. 1992. "Fewer U.S. Babies Dying, but Twenty-Three Nations Do Better." *Anchorage Daily News* (Associated Press) (February 7):A1.

Cartwright, Peter S., F. Joseph McLaughlin, Alfonso M. Martinez, Dorothy E. Caul, Indira G. Hogan, George W. Reed, and Michael S. Swafford. 1993. "Teenagers' Perceptions of Barriers to Prenatal Care." *Southern Medical Journal* 86(7):737–41.

"Census Heightens National Health Insurance Issue." 1991. *Nation's Health* May-June.

Cornelius, Llewellyn J. 1993. "Ethnic Minorities and Access to Medical Care: Where Do They Stand?" *Journal of the Association for Academic Minority Physicians* 4(1):16–25.

Council on Ethical and Judicial Affairs, AMA. 1990. "Black-White Disparities in Health Care." *Journal of the American Medical Association* 263(17):2344–46.

Ginzberg, Eli. 1991. "Access to Health Care for Hispanics." *Journal of the American Medical Association* 265(2):238–41.

Health Insurance Coverage in the U.S. 1989. U.S. Public Health Service. National Center for Health Services Research. National Medical Expenditure Survey. Washington, D.C.: USGPO.

Lillie-Blanton, Marsha, Rose Marie Martinez, Andrea Kidd Taylor, and Betty Garman Robinson. 1993. "Latina and African American Women: Continuing Disparities in Health." *International Journal of Health Services* 23(3):555–84.

McBride, David. 1993. "Black America: From Community Health Care to Crisis Medicine." *Journal of Health Politics, Policy, and Law* 18(2):319–37.

McKenzie, Nancy F. 1994. "The Real Health Care Crisis." *The Nation* (February 28):266–68.

Nazario, Sonia L. 1988. "Life and Death: High Infant Mortality Is a Persistent Blotch on Health Care in U.S." *Wall Street Journal* (October 19):A1, A16.

New York State Advisory Committee to the United States Commission on Civil Rights. 1964. *Report on the Buffalo Health Facilities.* Washington, D.C.: U.S. Civil Rights Commission.

Nsiah-Jefferson, Laurie. 1993. "Access to Reproductive Genetic Services for Low-Income Women and Women of Color." *Fetal Diagnosis and Therapy* 8(Suppl. 1):107–27.

Office of Technology Assessment. 1993. *The U.S. Ranks Low Internationally on Most Health Indicators*. Report brief. November.

"Report Cites Racial Discrepancies in Medical Care." 1990. *New York Times* (May 2):A1, A21.

Short, P., A. Monheit, and K. Beauregard. 1989. *A Profile of Uninsured Americans*. National Medical Expenditure Survey Research Findings 1, National Center for Health Services Research and Health Care Technology Assessment. Rockville, Md.: Public Health Service.

Smith, David B. 1990. "Population Ecology and the Racial Integration of Hospitals and Nursing Homes in the United States." *The Milbank Quarterly* 68(4):561–96.

Sullivan, Louis W. 1991. "Effects of Discrimination and Racism on Access to Health Care." *Journal of the American Medical Association* 266(19):2574.

Taravella, Steve. 1990. "Black Hospitals: Struggling to Survive." *Washington Post* (September 11):WH12, 13, 14.

U.S. Congress, Joint Economic Committee. 1989. Subcommittee on Education and Health. *Medical Alert*. Staff Report Summarizing the Hearings on "The Future of Health Care in America." 101st Cong., 1st sess.

U.S. General Accounting Office. 1993. *Long-Term Care Insurance: High Percentage of Policyholders Drop Policies*. Report to the Chairman, Subcommittee on Regulation, Business Opportunities, and Technology, Committee on Small Business, House of Representatives. August.

3

Physicians

Physicians are in turmoil. Their historical control of medicine is increasingly being challenged by outside forces, including government regulation, giant health insurance corporations, and salary-paying HMOs. Their practice of medicine is questioned by utilization-review companies, and their investments are scrutinized by state and federal regulators. The former hegemony of their principal professional organization, the AMA, has been shattered by loss of membership, internal dissension, and the creation of dozens of competing professional organizations. Pesky researchers question the ethics, cost, and efficacy of self-referral; point out the deficiencies of the traditional fee-for-service form of reimbursement; and uncover nepotism, sexism, and racism in medical schools. Other researchers focus on the widespread incidence of medical malpractice and the fundamental limitations of traditional tort reform legislation.

However, it is not just physicians who are in turmoil but the entire health care system in the United States. Physicians are being swept up in massive political-economic and social changes sweeping across the country. Ironically, the current state of health care in the United States in large part has stemmed from the historical ability of physicians to control the autonomy of their profession and to minimize outside regulation over it. This very control, serving their interests while largely ignoring the emerging consequences, has resulted in social repercussions that are now shaking up and transforming the profession. These social forces have been joined by others emanating from the highest levels of corporate America; together, these forces are irrevocably transforming health care for physicians, for all other health care providers, and for all of us who will need health care in our life times. Ultimately, the critical question that we as health care consumers must address is "transformation for the benefit of whom?"

The American Medical Association

Perhaps thirty-five years ago the AMA was a monolithic politically active trade organization at the apex of its power. In those days, the AMA represented 70 percent of all U.S. physicians. Joseph A. Califano, Jr., domestic-affairs assistant to President Lyndon Johnson in the late 1960s, has been quoted as saying, "We could shake hands with the AMA, and we had a deal with doctors" (Galen and McNamee 1993, 70). To be sure, the AMA is still a political force to be reckoned with; but its base has been growing narrower, and it is no longer monolithic. Today fewer than 42 percent of all U.S. physicians are members of the AMA.

There are a number of reasons why the association's constituency has eroded (Galen and Mike McNamee 1993). Rapidly escalating membership fees may have influenced declining membership. The AMA's image as a male-dominated, politically conservative organization has certainly driven away some potential members. Most importantly, however is the proliferation of dozens of other national medical specialty societies, some of which have tens of thousands of members. The AMA is an umbrella organization that has been less and less able to represent emerging divergent interests of physicians as a national group. Splits occur within AMA when, for example, Medicare proposes to raise reimbursement rates for certain types of physicians while lowering them for others. Another point of cleavage is that the AMA tends to represent the interests of physician-entrepreneurs whereas other physician's professional organizations are more likely to represent the interests of physicians on salary and physicians who do not engage in extensive entrepreneurial activities. A few of these organizations include the American College of Physicians, the American Society for Internal Medicine, Physicians for a National Health Program, and Physician's Forum.

The Politics of Free Enterprise

Without question, the AMA has been the premier political organization of the health care industry for much of the twentieth century. As a professional organization, the principle role of the AMA has been as defender of physician autonomy to maximize income. Not surprisingly, with minor exceptions the AMA has consistently fought all proposed U.S. legislation for single-payer and national health insurance systems in the twentieth century.

During the first couple of decades of the twentieth century the American Association for Labour Legislation (AALL) promoted state workers' compensation laws and national and state-based health plans based on the English and German models. As a social movement and a political force, the AALL was seriously stunted, during its existence, by a rather narrow professional constituency. However, during the 1912–1918 period in particular, the AALL and an AMA committee worked closely together developing progressive health care proposals for states to adopt. Catching itself before siding irrevocably against its own interests, the AMA then turned around to help defeat AALL health care reform legislation in fifteen states that sought to adopt it (Smith 1990, 488).

During the depths of the depression, AMA political arm-twisting forced President Franklin D. Roosevelt to cut health care from New Deal social programs. In the latter part of the 1930s President Roosevelt actively promoted a national health plan similar to the Medicaid program enacted in 1965. The AMA, along with the state medical societies, saw to it that the so-called Wagner Bill never came to a vote. During the next couple of decades the executive branch pushed various versions of national health insurance programs, frightening the AMA into decisive action by the time of the 1950 elections. In a precedent-setting $1.3 million campaign (the equivalent of $7.1 million in 1993 dollars), the AMA went after several senators who supported national health insurance, contributing to the defeat of at least three of them. Then-president Harry Truman's program for national health insurance was labeled a "Communist plot" by the AMA. In accordance with this ideological theme, association members sent letters of protest to the president on pink paper (Smith 1990, 489; Kemper and Novak 1993, 73).

In the late 1950s, when it became clear to the AMA that national health insurance proposals were popping up again and again, the organization seriously began to explore the formation of a political action committee (PAC). By 1960 the AMA was still equivocating and had not formed its own PAC, but that year it did spend $7,500 for a series of regional seminars to acquaint physicians with the power of local PACs (Smith 1990, 490). The AMA stopped equivocating with the 1961 election of President John F. Kennedy, who was widely known as a champion of fundamental health care reform: "Calling [Medicare] 'socialized medicine,' the AMA enlisted a Hollywood actor named Ronald Reagan to help block the program on Capitol Hill. 'If you and I don't stop Medicare,' Reagan warned on a phonograph record the AMA sent to doctors' wives, 'we'll spend our sunset years telling our children and children's children what it was like in America when men were free" (Kemper and Novak 1993, 73).

The AMA formed the American Medical Association Political Action Committee (AMPAC) the year that Kennedy was elected. "In 1961, AMPAC had 13,416 members; this had increased to 126,220 by 1974" (Smith 1990, 490). The goal of AMPAC was to support a strong, conservative bipartisan coalition in Congress, a coalition that would represent the interests of AMA members.

In less than one and one-half years, AMPAC had organized PACs in forty-five states, and by the late 1970s it was heavily involved in over 220 congressional races every two years (Smith 1990, 490). In recent years AMPAC has become a phenomenally successful PAC, funneling huge amounts of money to "their" legislators and funneling substantial amounts of money to legislators who do not toe the AMA line just to keep channels open. A revealing study by the consumer-oriented Common Cause organization details AMPAC expenditures from 1981 through mid-1991:

> [AMPAC] contributed $11,944,307 to congressional candidates during the period. The AMA PAC, which includes contributions from a number of state affiliates, also is one of the largest PACs overall.
>
> The AMA contributed to nearly every current Member of Congress—86 Senators and 401 Representatives—during the period. (Common Cause 1992, 627–28)

The Kusserow Letter. Funneling millions of dollars of PAC money to influence legislators is but one means in a sizable arsenal of weapons used by the AMA to influence public policy. There is, for example, the direct approach. In an unusually blunt maneuver, in 1990 the AMA wrote a letter to then-president George Bush requesting him to fire Richard P. Kusserow, inspector general in the Department of Health and Human Services (HHS)("Inspector General Under Fire" 1991). Kusserow was not an inconsequential government bureaucrat. At the time he had a staff of 1,400 and a budget of $90 million. His job was to go after fraud, abuse, and waste in HHS programs like Social Security, Medicare, and Medicaid. Moreover, he was good at it. According to the AMA, "Competent and honest physicians have been damaged, and many more have been unnecessarily harassed" ("Inspector General Under Fire 1991" 7). In any case, Kusserow was still at the helm of the Inspector General's Office the following year.

The Canada Campaign. Perhaps the greatest threat imaginable to the AMA on the health care reform horizon is the prospect of a Canadian-style single-payer health care program for the United States. In such a system, hundreds of private health insurance companies would disappear, to be replaced by a public "single payer," that is, one public agency that insures all residents and reimburses health care providers. The providers themselves would remain predominantly in the private sector just as they are today. What really worries the AMA is the prospect of a single purchaser of physician services. In a monopsony (a market situation with one buyer and many sellers), the government as the only buyer of physician services could wield a very big stick to keep reimbursements low, ultimately curbing provider profits and incomes.

In any case, responding to the threat of publicly financed health care for everyone, the AMA initiated a major anti–Canadian health care blitz late in 1989. The first stage involved repeated mailings to nearly 300,000 association members requesting "contributions of $200 (or more) payable to AMA." The predominant theme of the mailing was "Unless you want to risk rationing, income caps, reduction of your autonomy, and other burdens of a Canadian-type experience very soon, please help us" (quoted in Haiven 1991, 52–53). The total raised during this campaign has not been publicly divulged, but it must have been sizable because it was enough to launch the second stage of the campaign to discredit the Canadian health care system.

AMA-financed full-page advertisements vilifying the Canadian health care system blossomed in the pages of the "*New York Times, Washington Post, Wall Street Journal, U.S. News & World Report, Time,* and *Newsweek*" (Haiven 1991, 53). These ads presented distortions and half-truths about health care in Canada, comparing it in some respects to health care in "Third World" countries. Even conservative legislators such as Republican congressman Bill Gradison, a member of the House Budget Subcommittee on Health, had to admit that the anti-Canada campaign was "misleading." The anti-Canada campaign backfired. By February 1990 the AMA had officially pulled the plug on the ads.

The Ethics of Free Enterprise

The AMA is primarily a trade organization. As such, it has used the concept of "professional ethics" to promote its members' reputation as caring and responsible practitioners. For example, the concept is used to put vulnerable, dependent patients at ease. Sick people are encouraged to trust a physician's decision on the grounds that physicians are professionals with a code of ethics. In the face of the fact that a fee-for-service reimbursement system offers financial incentive for overtreatment, the professional code of ethics is presented as the guarantee that despite this financial conflict of interest the patient will not be exploited or abused. In addition the code of ethics acts as a shield to fend off outside monitoring and regulation of activities in the professional setting. Why, for example, would federal or state regulations be necessary to protect patients against physician conflicts of interest if a code of professional ethics is in place? These are some of the ideological uses of professional ethics. Historically, however, the concept of professional ethics has yielded easily to the invisible hand of the marketplace:

> Between the 1890s and the 1950s the AMA first ignored fee splitting [kickbacks to referring physicians] and other questionable commercial practices, then denounced them, but was never able effectively to enforce its policies. From mid-century until 1991, as new, more extensive and sophisticated commercial practices emerged, the organization's public stance weakened, its guidelines were chipped away, and the few clear prohibitions in its codes were abandoned in

favor of subjective standards. The AMA revised its ethical codes to allow practices previously forbidden. (Rodwin 1992, 704)

Studies by the American College of Surgeons and congressional investigations continued to find substantial evidence of various kickback schemes
throughout the 1950s and 1960s and into the early 1970s. The entrance of
the federal government into health care via Medicare and Medicaid in 1966
gave government, for the first time, a good reason to be concerned about
the costs of fee splitting, secret commissions, and other kickback schemes.
This led to 1972 federal legislation prohibiting kickbacks in the Medicare
program, legislation that has since been strengthened several times by additional legislation in the 1970s and 1980s. Nevertheless, contemporary financial conflicts of interest continue to flourish (Rodwin 1992, 719, 724–25;
Relman 1992, 102, 105). Some of these include:

Hospital incentives: Hospitals rent spacious offices to physicians and
   provide other amenities next to or near the hospital. Office rent may
   be subsidized. Hospital kickbacks to the physician are not necessary
   since the hospital guarantees a steady stream of patients by using
   these strategies.
Self-referral: A physician may own an interest in a laboratory, a rehabilitation facility, an X-ray unit, or some other medical service or facility.
   The problem arises when the physician refers his or her patients to
   these facilities, particularly without informing the patient of the financial conflict of interest.
Corporate consultancy: A respected physician is hired as a "consultant"
   to a drug company, for example, to write articles or give lectures
   about the company's products. The physician's ability to independently evaluate the drugs is compromised.
Honoraria to attend presentations: Fancy dinners, sums of cash, or free
   airline transportation are given to physicians who will come to hear a
   presentation from a drug company.

During the 1980s, in the context of the Reagan administration's ideological reliance on free market competition, the AMA made significant changes
to stated policies:

The 1980 AMA Principles dropped the injunctions against fee splitting and
earning income outside of services performed. No mention was made of other
economic issues, such as dispensing drugs and appliances, ownership of pharmacies and other providers, or deriving income from patents. Today's principles
contain no statement on the issues that were a focus of the AMA ethical concerns for nearly 80 years. Antitrust law now prevents the AMA from restricting
advertising and certain other commercial practices. It does not require that the

AMA abandon all its ethical positions; nor does it prevent the AMA from developing comprehensive conflict-of-interest policies. (Rodwin 1992, 727)

In the late 1980s and early 1990s a number of studies emerged documenting the relationship between physician referrals and financial conflicts of interest. In addition a court decision involving the Medicare antikickback statute clarified the potential legal liability for physician self-referral in existing physician-owned enterprises. Partly in response to these social forces, at the end of 1991 the AMA passed a resolution cautioning that self-referral to physician-owned facilities was "presumptively inconsistent" with the physician's ethical obligation to patients. An important caveat was that self-referral was acceptable if, in the eyes of the referring physician, there were no acceptable alternatives. However, six months later the AMA reversed its position and passed another resolution unequivocally allowing physicians to make self-referrals if patients are informed of the physician's financial conflict of interest and of available alternatives. A few months later the AMA reversed its position again, supporting the 1991 statement. Certainly there is more to come from the fractious AMA on this issue (Rodwin 1992, 727–32; Swedlow et al. 1992, 1502; Wolfe 1993a, 7).

In any case, the AMA has no mechanism to enforce this policy. The AMA is a voluntary organization. Physicians can continue to practice medicine even if they violate AMA ethical principles and are sanctioned by the association. In practice, discipline for violations of AMA ethical principles is usually left up to state medical societies; however, it is extremely rare for a state board to discipline a physician merely for a violation of ethics (Rodwin 1992, 731).

Self-Referral

With the passage of Medicare and Medicaid in the mid-1960s, Congress became increasingly interested in containing the cost of health care. Excessive profiteering spawned by government funding of fee-for-service physician-entrepreneurs led to the first of several attempts to regulate the hemorrhage of Medicare cash. In 1972 Congress outlawed kickbacks from any kind of business reimbursed under Medicare or Medicaid. This and subsequent regulations became moot in the shadow of a giant loophole in the regulations: Self-referral was left virtually unregulated. Two decades of anecdotal data and research exposing the financial impact of self-referral on Medicare and Medicaid pitted Congress against the AMA and other health industry lobbyists with vested interests in the profits of self-referral. The dam broke toward the end of the 1980s. Even a Republican administration friendly to the AMA and other health care industry trade organizations could not ignore the budget busting impact of self-referral on Medicare and Medicaid.

The Inspector General's Findings

Richard Kusserow, inspector general of the HHS, had been doing his homework in the mid-1980s, and by 1989 he had a lot to show for it. He released a report that year indicating that Medicare spent an extra $28 million in 1987 to cover excessive lab tests ordered by physicians with investments in clinical laboratories (Hyman 1992, 325). The same year Kusserow testified at congressional hearings that physician-entrepreneurs who owned or invested in freestanding clinical laboratories ordered 45 percent more lab work for Medicare patients than did physicians with no such investments (Iglehart 1990, 1685). He researched the magnitude of the self-referral problem and found that 27 percent of freestanding physiological labs (that is, rehabilitation labs), 25 percent of freestanding clinical laboratories, and 8 percent of durable medical equipment suppliers nationwide were fully or partially owned by referring physician-entrepreneurs (Hudson 1990). Kusserow issued a "fraud alert on joint ventures," noting too that some investment relationships that do not involve self-referrals may also be illegal according to current federal law. Finally, to cap an extraordinarily active year, the inspector general announced late in 1989 "that SmithKline Beecham Clinical Laboratories had agreed to pay the federal government $1.5 million to settle an investigation into alleged kickbacks to physicians affiliated with the Hanlester Network [of clinical laboratories] in California. Kusserow's investigators alleged that more than 100 physicians were rewarded with thousands of dollars for referring Medicare and Medicaid patients to clinical laboratories in which they were limited partners" (Iglehart 1990, 1686).

At the very end of 1989 President Bush signed into law the Omnibus Budget Reconciliation Act. This legislation contained provisions prohibiting physician-entrepreneurs under most circumstances from referring Medicare patients to any clinical labs in which the physicians have investments or any other financial interests. The original proposed legislation authored by Representative Fortney H. (Pete) Stark, Democrat from California, was much broader: It would have banned Medicare referrals to most freestanding health care facilities in which a physician-entrepreneur had a financial interest, not just clinical labs. The broader proposal was defeated in committee by legislators heavily lobbied by the AMA and other "medical-industrial complex" vested interests. The resultant legislation, which became fully effective in 1992, was severely compromised (Iglehart 1990). By 1993, however, more data about the excesses associated with self-referral, together with the growing fiscal crunch in health care, prompted legislative proposals from both Democrats and Republicans to expand self-referral limitations to most kinds of medical services. Moreover, the proposed ban on self-referrals would pertain to all patients, not just to Medicare recipients (Abelson 1993, 43).

Fee-for-Service Versus Salary

Apart from investment income, physicians in the United States are typically reimbursed in one of three ways for the practice of hands-on medicine: Some have a fee-for-service practice in which they are paid for every medical procedure performed. Many, particularly those in public service, are reimbursed purely by salary, that is, by a fixed paycheck that does not vary according to medical decisions they make during the course of their practice. Others, the growing majority of physicians during this transitional time in history and notably those employed by private, corporate-owned HMOs, are typically reimbursed by some combination of salary, capitation, and various financial incentives. Capitation is a set amount of reimbursement based on the number of patients a physician sees, but the amount is not related to the quantity or type of medical procedures provided those patients. Under a pure capitation form of payment, additional income for the physician is dependent solely on seeing more patients. The purpose of additional financial incentives is to influence physician behavior to keep expensive medical procedures down and corporate profits up. In a manner of speaking, the less physicians do the more they are paid. The questions of principal concern are these: When a physician who is not strictly on salary makes a medical decision, has the medical integrity of that decision been compromised by concern for personal gain? If so, what are the individual and collective consequences?

Sometime around 1980 health care in the United States passed a historic benchmark. In or near that year, for the first time ever, more of the nation's physicians worked for a salary than on a fee-for-service basis (Orris 1982). This benchmark is important in the United States for at least two reasons: (1) The trend toward the salaried physician is an integral part of larger, fundamental changes occurring in the health care system, and (2) forms of physician compensation significantly influence cost and quality of health care.

The explosion of expensive medical technology led to the emerging focus of health care in the hospital and in the freestanding technology-based facility and to the concentration of ownership of health care systems by corporate enterprises. Together, these social processes have ousted the physician from traditional fee-for-service solo practice. Salaried physicians include residents, administrators, researchers, educators, and those who work for insurance companies or legal institutions. Many work in the public sector. By far the largest group of salaried physicians, however, are clinicians working in private and public positions. While the trend toward salaried physicians is quite clear, fee-for-service medicine will continue to be a powerful force for some time to come because of its prevalence and because the AMA is the premier political organization representing the interests of fee-for-service physicians.

Financial Incentives and the Salaried Corporate Physician

HMOs vary considerably in how they reimburse physicians (Hillman 1990). They may use one or any combination of fee-for-service, salary, or capitation. Most HMOs, however, mix in various financial incentives to influence physician behavior in order to maximize corporate goals. For example, about two-thirds of all HMOs set aside a portion of the basic salary or capitation payment received by a physician. Physicians as a group who exceed their budgeted amount for expensive referrals or hospital services lose the withheld portion of their income. Those who together meet corporate goals to minimize referrals and the use of hospital services receive all withheld amounts and perhaps a bonus payment as well. About 18 percent of HMOs hold physicians personally accountable when their own patients, versus the collective patients of a group of HMO doctors, exceed the budgeted amount. In this case, over-budget physicians lose the withheld cash while under-budget physicians in the same clinic get the cash plus a bonus.

About 30 percent of HMOs use financial incentives that place even greater financial risk on the physician than simply withholding a portion of income. A common strategy is to place a lien on future income of physicians who have exceeded corporate goals for referrals and use of hospital services. Approximately 40 percent of the capitated primary care physicians employed by HMOs are required to pay for outpatient laboratory tests from their capitation payments. This particularly draconian scheme reduces the physician's income by $100 for every $100 spent on lab tests for his or her patients. Congress, the GAO, and other agencies have expressed concern about quality of care under physician behavior modification schemes like this which put individual physician incomes at risk. Curiously, neither Congress nor any federal agencies have ever investigated the traditional fee-for-service means of payment on the basis of similar concerns (Hillman 1990).

Financial Incentives and Fee-for-Service Physicians

Fee-for-service physicians have a wide array of means at their disposal to increase income (Novack 1991). One method is to simply raise fees. Another is to perform additional or more high-tech and therefore more expensive medical procedures such as lab tests, diagnostic imaging, and surgery. Diagnostic tests are profitable when the physician has the testing equipment in his or her office or when the physician refers patients to outside facilities owned by the physician. Billing upgrades increase income by billing for a more time-consuming office visit than actually occurred. For example, "brief" visits billed to Medicare between 1985 and 1988 fell 8 percent a year, but during the same period of time "extended" office visits increased 13 percent per year. In the same manner, minor surgery may be fraudulently billed as more complex surgery. These kinds of strategies inflate physicians' bills by up to 20 percent, but fee-for-service physicians can maintain very good incomes without padding their bills. As an example, Medicare pays about $1,500 for cataract surgery that takes as little as twelve minutes to perform. Private insurers and those paying with cash for cataract surgery typically pay even more.

The Consequences of Financial Incentives

A comparison of medical treatment by salaried or capitated HMO physicians, on the one hand, with medical treatment by fee-for-service physician-entrepreneurs, on the other, generally yields the expected results: HMO physicians provide less medically intense treatment for both outpatient and inpatient care. A major study comparing HMO and fee-for-service treatment found that HMO patients were hospitalized 40 percent less often than a comparable fee-for-service group of patients. Moreover, the proportion of inappropriate hospitalizations was lower among the HMO group than among the fee-for-service group. Despite the differences in medical treatment, the medical outcomes of the two groups were similar (Franks, Clancy, and Nutting 1992, 425). Another classic study compared rates of surgery by British surgeons, typically on salary or capitation, with American fee-for-service surgeons. The study found the per capita rates of surgery in England were nearly half those in the United States (Bromberg and Price 1990, 131).

Research indicates that common excessive medical treatments encouraged by fee-for-service physicians include major procedures such as cesarean sections, heart surgery, and hysterectomies as well as diagnostic imaging and lab tests of all kinds. Adverse consequences of the vast amount of unnecessary medical treatment arising from fee-for-service treatment include increased costs and risks to health. Annual costs for excessive treatment are measured in the scores of billions, and perhaps in the hundreds of billions, of dollars. The risks to health of excessive treatment requiring hospitalization is that approximately 370 of every 10,000 hospitalizations result in adverse medical consequences, including additional hospitalization, temporary or permanent disability, or death (Brennan et al. 1991; Saks 1993, 9).

The evidence overwhelmingly indicates that Americans pay an enormous price to maintain the tradition of a large fee-for-service health care sector.

Medical Malpractice

Medical malpractice is the negligent treatment of patients by health care providers, including physicians. Negligent health care providers may be drunk, drug impaired, incompetent, or otherwise unable to exercise adequate judgment or skill in the treatment of patients. The consequences of physician negligence range from no effect to full, permanent disability or death. From a public health perspective, the key issues involve the negligence of the physician and the consequences for the patient: In other words, what social structures or processes detect and deter medically negligent physicians from harming their patients and what structures act as obstacles to the detection and deterrence of negligent physicians? What patients are at risk as victims of malpractice, and what are the consequences for those patients?

The media image of medical malpractice has been predominantly formed and conditioned not by the public health perception of malpractice but, rather, by the institutions involved with the financial consequences of medical malpractice, primarily the private insurance industry and physicians through their professional organizations. As a result, medical malpractice is commonly discussed in the context of reducing the high cost of malpractice insurance premiums and implementing tort reform rather than gaining effective control of negligent physicians and reducing the toll they take in medical injury and human suffering.

Public health institutions in both the private and public sectors are starved for resources and have minimum access to the powerful media machines that churn out public opinion. On the other hand, the $1.8 trillion insurance industry (Weiss 1992, 17) and the AMA engage legions of public relations flacks, hundreds of lobbyists, and scores of millions of dollars each year to influence the media and public opinion. This uneven access to the media during the last couple of decades has resulted in a highly skewed public perception of the various issues related to medical negligence and malpractice. As a result, the public discussion has been heavily weighted by vested interests wielding ideological arguments.

Magnitude of the Medical Negligence Problem

The Harvard Medical Practice Study (Hiatt et al. 1989) selected a random sample of approximately 31,000 records from fifty-one hospitals in the state of New York in the year 1984. Teams of physicians evaluated these records

TABLE 3.1   Negligent Injury and Resulting Litigation (per 10,000 hospital patients)

9,630	will experience no adverse events, and
370	will suffer adverse events, but
270	of those will be without negligence. Of the
100	negligent adverse events, in
98	no claims for compensation will be made. Of the
2	claims made, only
1	will receive any compensation

Source: Based on findings of the Harvard Medical Practice Study, reported in Saks, Michael J. 1993. "Malpractice Misconceptions and Other Lessons About the Litigation System." *The Justice System Journal* 16(2):9

to uncover injuries caused by medical negligence, that is, "the failure to meet standards reasonably expected of the average physician, other provider, or institution" (Hiatt et al. 1989, 481).

The Harvard study revealed a medical negligence rate of 10 in every 1,000 hospitalizations. The injuries included in the study were at least serious enough to result in a longer hospital stay, disability upon discharge, or death. Further, projecting their findings to the entire state of New York in the year of the study, the researchers estimated over 27,000 serious injuries due to medical negligence among 2.6 million patients discharged from acute care hospitals. These projected injuries included nearly 7,000 deaths and almost 900 cases of permanent and total disability. Table 3.1 summarizes the relationship between adverse events (injuries or illnesses caused by medical intervention) not resulting from negligence, adverse events resulting from negligence, and the resulting litigation.

People sixty-five years of age and older were particularly likely to be victims of medical negligence regardless of the severity of their initial illness (Brennan et al. 1991, 373), indicating a greater propensity among the elderly to be treated by substandard medical practitioners. In addition, "there was more negligence among the Medicaid patients than the privately insured, and much, much more among the uninsured" (Hiatt 1992, 258). In other words, there is an inverse relationship between wealth and negligent medical treatment.

While a California study (Danzon 1985) found that an estimated 90 percent of those injured by medical negligence never filed a claim, the Harvard Medical Practice Study found that more than 98 percent of all the injuries caused by medical negligence were not followed by a malpractice claim (Localio et al. 1991). In summary the investigators observed that "the civil-justice system only infrequently compensates injured patients and rarely identifies and holds health care providers accountable for substandard medical care.

....The abandonment of malpractice litigation is unlikely unless credible systems and procedures, supported by the public, are instituted to guarantee professional accountability to patients" (Localio et al. 1991, 250).

Detection and Deterrence

There is an extensive array of institutional structures across the nation with the nominal purpose of deterring, limiting, or terminating the practices of negligent physicians. Nevertheless, nationwide projections based on the Harvard Medical Practice Study (Brennan et al. 1991) as well as other studies (Wolfe 1992) indicate that physicians cause 100,000 to 300,000 serious injuries and deaths every year from medical negligence. Clearly these facts put in serious question the actual effectiveness of existing institutional safeguards.

Hospital Peer-Review Committees. The members of hospital peer-review committees have the benefit of knowing the professional strengths and weaknesses of the physicians with whom they share hospital privileges. The intimacy of the hospital setting, however, makes effective self-regulation among friends and colleagues unlikely. The threat of suits against individuals sitting on the peer-review committees adds to the obstacles inhibiting effective detection and deterrence of negligent physicians by these committees (Schwartz and Mendelson 1989, 1342). In 1991, for example, American hospitals sanctioned only 750 physicians with restrictions lasting longer than one month (Wolfe 1992, 1). This is the equivalent of 1.25 such sanctions for each 1,000 physicians. Contrast this rate with the rate at which physician-owned malpractice insurance companies terminated insurance because of medical negligence: 6.6 terminations per 1,000 physicians (Schwartz and Mendelson 1989, 1345). In the latter case physicians are personally liable for a colleague's malpractice; in the former case they are not.

State Licensing Boards. At the state level, licensing boards have the authority to investigate and discipline physicians for medical negligence as well as for other problems relating to their practice of medicine. A maximum of 5 per 1,000 physicians nationally have been disciplined by state boards in any recent year, and the figure is a fraction of that for serious disciplinary actions such as license revocation or suspension. Moreover, only about 12 percent of all disciplinary actions actually relate to medical negligence. The rest have to do with criminal behavior, overprescribing drugs, ethics issues, and so on. The most aggressive states discipline about 10 physicians per 1,000 annually, and the most reticent discipline about 1 per 1,000. In 1991 state medical boards disciplined only 3,034 physicians, whereas in that same year an estimated 150,000 to 300,000 serious injuries or deaths occurred due to physician negligence in hospitals. These figures do not include estimates of medical negligence that occur in physicians' office settings outside the hospital (Wolfe 1993b).

Apart from the regularly occurring problem of friends and colleagues being reluctant to enforce sanctions against each other, most of these boards face a number of additional obstacles. One very difficult one is the standard of proof state boards are required to use to identify and manage negligent physicians. "Clear and convincing evidence" must be produced rather than the less-stringent "preponderance of evidence" that is typically used in other settings such as state courts (Schwartz and Mendelson 1989, 1345). Another serious obstacle is the widespread shortage of investigators and of resources necessary for boards to effectively conduct investigations. As a result of these shortages, boards often have backlogs of hundreds of cases. A third obstacle is that state boards generally do not have extensive peer-review capabilities, inhibiting the quantity and quality of information received during an investigation. Finally, cases in which an accused physician fully contests state licensing board charges typically drag on six to eight years. The physician may remain in practice that entire time. One public interest lawyer wryly noted that "this system is so slow, so meager, and so trivial that death is weeding out incompetent physicians much faster than is the board" (quoted in Chesteen and Lally 1991, 37).

Physician-Owned Insurance Companies. Approximately 40 percent of all physicians in patient care are insured against medical negligence claims through physician-owned insurance companies (Schwartz and Mendelson 1989). Unlike the physicians covered by the alternative of commercial insurance and unlike the members of either state licensing boards or hospital peer-review committees, members of physician-owned insurance companies are personally liable for claims made against any of their co-owners. As a result of this financial accountability, applicants to physician-owned insurance companies are often carefully screened for competence by a committee of members prior to admission. Once admitted, members who have had claims for malpractice filed against them may be rigorously evaluated by peers, outside consultants, and underwriters.

Sanctions against negligent physicians may include additional surcharges on their insurance premiums, deductibles in the event of successful claims, restrictions on practice, the requirement of additional training, or the termination of insurance. In about a third of the cases, however, the last sanction takes the form of a resignation from part ownership in the insurance company (and therefore termination of coverage) under pressure from the insurance company. Schwartz and Mendelson (1989, 1345) estimate that in 1985 state boards suspended or revoked the licenses of about 0.08 percent of all practicing physicians, less than one per 1,000, because of incompetence or negligence. During the same year physician-owned insurance companies terminated coverage for 6.6 per 1,000 member physicians due to medical negligence. In other words, the maximum sanction was applied by the physician-owned insurance companies more than eight times as frequently than the maximum sanction applied by state boards.

Certainly it can be argued that since suspension of license is considerably more serious than loss of insurance, the penalties are not comparable. However, lesser sanctions for negligence were levied by the physician-owned insurance companies about thirteen times as frequently as lesser sanctions applied by the boards. There is a strong suggestion in these research findings that structurally the physician-owned insurance companies, characterized by personal financial liability, are far more effective at weeding out negligent physicians than are the state licensing boards.

The occasional revocation of a physician's license by the state board due to negligence, the board's ultimate sanction, may effectively prevent a physician from endangering the people of a particular state. However, that same negligent physician is free to start a practice in another state, whose licensing board may be entirely unaware of the physician's history of incompetence. Physician-owned insurance companies administer their ultimate sanction, termination of insurance, far more frequently than boards revoke or suspend licenses; however, the social result is the protection of member-physicians' finances rather than protection of the public's health. The sanctioned physician is relatively free to continue his or her flawed practice of medicine with commercial insurance or without insurance coverage at all. In addition, he or she may be accepted to practice in the military or in a state or municipal hospital.

National Practitioner Data Bank.   In the fall of 1990 the Department of Health and Human Services initiated the National Practitioner Data Bank. The nominal purpose of this data bank is to collect and disseminate information about medical malpractice payments and a range of adverse professional actions involving physicians and other health care practitioners:

> This system . . . was created to help meet a national need to restrict the ability of incompetent practitioners to move from state to state without disclosure or discovery of the practitioner's previous damaging or incompetent performance. The data bank contains information on adverse actions taken against a practitioner's license, clinical privileges, and professional society memberships, as well as information on malpractice payments resulting from judgements or settlements. (U.S. General Accounting Office 1992b, 2)

Unfortunately, the political compromises made during the formation of the data bank legislation have seriously inhibited the use of this information to protect the public's health. Congress refuses to allow disclosure to consumers of any information that might reveal the identity of an individual practitioner. The only organizations allowed to obtain this information are hospitals and other health care entities, professional societies, state licensing boards, and individual practitioners. Of these, only hospitals are actually re-quired to query the data bank when hiring, granting clinical privileges, or evaluating physicians. Despite the stated major purpose of the data bank, state licensing boards are not required to evaluate data bank information prior to granting new licenses. A 1993 study by the GAO found that the data bank's effectiveness is further hampered by long delays in providing re-quested information, lax security regarding sensitive information, inadequate federal monitoring of the data bank contractor, and poor planning for the data bank's future (U.S. General Accounting Office 1993).

Verifying Physicians' Credentials. There is no single, public source for in-formation about physicians who have been disciplined because they were drug impaired, incompetent, negligent, unethical, or engaged in criminal behavior. Most state medical societies will release a list of names of physi-cians that they have disciplined, but that list will not contain the names of physicians who have been disciplined by a myriad of federal agencies, other state medical boards, hospital peer-review boards, or a number of other insti-tutions. The closest thing to such a list that may be as accessible as the local library is a book updated every couple of years under the title Questionable Doctors (Van Tunen 1991), produced by the Public Citizen Health Re-search Group, a consumer advocacy Ralph Nader spin-off group. This publi-cation lists in one source physicians who have been disciplined by several federal agencies and most state medical societies.

Although it is almost impossible to find out if a particular physician has been disciplined by all of the institutions that potentially might do so, it is even more difficult for a person seeking health care to verify that a physician has the training and experience that he or she claims. A study conducted by Julia Reade and Richard Ratzan (1989) led to the conclusion that "obtain-ing access to complete, up-to-date, and verified information about physi-cians is all but impossible" (1989, 468).

Sleep-Deprived Medical Residents. Residents are recently graduated med-ical students who are doing one to four years of additional clinical training, usually on the house staff of a hospital. Residents are terribly exploited, working 100 to 120 hours per week or more and often working up to thirty-six hours straight with no more sleep than a quick nap (U.S. General Ac-counting Office 1992a). A substantial body of research dating back to the early 1970s supports the commonsense assumption that fatigued residents are probably more prone to medical negligence than well-rested physicians.

The Accreditation Council for Graduate Medical Education (ACGME) accredits the nearly 7,000 residency programs across the United States. For several years during the late 1980s, the ACGME, the AMA, and the AAMC worked together to develop accreditation standards that would limit the ex-cessive hours typically worked by medical residents. These efforts were opposed by the American Boards of Medical Specialities (ABMS), in particular the six surgical specialty areas of the twenty-four medical specialities in the ACGME. Only one of these six surgical specialities restricted the maximum number of hours a resident could work per week, only one of them limited the number of days per week a resident had on-call duty, and only one of them required a minimum of one day per week off (U.S. General Accounting Office 1992a, 45). The surgical specialities wanted virtually no restrictions on their exploitation of medical residents.

Nevertheless, as a compromise the ACGME finally adopted the following policy statement at the end of 1991: "It is desirable that residents' work schedules be designed so that on the average, excluding exceptional patient care needs, residents have at least one day out of seven free of routine responsibilities and be on-call in the hospital no more often than every third night" (U.S. General Accounting Office 1992a, 3).

This sounds like a mushy equivocating statement because it is. Under these guidelines, residents can still work ninety-six hours or more per week. The guidelines are the compromised remnants of a more meaningful policy opposed by the surgical specialities of the ACGME, the American Board of Surgeons, and the American College of Surgeons. Surgeons objected to any ACGME regulations on the basis that "such limits interfere with the development of the resident's sense of commitment to the patient and impede the continuity of care necessary for patient safety" (U.S. General Accounting Office 1992a, 3). Apparently severe fatigue and stress, and the resultant increased risk of medical negligence, was not thought to interfere with "patient safety."

New York State is the only state that attempts to regulate the number of hours residents work. The impetus for this regulation arose from a 1986 New York grand jury investigation of the suspicious death of a teenager admitted to New York Hospital who was treated by two overworked and undersupervised residents. New York limits residents to eighty hours work per week, averaged over a four-week period. The state also requires one full day off each week, a minimum of eight hours off between scheduled on-duty assignments, and a specific level of supervision. The additional personnel required to replace the medical residents now limited to "only" eighty hours per week cost the hospitals of the State of New York an estimated $227 million the first year. This cost projection, along with others, indicates how significant the exploitation of cheap, abundant medical resident labor is to the current practice of hospital-based health care nationwide (U.S. General Accounting Office 1992a, 32–36).

Summary and Discussion

Other than having similar training, physicians are not a homogeneous group. Source and form of income differentiate physicians in some very important ways. The growing majority of physicians are compensated primarily by salary, although a large but shrinking minority practice on a fee-for-service basis. This distinction is crucial because the evidence indicates that fee-for-service physicians tend to run up far greater costs than their salaried colleagues and tend to conduct a much larger number of unnecessary and inappropriate medical procedures, with possible adverse consequences for their patients and for the practice of medicine in general.

Physicians are also distinguished by their financial relationship with facilities to which they refer patients. In Florida 40 percent of all practicing physicians have investments in such facilities. Although there is no definitive research on the question, one may estimate that nationally perhaps 10 to 20 percent of all physicians self-refer; however, this way of describing the situation blurs a very important distinction. Generally speaking, physicians on salary cannot and therefore do not self-refer. In other words, a resident in a hospital or a physician-employee of an HMO is unlikely to be able to refer a patient outside the system to a facility in which he or she invests. As a result, it is probable that nearly all self-referring physicians are also fee-for-service physicians. As a group self-referring physicians tend to provide much more medical treatment than non-self-referring, the treatment tends to cost more, and the treatment is more likely to be unnecessary or inappropriate. There is also some evidence that physician-owned freestanding facilities tend to provide lower-quality medical care than independently owned facilities.

The AMA is a professional/trade organization representing a sizable minority of American physicians. It appears to represent primarily the interests of physician-entrepreneurs, whereas certain other physician associations tend to represent salaried physicians or fee-for-service physicians, who are less likely to be involved in joint ventures. As a political organization, the AMA has historically acted to maximize physician income and autonomy and to reduce accountability to the public and public regulation of its membership.

The issues of medical malpractice and tort reform have been blurred and distorted by decades of ideologically driven public relations campaigns by the AMA, the insurance industry, and others intent on obscuring the issues for their own ends. Medical negligence is widespread in American medicine, yet only about 1 percent of its victims are ever compensated for serious injuries. None of the means commonly used in the United States to detect and deter negligent physicians are particularly effective.

References

Abelson, Alan. 1993. "You'd Be Smiling, Too, If You Had Their Stocks." *Barron's* (January 25):1, 43–44.

Brennan, Troyen A., Lucian L. Leape, Nan M. Laird, Liesi Hebert, A. Russell Localio, Ann G. Lawthers, Joseph P. Newhouse, Paul C. Weiler, and Howard Hiatt. 1991. "Incidence of Adverse Events and Negligence in Hospitalized Patients." *The New England Journal of Medicine* 324:370–76.

Bromberg, J. and M. R. Price. 1990. The Impact of the Fee-for-Service System on the Utilisation of Health Services." Part I: "A Review of the Determinants of Doctors' Practice Patterns." *South African Medical Journal* 78(August 4):130–32.

Chesteen, Susan A., and Joan M. Lally. 1991. "Physician Licensing Boards: Saints or Sinners in the Public Eye?" *Business Forum* (Winter Special):36–40.

Common Cause. 1992. "Why the United States Does Not Have a National Health Program: The Medical-Industrial Complex and Its PAC Contributions to Congressional Candidates, January 1, 1981, Through June 30, 1991." *International Journal of Health Services* 22:619–44.

Danzon, Patricia M. 1985. *Medical Malpractice: Theory, Evidence, and Public Policy.* Cambridge, Mass.: Harvard University Press.

Franks, Peter, Carolyn M. Clancy, and Paul A. Nutting. 1992. "Gatekeeping Revisited: Protecting Patients from Overtreatment." *The New England Journal of Medicine* 327(6):424–29.

Galen, Michele, and Mike McNamee. 1993. "The AMA Is Looking a Bit Anemic." *Business Week* (April 12):70–71.

Haiven, Judy. 1991. "A Canadian Takes on the AMA's Line of Bull Against Her Country's Health-Care System." *Mother Jones* (April):50–53, 67–70.

Hiatt, Howard H. 1992. "Medical Malpractice." *Bulletin of the New York Academy of Medicine* 68:254–60.

Hiatt, Howard H., Benjamin A. Barnes, Troyen A. Brennan, Nan M. Laird, Ann G. Lawthers, Lucian L. Leape, A. Russell Localio, Joseph P. Newhouse, Lynn M. Peterson, Kenneth E. Thorpe, Paul C. Weiler, and William G. Johnson. 1989. "A Study of Medical Injury and Medical Malpractice." *The New England Journal of Medicine* 321:480–84.

Hillman, Alan L. 1990. "Health Maintenance Organizations, Financial Incentives, and Physicians' Judgments." *Annals of Internal Medicine* 112:891–93.

Hudson, Terese. 1990. "Fraud and Abuse Rules: Enforcement Questions Persist." *Hospitals* (March 5):36–37.

Hyman, David A. 1992. "Professional Profiteering? The Ethics of Physician Entrepreneurship." *Perspectives in Biology and Medicine* 35(3):317–29.

Iglehart, John K. 1990. "Congress Moves to Regulate Self-Referral and Physicians' Ownership of Clinical Laboratories." *The New England Journal of Medicine* 322:1682–87.

"Inspector General Under Fire." 1991. *Modern Maturity* (April–May):7.

Kemper, Vicki, and Viveca Novak. 1993. "What's Blocking Health Care Reform?" *International Journal of Health Services* 23:69–79.

Localio, A. Russell, Ann G. Lawthers, Troyen A. Brennan, Nan M. Laird, Liesi E. Hebert, Lynn M. Peterson, Joseph P. Newhouse, Paul C. Weiler, and Howard H. Hiatt. 1991. "Relation Between Malpractice Claims and Adverse Events Due to Negligence." *The New England Journal of Medicine* 325:245–51.

Novack, Janet. 1991. "Upgrades." *Forbes* (May 27):125–26.

Orris, Peter, ed. 1982. *The Salaried Physician.* New York: Academy Professional Information Services.

Reade, Julia M., and Richard M. Ratzan. 1989. "Access to Information: Physicians' Credentials and Where You Can't Find Them." *The New England Journal of Medicine* 322(6):409–10.

Relman, Arnold S. 1992. "What Market Values Are Doing to Medicine." *Atlantic Monthly* (March):99–106.

Rodwin, Marc A. 1992. "The Organized American Medical Profession's Response to Financial Conflicts of Interest: 1890–1992." *The Milbank Quarterly* 70:703–39.

Saks, Michael J. 1993. "Malpractice Misconceptions and Other Lessons About the Litigation System." *The Justice System Journal* 16(2):7–19.

Schwartz, William B., and Daniel N. Mendelson. 1989. "The Role of Physician-Owned Insurance Companies in the Detection and Deterrence of Negligence." *Journal of the American Medical Association* 262:1342–46.

Smith, James P. 1990. "The Politics of American Health Care." *Journal of Advanced Nursing* 15:487–97.

Swedlow, Alex, Gregory Johnson, Neil Smithline, and Arnold Milstein. 1992. "Increased Costs and Rates of Use in the California Workers' Compensation System as a Result of Self-Referral by Physicians." *The New England Journal of Medicine* 327:1502–6.

U.S. General Accounting Office. 1992a. *Reduction in Resident Physician Work Hours Will Not Be Easy to Attain.* GAO/HRD–93–24BR. Washington, D.C. November.

———. 1992b. *National Practitioner Data Bank.* GAO/IMTEC–92–56. Washington, D.C. July.

———. 1993. *Health Information Systems: National Practitioner Data Bank Continues to Experience Problems.* GAO/IMTEC–93–1. Washington, D.C. January.

Van Tunen, Ingrid. 1991. *Questionable Doctors.* Washington, D.C.: The Public Citizen Health Research Group.

Weiss, Lawrence D. 1992. *No Benefit: Crisis in America's Health Insurance Industry.* Boulder, Colo.: Westview Press.

Wolfe, Sidney M., ed. 1992. "Only 750 Restrictions on Doctors' Hospital Privileges Reported in First Year of Data Bank Operation." *Health Letter* (August):1–3.

———. 1993a. "Buying and Selling Patients: An Update." *Health Letter* (January):6-7, 15.

———. 1993b. "Keeping Doctors Honest: Most Medical Boards Fail the Test." *Health Letter* (March):4–7.

4

Nurses

The history of nursing in the United States is marred by sexism and racism. In addition, nursing has struggled against physicians for over 120 years to fend off professional domination and control. Now this profession is undergoing a variety of fundamental changes as the medical industry continues its transformation from small-time entrepreneurs in local businesses to mammoth international corporate chains dominated by regional monopolies and national oligopolies (that is, where the market is dominated by a few large health care corporations).

History of the Profession

Prior to the 1870s nurses were untrained menial workers recruited from the poorer elements of the working class. The impetus for change came from wealthy women who were horrified at the filthy conditions of patients in hospitals and who wanted to establish nurse-training schools to improve hospital-based health care. Ultimately these women were successful, but they first had to engage in a mighty political struggle with physicians, who were threatened by nurses who might become knowledgeable, relatively independent, and not sufficiently subservient. By the turn of the century hundreds of nursing schools had been established. Nursing students were exploited as cheap labor by physicians and hospitals alike (Starr 1982, 155–56). Until the development of the modern hospital in the early decades of the twentieth century, nursing was something of a cottage industry. After training, nurses were typically hired by individual families to care for the sick in private homes. The bulk of nursing employment shifted to the growing number of hospitals as the twentieth century wore on (Smith 1992, 392).

During the next few decades sexism in the workplace continued to restrict working women to a few low-paying occupations, one of which was nursing. Since most nursing positions were in hospitals, which were also integrally involved in the training of nurses, hospitals were able to keep nursing wages depressed. After World War II, however, fundamental structural changes in the nursing market altered the profession. These changes are evolving to this day. The introduction of Medicare and Medicaid in the early 1960s exacerbated a shortage of nurses because more nurses were needed for the influx of new patients and because the emerging technology of medicine required more nurses. Federal and state subsidization of nursing costs via Medicare and Medicaid reimbursement to providers resulted in rising salaries. The federal government jumped in to help contain rising compensation costs for nurses by passing the Nurse Training Act of 1964, which granted funds to schools of nursing and loans to nursing students. The idea was to stimulate the flow of nurses into the marketplace, thereby restricting increases in salaries and benefits (Newschaffer and Schoenman 1990).

Theories Explaining Cyclical Nursing Shortages

Since the 1960s the demand for nurses has periodically outgrown the supply, hesitatingly but ultimately driving up salaries in the nursing profession. In response to the recurring nursing shortage, the federal government reauthorized the Nurse Training Act and has authorized new legislation such as the Nursing Shortage Reduction Act of 1988, which extended previous federal assistance and added additional funds for nurses working in areas of extreme nursing shortages. The last severe cyclical nursing shortage, during the last half of the 1980s, was preceded by a 12-percent drop in enrollments in licensed practical nurse (LPN) programs from 1983–1986 and a 19-percent drop in registered nurse (RN) program enrollments during the same period. During the mid-1980s the average hospital claimed to have a 14-percent vacancy rate for full-time RN positions (Sullivan and Brown 1989; Newschaffer and Schoenman 1990). Despite the fact that the shortage of nurses resulted in higher salaries, nursing salary increases should not be overstated. After inflation, beginning salaries for nurses in 1987 were lower than in 1977 (Chernomas and Chernomas 1989, 642).

Theories abound regarding the causes of the periodic nursing shortages. Some analysts claim that the cyclical nursing shortages result from classic supply-and-demand economic theory. In other words, low nursing wages result in fewer students going into training, coming out of training, or staying with nursing as a profession. As a result, after a lag time of a few years wages rise, more students are attracted to schools of nursing, and more nurses are drawn back into the field. The raises stop, the salary falls behind, and the cycle starts all over again (Newschaffer and Schoenman 1990). Looking beyond the theories, two analysts of the cyclical nursing shortage issue, Robert and Wanda Chernomas, have summed up the literature rather nicely regarding the views of nurses themselves on this issue:

> What do nurses want?: respect for their judgment, determination of standards of quality of care and staffing needs, control over their work schedule, educational support, and participation with a full vote in establishing policies related to patient care. Problems with administrators, a lack of stimulation, and absence of control over scheduling, a desire for new experiences, and problems in staff interpersonal relations were major factors associated with nurse turnover. Hospitals with low job satisfaction scores have higher turnover and absenteeism rates. Magnet hospitals, so described by the American Academy of Nursing, experience much less difficulty attracting and retaining nurses. These hospitals have been described by nurses as those in which there is administrative support for nursing, nursing participation in control over working conditions and practice, support for professional advancement, and, often, good collegial relationships with physicians. Giving autonomy to staff nurses and allowing them to utilize their knowledge base increases job satisfaction, reduces absenteeism and turnover, and appears to improve the quality of care. (Chernomas and Chernomas 1989, 645)

Registered Care Technologist: AMA Response to the Nursing Shortage

Several issues have shaped the AMA response to the cyclical shortage of nursing personnel. During the development of modern, professional nursing in the late 1800s, physicians tried to exert complete control over nursing, similar to the total control physicians currently have over most of the allied health professions. The leaders of the historical movement developing trained nurses, however, were able to outfox both the AMA and state medical societies in order to win major victories against the physicians. For example, the training of modern nurses and the accreditation of their educational institutions are largely controlled by nurses rather than by physicians. On the other hand, on the hospital floor and at the front lines of medical care, physicians remain in control and nurses have little professional autonomy. This inconsistency between professional autonomy and professional control has led to chronic stress in the relationship between nurses and physicians.

In recent decades the AMA has struggled to prevent mid-level health care providers, such as nurse practitioners, from receiving direct reimbursement from insurers and from practicing independently from physician oversight. Clearly, however, these attempts to limit competition have not been uniformly successful. Nurse practitioners and other mid-level providers have made very significant gains over the years in terms of independent practice with little or no physician oversight. Furthermore, under the conditions of health care reform, these gains will probably accelerate. Physicians as employers of nurses have also been very interested in programs to increase the numbers of nurses in training because larger numbers of nurses applying for jobs will put downward pressure on future salary increases.

Early in 1988 the AMA Board of Trustees approved a proposal to develop a new allied health profession, the registered care technologist (RCT). The proposal for a nonnurse bedside technologist was developed specifically in response to the nursing shortage, then near its cyclical peak. The AMA proposed to focus recruitment of RCTs among low-income minority high school students. With as little as two months hospital-based training, the "assistant RCT" could work with patients. RCT training would focus on practical medical protocols and technical skills for use at the bedside. The "basic RCT" would receive nine months of training, and the "advanced RCT" would receive a total of eighteen months of training. Like that of many other allied health professionals, RCT training would be firmly in the hands of physicians, and RCTs on the floor would report to physicians rather than to nursing supervisors. During the two years after AMA approval of the RCT proposal, the association spent half a million dollars developing the proposal and looking for two facilities at which to test the RCT curriculum ("Claiming 'Success'" 1990; Sullivan and Brown 1989).

The RCT proposal would have met the needs of physicians perfectly. Since physicians were to have controlled both the training and the practice of RCTs, the technologists would have remained firmly and permanently subservient to physicians. Minority students with no more than high school educations, permanently suffering particularly high levels of unemployment, would have been an especially pliant target group. (Parenthetically, it is unfortunate that the AMA has not shown as much enthusiasm for targeting minorities as medical students.) RCTs, with limited education and entirely subservient to physicians, would never have been able to practice independently of physician oversight and therefore would never have become competition to physicians as have nurse practitioners and other mid-level practitioners. Hospital administrators and physician employers would have realized higher profits by replacing better-educated nurses with lower-cost RCTs.

As might be expected, none of these points escaped notice by nurses. The American Nursing Association (ANA), together with more than a hundred other nursing organizations, consumer groups, and health care reform organizations, led a vigorous nationwide campaign to defeat the proposal and to discourage tentative selected RCT test sites from starting up. Nurses and their allies described the RCT program as unnecessary; as fragmenting to the health care system; as redundant, duplicating already existing allied health professions; as not cost effective; and as threatening to the quality of bedside care; furthermore, they claimed, it would leave RCTs so poorly paid as to defeat recruitment goals ("Claiming 'Success'" 1990; "Defending Nursing's Turf" 1990).

At the federal level, nurses were well prepared for the battle against RCTs as well as for the achievement of other political goals. During the ten-year period ending in 1993 nurses' organizations gave $1.5 million in campaign contributions. In 1992 the ANA moved its headquarters from the Midwest to Washington, D.C., to beef up its lobbying efforts. The association has eight lobbyists doing battle on the front lines of politics, and these are joined by additional lobbyists representing about thirty other nursing organizations. The ANA was the first major medical organization to back Bill Clinton's bid for the presidency, and it threw significant resources into the campaign. As a result, nurses' interests are heard sympathetically in the Clinton administration. The ANA also donated $330,000 in 1992 elections to over 250 legislators at the state level (Weisskopf 1993).

As the struggle against the RCT proposal wore on, the Kentucky Nursing Association (KNA) had a particularly full plate: The AMA chose Parkway Medical Center, a long-term care facility in Louisville, as the site of the first RCT program. In what has been termed "furious opposition," the KNA and their allies forced Parkway to reverse its position and decline the AMA offer ("Claiming 'Success'" 1990). By the summer of 1990 a battered and unsuccessful AMA threw in the towel. The AMA House of Delegates voted to cease efforts to find health care facilities willing to be pilot training sites for RCTs. Meanwhile, the ANA drew up a list of recommendations to more effectively recruit and retain nurses to blunt the effects of the cyclical nursing shortages. Some of these recommendations included freeing nurses from nonnursing duties by better utilization of supportive staff, providing better benefits and working conditions, raising salaries and improving compensation for experience, and providing financial support for schools of nursing (Meehan 1990).

Some nursing organizations have recommended the establishment of "nurse extenders" or "acute care technologists" under nurse supervision. Some of these proposals or operating programs utilize nurse extenders who are accountable to the head nurse but who are not involved in patient care. These nurse extenders keep the clinical environment clean and orderly, order supplies, take messages, and do related tasks to support nurses and give them more time to do their work. Other nurse extender programs involve the nurse extender in direct patient care such as monitoring patients' signs and symptoms, performing tracheal suctioning, and performing electrocardiograph testing as well as checking technical equipment (Sullivan and Brown 1989, 559–60).

Nurses in Unions

Approximately 350,000 registered nurses are members of labor unions. That is about one of every five registered nurses in the labor force (Lippman 1991, 67). A study of union representation elections for hospital-based nurses compiled for the years 1981 through 1985 showed 619 such elections, with the unions winning nearly 50 percent of them (Scott and Simpson 1989). About one-quarter of the elections involved local independent unions, but the rest included major national unions such as Service Employees International Union (SEIU); Retail, Wholesale, and Department Store Union (RWDSU); United Food and Commercial Workers (UFCW); the ANA; and the Teamsters Union. During this period approximately 42,000 registered nurses were added to the ranks of organized labor. During the same period 5,600 registered nurses were dropped from labor union representation due to union decertification elections; however, nurses unions are only half as likely to decertify as are unions in general (Scott and Simpson 1989).

Pay, particularly in recent years, has been somewhat superseded by working conditions and quality of care issues as the major reasons that nurses resort to a strike. Nursing union leaders interviewed by *RN* magazine reported that "patient care problems such as short-staffing and floating without adequate orientation" and "equitable staffing, scheduling, and promotion policies" were more likely to provoke nurses to organize than were salary issues (quoted in Lippman 1991, 68).

Most labor leaders agree that the organizing activity in the early 1990s was just the beginning of a new wave of unionization among nurses and other hospital employees, and a 1991 survey by a group affiliated with the AHA confirms it. A survey of nearly five hundred hospital administrators from across the country indicated that fully 22 percent of their facilities had union organizing activity going on at the time, and nurses were involved in about one-quarter of these organizing drives. According to hospital administrators, the main issues contributing to employee interest in union organizing were wages, management issues, job security, staffing levels, and communication problems. State nurses associations were organizing most of the nurses, while other hospital employees were being organized by SEIU, Teamsters, Local 1199, and a host of smaller unions. At least one employee relations consultant is predicting that the new National Labor Relations Board (NLRB) regulations will allow hospital employee organizing drives to win about 70 percent of the elections, compared to the average of about 50 percent prior to the ruling (Eubanks 1992).

Nurses as Entrepreneurs and Independent Practitioners

Poor working conditions, concerns about the quality of patient care, low salaries, and lack of autonomy among nurses can lead to one of two types of responses. The first is the class or social response: A group of workers can organize to confront management and negotiate better conditions. This response gives rise to organizations for collective representation—unions. The second major type of response is individualistic: An individual nurse can try to improve his or her work situation by attempting to impress management and get better treatment, more pay, or a promotion. A nurse can switch jobs and hope things work out better with a new employer, get more education to land a better job in or out of nursing, or escape wage labor altogether to become an entrepreneur in business or an independent practitioner.

Nurse Practitioners

The concept of nurse practitioners originated in the mid-1960s. The original idea was to provide additional training to nurses so that they could provide primary care services in areas where physicians were scarce, but over the years nurse practitioners have worked in a wide variety of settings. The federal government has supported the development of advanced-practice nurses, including nurse practitioners, clinical nurse specialists, and nurse midwives, since the late 1960s due to the declining number of primary care physicians being trained. Family physicians have dropped from 17 percent of all physicians in 1978 to 11 percent in 1990. Currently there are about 100,000 advanced-practice nurses of all kinds in the United States. There are two hundred nurse practitioner (NP) training programs across the United States; these programs typically offer masters' degrees (Jonas 1992; Galen 1993; Khanna 1992).

NPs can do 80 to 90 percent of what a family physician does. In addition, in over thirty states NPs and other mid-level practitioners, such as physicians assistants, have the authority to write prescriptions without a physician's signature. NPs are less expensive to hire than physicians, charge less as independent practitioners, and practice less-expensive medicine. In 1990 the average family physician's salary was $103,000, whereas the average NP salary was $42,000. NPs tend to select lower-cost treatments, prescribe fewer drugs, and order fewer tests. In accordance with their original mission, NPs are more likely to practice in areas that suffer from shortages of physicians. About 20 percent of all NPs work in rural America, and 50 percent work in inner-city communities (Aiken and Fagin 1993; Galen 1993; Khanna 1992).

The fact that NP's services are relatively inexpensive has opened doors for them in recent years that had previously been nailed shut. For example, NPs have expanded into acute-care neonatal intensive-care units, where they perform sophisticated medical procedures on infants. In New York, where the hours of overworked medical residents have been limited by legislation, consideration is being given to hiring NPs to fill former resident positions in hospitals (Jonas 1992). In California, draconian budget cuts in the Department of Health Services have resulted in the proposed use of advanced-practice nurses and physician assistants to replace more expensive physicians (Khanna 1992). Future prospects for nurse practitioners and other advanced-practice nurses look rosy indeed; however, the AMA has not been at all happy about this emphasis on the expanded role of nurses. According to medical ethicist Art Caplin from the University of Minnesota,

> The resistance is dressed up in language about inadequate training, inappropriate preparation and lack of skills, but the bottom line is that it's a fight over turf.
> . . . [In addition,] rattling in the background are the bones of about 100 years of sexism, in which nurses were basically mistreated, underappreciated, taken for granted and viewed by too many doctors as being third-rate citizens. (Cimons 1993, A12)

Changing Composition of the Nursing Labor Force: Blacks, Men, and Immigrants

Black and White: The Integration of Nursing

The National Association of Colored Graduate Nurses (NACGN) was founded in 1908 to fight racism and advocate the integration of African-Americans into professional nursing organizations, hospitals, and other health care facilities. This was a brave and tremendously difficult undertaking at the time, as it was for decades into the future. African-American nurses were not allowed membership in local and state chapters of the ANA. As late as 1951 ANA chapters in four states and the District of Columbia barred African-American nurses from membership (Smith 1992, 388).

Hospitals proliferated in the first few decades of the twentieth century, but they were typically unable or unwilling to pay high enough salaries to recruit or retain sufficient numbers of nurses. Shortages of nurses were common in the 1930s and, particularly, in the 1940s due to competing industrial and military demands for personnel during World War II. It was in this period of extreme labor shortage that racist bars to employment began to weaken as African-Americans were increasingly hired in hospitals and elsewhere. During the 1950s hospitals continued to be integrated, but not without racist incidents. Occasionally racist white employees would walk out on strike, trying to force management to fire recently hired African-American nurses. Management steadfastness or countervailing black–white unity among nurses during the walkouts often successfully broke obstructionist tactics (Smith 1992, 392–93).

During the 1940s the NACGN and the ANA worked closely together fighting racism in the nursing profession. ANA state chapters increasingly abolished segregationist practices while the national organization tried to undermine those chapters that persisted (Smith 1992, 393).

The last national convention of the NACGN was held in 1951. In response to over a decade of joint NACGN-ANA cooperation fighting racism and promoting integration of hospitals, the 250 delegates at the convention unanimously voted to dissolve the NACGN and join the ANA or the Nursing League of America as individuals. In the mid-1990s, a little over 7 percent of all registered nurses are black. Compared to black representation in the total workforce of 10.1 percent, blacks remain significantly underrepresented in the profession.

Men in Nursing

In 1983, 4.2 percent of all registered nurses were men. Eight years later, the percentage of men had climbed by only one point, to 5.2 percent. Nevertheless, the transformation of this historically feminine occupation into one with a significant number of men is well on its way. In 1988 about 6 percent of all student nurses were men, but by 1992, 10 percent of all student nurses were men. Although no formal studies have been reported in the literature, the general consensus is that men are attracted by money, benefits, and job security. Shortage-induced nursing wage increases in the mid-1980s have pushed nursing wages into the $25,000 to $50,000 wage bracket—considerably higher than those of many remaining factory jobs and certainly higher than those of many other service-sector jobs. In addition nursing benefits tend to be good, and the recurring shortage of nurses translates into relative job security. Anecdotal evidence appears to indicate that men gravitate toward the exciting high-tech environments of emergency rooms and intensive-care units rather than nursing homes or other hospital floors (Kilborn 1992).

Immigrant Nurses

The United States has a long history of bringing in cheap labor from foreign shores to fuel the engine of capitalist development. It is consistent in this historical context that the hospital industry would lobby for the importation of foreign nurses as one of several strategies to contain upward pressures on nursing salaries, benefits, and working conditions. A law passed in 1989 allowed foreign nurses in the United States to temporarily extend their visas. At the time there were about 25,000 foreign nurses working in the United States, and about 70 percent were from the Philippines. Since that law expired at the end of 1989, former president Bush signed the Immigration Nursing Relief Act before the end of the year; this act extended the provisions of the older law and made some important additions ("Bush Signs Bill Allowing Foreign Nurses" 1990).

Even though the policy of recruiting foreign nurses may appeal to hospital administrators and to legislators, some of the consequences of such a policy should be considered. On the one hand, legislators are happy to avoid putting money into the education of more domestic nurses. However, by pursuing this policy the United States is avoiding the construction of the educational infrastructure necessary to train nurses well into the twenty-first century. What will the future consequences be of the steady deterioration of our nation's ability to educate nurses? Another very important issue involves the consequences of this policy for those countries exporting nurses to the United States. Canada and the Philippines, for example, expend vast resources to train nurses only to have many of them recruited by the United States. In effect, the United States exports the expense of training nurses to countries that can ill afford to subsidize America's health care system (Bashi and Domholdt 1993, 433).

Summary and Discussion

From the earliest years of modern nursing the profession was forged and shaped in a struggle for professional autonomy and against physician domination. That struggle has continued into the current period, the latest example being the AMA attempt to bring into existence the profession of registered care technologist. In addition, this attempt was one of several responses by management to cyclical nursing shortages. Other responses have included higher salaries, better working conditions, the employment of nurse extenders under nurse supervision, more professional autonomy, the employment of immigrant nurses, encouragement of male nurses, and lobbying for more federal funds for nurse training. Collective responses by nurses to low pay and poor working conditions have included organizing unions and putting forth alternative responses to nurse shortages, such as demands for more government funds for nurse training, and the use of nurse extenders under nurse supervision. Individualistic responses to poor working conditions and low pay have included additional education leading to advance-practice nursing, changing jobs, becoming self-employed, and trying to please management.

The future need for nurses seems quite clear, but preparation for that need is another matter. University and community college budgets are being stabilized or cut back in nearly every state. Federal support for nursing has been up and down, but in any case it has not been sufficient. The use of immigrant nurses has negative consequences for their countries of origin, and the compensation made by organized nursing. It seems likely that the direction of health care reform, the increasing centralization of ownership of medical facilities, and the success of nurse-initiated unions and political activism will be most influential in determining the future of nursing.

References

Aiken, Linda, and Claire Fagin. 1993. "More Nurses, Better Medicine." *New York Times* (March 11):A23(L).

Bashi, Harriette L., and Elizabeth Domholdt. 1993. "Use of Support Personnel for Physical Therapy Treatment." *Physical Therapy* 73(7):421–36.

"Bush Signs Bill Allowing Foreign Nurses to Apply for Permanent Residency." 1990. *Pennsylvania Nurse* 45(4):7, 9.

Chernomas, Robert, and Wanda Chernomas. 1989. "Escalation of the Nurse-Physician Conflict: Registered Care Technologists and the Economic Crisis." *International Journal of Health Services* 19(4):635–50.

Cimons, Marlene. 1993. "Health Reform May Expand Role of Advanced Nurses." *Los Angeles Times* (June 28):A1.

"Claiming 'Success,' AMA Members Vote to Abandon the RCT Idea." 1990. *American Journal of Nursing* 90(8):75.

"Defending Nursing's Turf: Kentucky Nurses Fight RCTs; New Threat Is MLPs." 1990. *The American Nurse* 22(6):29.

Eubanks, Paula. 1992. "ASHHRA/OMNI Labor Survey: Significant Union Activity in Pre-Petition Stages." *Hospitals* (May 20):50–54.

Galen, Michele. 1993. "Cheaper Primary Care: Nurses May Be the Answer." *Business Week* (April 12):71.

Jonas, Gabrielle. 1992. "The Widening Scope of NP Practice." *Health Letter* (October):11.

Khanna, Prerna Mona. 1992. "While Physician Extenders Proliferate, Doctors Worry About Competition, Care." *Wall Street Journal* (August 5):B1(W).

Kilborn, Peter T. 1992. "As Pay for Nurses Increases, So Does the Number of Men Entering the Field." *New York Times* (October 29):A22(L).

Lippman, Helen. 1991. "Expect to Hear About Unions." *RN* (October):67–72.

Meehan, Joan B. 1990. "AMA Votes to Abandon Plan to Create RCT." *The American Nurse* 22(7):25.

Newschaffer, Craig J., and Julie A. Schoenman. 1990. "Registered Nurse Shortages: The Road to Appropriate Public Policy." *Health Affairs* 9(1):98–106.

Scott, Clyde, and Jim Simpson. 1989. "Union Election Activity in the Hospital Industry." *Health Care Management Review* 14(4):21–28.

Smith, David B. 1992. "The Racial Integration of Medical and Nursing Associations in the United States." *Hospital and Health Services Administration* 37(3):387–401.

Starr, Paul. 1982. *The Social Transformation of American Medicine.* New York: Basic Books.

Sullivan, Patricia A., and Timothy Brown. 1989. "Unlicensed Persons in Patient Care Settings." *Nursing Clinics of North America* 24(2):557–69.

Weisskopf, Michael. 1993. "Doctors' Pressure Rises as Nurses Make House (and Senate) Calls." *Washington Post* (May 16):A1, A16.

5

Hospitals

The literature often classifies hospitals into three main groups: private for-profit (increasingly found as members of corporate-owned chains of hospitals), private nonprofit (also increasingly part of larger chains of nonprofits), and public nonprofits, typically owned by counties, states, or municipalities. In some ways, however, it makes more sense to classify hospitals into two main groups: private and public. Private hospitals, both for-profit and nonprofit, are increasingly concerned about costs and profitability. Everything possible is done to attract well-insured patients and to discourage or eliminate uninsured patients, indigents, and those insured by lower-reimbursing government-assisted forms of health insurance. These patients are covertly and overtly steered to the increasingly stressed and underfunded public sector for health care: public hospitals and federally funded health centers. The social and economic forces driving the transformation of hospital care is resulting in a two-track system.

For better or for worse, hospitals are the focal point of health care in the United States. They represent the largest single category of health care spending, at 44 percent of the national total. Not counting federal facilities, 5,342 community hospitals employ 3.5 million people in the United States. Of the total number of hospitals, almost 60 percent are private nonprofit, nearly 27 percent are public nonprofit, and the rest are for-profit. The United States has patient-per-day and patient-per-hospital-stay costs far higher than those of any other industrialized nation. In addition, compared to most other industrialized countries, U.S. hospitals are characterized by fewer beds per thousand population, a lower admission rate, and a shorter length of stay. On the other hand, compared to these same countries, the United States typically has more employees per bed (Iglehart 1993, 372–73).

Between 1980 and 1990 over 550 community hospitals failed, and several hundred others merged. During approximately the same period, community hospital admissions dropped from 36.4 million to 31.1 million. Between the years of 1983 and 1991 the number of beds in community hospitals fell from 1,003,700 to 924,000, a decline of nearly 8 percent. Part of this decline is related to the explosive growth during this period in the number of outpatient centers performing procedures formerly done in hospitals. Other important factors include changing federal and private insurance reimbursement policies and the rise of investor-owned hospital chains. However, fewer hospitals has not meant lower profits. A survey of 167 large hospital chains showed that between 1988 and 1993 operating profits were up 28 percent (Iglehart 1993, 372–73; Lindorff 1992, 29; Freudenheim 1993).

In addition, the downsizing of the industry as a whole has been accompanied by a simultaneous process of concentration of ownership. In other words, while the total number of hospitals and beds has been declining for several years, those that remain are falling under the control of fewer and fewer corporate owners. For example, in 1989 Columbia Hospital Corporation was a scrawny upstart chain with just four hospitals. A few years later, in summer 1993, Columbia merged with Galen Health Care Inc., a spin-off of Humana Corporation, creating a $5 billion merger with ninety-nine hospitals and 22,000 beds. Now the new corporate entity, Columbia Health Care Corp., is tied for first place among hospital chains with Hospital Corporation of America (HCA). Columbia cofounder Richard E. Rainwater calls his successful strategy for hospital empire building "the Wal-Mart approach to health care" (quoted in Zellner, McNamee, and Greising 1993, 33). His next task will be to eliminate competition by buying out and often closing competing hospitals in metropolitan areas with Columbia facilities. The consolidation of local and regional monopolies will be complete with the vertical integration of health care facilities in the same area, that is, with the purchase of home health care services, outpatient diagnostic centers, and perhaps feeder satellite clinics (Zellner, McNamee, and Greising 1993).

Brief History of Hospitals

The foundation of the modern hospital can probably be traced to the massive system of hospitals built by the Union during the Civil War and their operation on relatively new principles of hygiene formulated by Florence Nightingale. The development of schools to train nurses and the acceptance of new practices of antiseptic surgery and aseptic cleanliness during surgery in the closing decades of the nineteenth century added immeasurably to the emergence of the modern hospital. The development of anesthesia midcentury and the invention of X-rays near the end of the century combined with other advances to lead to a proliferation of surgery by the beginning of the twentieth century. "Growth in the volume of surgical work provided the basis for expansion and profit in hospital care" (Starr 1982, 154–58). As hospitals become flooded with private patients requiring surgery (thereby displacing remunerative home visits), physicians increasingly began charging for hospital procedures. Prior to this time a physician's hospital work had usually been considered a charitable donation and had been unpaid.

Over time, improving survival rates, cleaner appearances, and better architecture distanced hospitals from their squalid, shunned origins as poorhouses. Whereas earlier hospitals had consisted primarily of huge wards to treat poor people, newer hospitals increasingly included a larger proportion of private and semiprivate rooms to treat the wealthy and middle classes on a fee-for-service basis. By 1908 wards included only 28 percent of all beds while the proportion of beds in single rooms had climbed to 40 percent, and the trend continued. With the growing emphasis on surgery and acute illness, the average length of stay in a hospital dropped from nearly a month in 1870 to 12.5 days in the early 1920s. Long-term recuperating patients and the chronically ill were released earlier, often to the care of convalescent homes, an emerging health care institution.

During this period hospitals became far more expensive to build, to equip, and to maintain due to improvements in building codes, increasing technology in medicine, and increasing staffing requirements. Their costs outstripped charity's ability to support them. Voluntary hospitals were escalating in number and were also going bankrupt more often than ever before. By 1920 there were over 4,000 hospitals in the United States, with an average capacity of seventy-eight beds. Hospital boards of directors increasingly opened up once-exclusive hospitals for use by more and more physicians in order to encourage them to bring in patients to improve hospital revenues. Profit-making proprietary hospitals started by physicians and corporations boomed after 1890. Nevertheless, minority physicians—such as African-Americans, Jews, and members of selected ethnic groups—were commonly barred from hospital privileges (Starr 1982, 162–70).

Private for-profit hospitals attracted paying patients for acute care, often surgery-related. There was little profit in patients with chronic illnesses, so they were left to the public and charity hospitals. Discrimination against various religions and ethnic groups by the physicians of major hospitals resulted in a plethora of ethnic and religious hospitals. Since hospital construction followed no central or even regional plan, too many small hospitals were built. The economic depression of the 1930s eliminated many of them and encouraged others to find innovative ways to bring in revenue. The most famous of these innovations was the founding of Blue Cross, a prepaid insurance system designed to keep revenue flowing to hospitals even during a severe economic downturn.

In the 1940s and 1950s hospitals dramatically increased their use of house staff (physicians employed by the hospital) because they were profitable both for the hospital and for private physicians with hospital privileges. During this period, however, despite an increased demand for physicians, medical schools were not expanding. As a result, medical schools increasingly affiliated with specific hospitals in metropolitan areas to improve training of medical students and residents and to lock the residents in as house staff. Ultimately these affiliations grew into the currently existing major medical centers (Starr 1982, 360–62).

Well past midcentury the typical general hospital in the United States was freestanding—that is, it was not part of a corporate chain of hospitals—but the situation was about to change. In 1961 there were a mere five consolidations of hospitals, but a dozen years later there were about fifty per year. By 1980, according to a survey by the AHA, there were 245 multihospital chains, with 301,894 beds, at that time about 30 percent of the nation's community hospital beds. Nonprofit multihospital systems controlled 57.6 percent of the beds, state and local public hospitals controlled 7.3 percent, and investor-owned multihospital systems controlled 35.1 percent of the beds and were by far the fastest growing segment of the multihospital chains. Their growth has been stoked in large part by the proliferation of private health insurance and Medicare. The significance of the explosion of investor-owned systems should not be missed: "The rise of the for-profit chains has, for the first time, introduced managerial capitalism into American medicine on a large scale" (Starr 1982, 431).

Meanwhile, the private nonprofits had some setbacks in the 1970s and 1980s. Money for capital investment increasingly dried up. Federal reimbursement policies and private HMOs have been demanding discounts and mandating frugal reimbursements. Hospitals are competing against other hospitals and against physicians moving into the provision of new services. The result has been that some nonprofits have been scooped up by expanding investor-owned chains while others have diversified to increase revenue. Hundreds of nonprofits have reorganized their corporate structure to allow them to operate profit-making subsidiary businesses while maintaining the core hospital's nonprofit status. Others have expanded their range of services within the nonprofit structure to increase revenue. For these and other reasons, the lines between nonprofit "volunteer" hospitals and investor-owned for-profit hospitals are blurring (Starr 1982, 436–38).

Investor-Owned Hospital Chains

Brief History

Through the 1950s cost shifting masked the growing underlying problems of financing hospital care. Poor people who sought care at hospitals were often treated at little or no cost to them. The costs were shifted to those who could pay. But poverty in America was overwhelming and growing, and increasingly the poor were refused treatment. As a result Medicare and Medicaid, public health insurance systems, were introduced in the mid-1960s to funnel public money to private hospitals and physicians to care for the poor and elderly. Ironically, both these programs were opposed at the time by the AHA and the AMA, although since then both these programs' constituents have profited handsomely from them. By the mid-1980s Medicare was the source of over half the revenue of many hospitals and was the major source of physician revenue. The advent of Medicare plus tax benefits existing at the time also gave birth to the huge multinational, investor-owned for-profit hospital chains (Lindorff 1992, 21–22).

There have been proprietary hospitals—that is, for-profit hospitals—in the United States since the late 1800s. Typically, these were relatively small hospitals owned by one or more physicians, initially established as a place where they could practice medicine. The business of buying dozens of hospitals as investments amassed under the roof of one for-profit corporation, however, did not start until the mid-1960s. Once investors realized the profits that could be made as a result of Medicare, hospital chains were formed, bought, and merged with dizzying rapidity. The rush to concentration of ownership of private hospitals was unabated by two recessions. In 1973 President Richard Nixon instituted price controls to curb inflation, and the bottom temporarily fell out of the hospital-chain acquisition business. Business picked up again, however, until 1977, when threats by the Carter administration to establish a national health program caused the price of hospital chain stocks to drop by 20 percent. The threats proved hollow, and business thrived as never before. The period 1978 to 1985 was hotter than ever for the burgeoning hospital chains. In 1978 there were 445 corporate-owned hospitals, but by 1984 the number had grown to 955, a 215 percent jump in just six years. Changes in federal reimbursement policies in the last half of the 1980s together with market forces cooled the rate of chain growth, but by 1991 the chains owned 1,382 hospitals in the United States, and another seventy-five in other countries. This represented chain ownership of 25 percent of all nonfederal hospitals in the United States. If contract management by chains of nonchain hospitals were included, chains controlled about 30 percent of all U.S. hospitals, and about one of every seven physicians worked in a chain-owned hospital. In 1988 investor-owned chains generated $6.35 billion in pretax profits (Lindorff 1992, 38, 47–49, 266).

For-Profits Versus Nonprofits

For-profit chains are established to maximize profits. A number of the strategies they have adopted to do so have a negative impact on both private and public nonprofit hospitals, thereby jeopardizing the last stop for health care for those who cannot otherwise afford it. For-profit chains tend to locate in states and neighborhoods with well-insured populations, scrupulously avoiding low-income areas. Often for-profits will build hospitals without some rather common facilities like emergency rooms (ERs), neonatal intensive-care units, or burn units. These facilities are often money losers, and in low-income neighborhoods emergency rooms simply attract too many charity and Medicaid patients, who are hazardous to the financial bottom line. For-profit hospitals that do have emergency rooms dump tens of thousands of patients a year on the doorsteps of public hospitals. That is, they may minimally "stabilize" poor patients who show up at the ER, but as soon as possible they transport them to a public hospital to avoid having to provide more extensive treatment for little or no reimbursement. All these strategies divert an ever increasing proportion of poor and uninsured patients to nonprofit hospitals (Lindorff 1992, 71, 194, 214–15).

Nonprofits are increasingly unable to handle the flood of charity and Medicaid patients that were once better distributed among the older proprietary hospitals (for example, private for-profit hospitals that were not part of a chain). Public funding for nonprofits declined precipitously during the 1980s and early 1990s, the conservative era of "getting government off the backs of the people," and the fiscal crisis continues. Nonprofits have been forced to deal with record-breaking patient loads during a period of flat or declining budgets. The problem has been exacerbated by for-profit "cream skimming," the practice of attracting well-insured patients away from other hospitals, in particular the nonprofits. For-profit chains spend hundreds of millions of dollars a year in advertising to lure well-insured patients away from other facilities. These well-insured patients in the nonprofits help subsidize medical care provided to the large number of indigents. As the insured patients are drained off by the for-profits, resources to treat the poor are simultaneously depleted in the nonprofits (Lindorff 1992, 65, 205–206).

As the for-profits gain strength in various communities, public and private nonprofit hospitals are pushed closer and closer to the brink of insolvency. As a result they are forced to change their methods of operating in order to stay afloat, and they start acting increasingly like for-profits. Although a consistently larger percentage of the nonprofits' patient load than of the for-profits' patient load is made up of indigents and Medicare patients, some nonprofits have begun limiting or discouraging treatment of poor patients. Many nonprofits have organized into chains, resulting in the threat that decisions affecting local communities will be made in distant administrative office suites. In sum, nonprofit hospitals are losing some of the features that most distinguish them from the for-profits as a result of for-profit dominance in communities and regions (Lindorff 1992, 206–11).

The Disappearing Nonprofits.   For-profit chains are scooping up both public and private nonprofit hospitals across the country in a splurge of purchases and leasing agreements. There is a very simple bottom-line reason for this. Earl Holland is executive vice president and chief operating officer of Health Management Associates, a for-profit chain that purchased or leased eight nonprofits between 1986 and 1993. He has been quoted as saying quite straightforwardly that nonprofits represent "the bulk of our future growth opportunities" (quoted in Lutz 1993, 49–50). Many nonprofits have been hit hard by the competitive tactics of the for-profits and the unfavorable impact of federal and state reimbursement programs.

In addition, public nonprofits often have been politically weak victims of budget-slashing binges by state legislators, county boards, and municipal assemblies. County or city officials may be especially pleased when substantial taxes are paid every year by a hospital that converted from nonprofit to for-profit status. If the hospital had been public nonprofit, local officials might be even more pleased that a public hospital in the red no longer needs to be subsidized by local taxes. Nonprofits frequently have a monopoly or near-monopoly presence in an area, and they can be purchased relatively inexpensively—perfect criteria for acquisition by a for-profit chain. Moreover, the rate of acquisition of nonprofits by for-profits is rapidly increasing (Lutz 1993).

Nonprofits That Should Not Be.   Nonprofit hospitals are very big business. Although they account for less than 1 percent of all nonprofit institutions in the United States, in 1990 they brought in $115 billion in revenue, fully 43 percent of all revenue generated by all nonprofits. In 1990 the GAO estimated that the federal government lost about $4.5 billion in taxes not paid by nonprofits, and state and local governments lost an additional $3.5 billion in taxes. As a result, the Internal Revenue Service (IRS) and investigators from state and local governments have been launching investigations across the country to see if nonprofit hospitals really deserve tax breaks. It turns out that many do not. For example, the GAO found that 71 percent of the nonprofit hospitals in California "provided charity care worth less than they would have paid in Federal and state taxes if they were not exempt" (Pear 1990, B17). The same held true for 43 percent of all nonprofit hospitals in New York. At least twelve states have attempted to revoke tax exemptions from nonprofit hospitals for a variety of reasons, usually relating to inadequate provision of service to indigents. IRS investigators look at situations, for example, in which nonprofits offer financial incentives such as cash, loans, or discounted office space to attract physicians who will bring patients to the hospital. Such actions often violate the federal prohibition against nonprofits diverting net earnings to the benefit of individuals (Pear 1990).

For-Profit Hospitals Are More Expensive

Research consistently shows that medical care in for-profit hospitals is more costly than in nonprofit hospitals. There are a number of reasons for this. One of the most important contributors to higher costs among the for-profits are administrative costs incurred by the home office. Frequently for-profits locate in areas where they have a regional monopoly because they bought the only hospital in the community or they closed down their competitors. Often prices rise dramatically once the monopoly is secured. For-profits often employ various covert and overt methods to aggressively weed out physicians who do not refer enough patients or order enough tests. For-profit chains feel compelled to purchase unneeded high technology, to remodel and refurbish for strictly cosmetic reasons, and to build when there is no clear need for additional beds—all in the name of competition and profit maximization. These unnecessary and extravagant expenditures are passed on as "health care" expenses (Lindorff 1992, 123–45).

For-profits have much higher advertising budgets than nonprofits, resulting in hundreds of millions of dollars in unnecessary marketing costs being passed on as "health care" costs. In 1989 the combined advertising and marketing budget for all U.S. hospitals was over $1.5 billion. A study in the late 1980s found that the average advertising expenses of for-profit hospitals were about 50 percent more than those of nonprofit hospitals.

Trends in Vertical Integration

A company experiences "horizontal growth" by acquiring or building more businesses of the same kind. "Vertical integration," on the other hand, refers to the acquisition of businesses whose products are used by the "core" company or that themselves use the core company's products; they operate "before" and "after" the core company, so to speak. In the area of health care services and facilities, for example, at the "before" end a hospital might acquire primary care clinics and "doc-in-the-box" strip mall walk-in clinics to act as feeders for referrals to the hospital. At the "after" end, a hospital might acquire or establish outside diagnostic imaging centers, long-term-care facilities, or home health care operations in order to capture the markets for medical services formerly offered outside the hospital or after hospitalization. Horizontal growth and vertical integration are key strategies for investor-owned chains to develop local and regional monopolies and to develop comprehensive networks for this new era of managed care and prepaid HMOs.

A major form of vertical integration involves hospital expansion into ambulatory care, thereby expanding services and displacing freestanding facilities unaffiliated with hospitals. A survey by *Healthcare* indicated that chain-affiliated hospitals in 1990 had 2,224 ambulatory centers, whereas hospitals operated by non-hospital-affiliated corporations had 430 centers. These centers provided a wide range of medical services, such as urgent care, occupational care, diagnostic imaging, surgery, and primary care. In 1990 hospital-based ambulatory care services generated 21–25 percent of total patient revenues, and this percentage has continued to grow. More than half of all hospitals surveyed in 1990 indicated that they expected to expand into one or more of several ambulatory services in the near future. Compared to public and private nonprofits, investor-owned hospital chains have relatively few freestanding ambulatory centers, but they are expanding at a far faster rate. Between 1989 and 1990 for-profit ambulatory centers grew by 28 percent to 183 centers, although as of 1990 well over 90 percent of such centers were operated by nonprofits (Lutz 1991).

The vertical expansion of hospitals into direct ownership of services such as diagnostic imaging centers, combined with a push to retain more of the revenues generated by some specialists with hospital privileges, has pitted hospitals directly against the financial interests of some physicians—with the expected consequences of legal fireworks. Hospitals have been sued for hiring their own radiologists, for example, and bypassing more expensive contracted radiological services. If hospital employees provide services, hospitals can retain more of the revenue stream and are able to make sure fewer of their potential patients are siphoned off by outside contractors. Hospitals have also been sued by anesthesiologists who felt jilted when the hospitals made an exclusive contract with others who were not so expensive. Many hospitals have even begun to charge radiologists and other specialists for the privilege of using hospital equipment to generate cash for both the hospital and the specialist. Some physicians allege that these and related practices are simply illegal kickback schemes (Freudenheim 1990).

Hospital Costs

During the 1970s and 1980s the rate of increase of U.S. hospital costs has greatly exceeded the nation's rate of inflation. Increased patient volume was not the cause, since during the same period the growth in cost per admission also exceeded the rate of inflation. During the 1980s alone, hospital operating costs shot up 63 percent over and above the rate of inflation. A bit less than half that increase was due to increased labor costs, and the rest was due to other factors. Contrary to myths cultivated by the AHA and other vested interests, AIDS was not a significant factor in the rising cost of hospital care. AIDS infection-control procedures adopted in the late 1980s accounted for 0.2 percent of 1987 overall hospital costs. Once these procedures were instituted, they did not continue to raise the base cost of running a hospital in subsequent years. Malpractice insurance costs added only about 0.2 percent to the average annual rise in hospital costs, even during the mid-1980s when they were increasing at a rate of 20 percent per year. During that period malpractice insurance represented about 1 percent of total hospital costs, but since then it has declined as a proportion of total hospital costs through

1990 and probably continues to do so (U.S. General Accounting Office 1992).

The average rate of growth for hospital costs from 1946 to 1983 was 8 percent, but that fell sharply to about 2 percent for a couple of years after 1983, then rose steadily back up to 7 percent by 1988. Prior to 1983 Medicare paid for all allowable costs incurred while treating Medicare patients. The brief drop in growth rate in the mid-1980s was made by the federal institution of payment according to diagnostic related groups (DRGs), a method of payment under Medicare that pays a flat rate for hospital stays based on a patient's diagnosis regardless of actual costs to the hospital. The idea was to force hospitals to more efficiently care for patients by reducing their hospital stay to a minimum. The DRGs had a dramatic if not long-lasting effect:

> From 1983 through 1989, hospital capacity declined 8 percent, and the average length of stay declined from 7.6 days per admission to 7.1 in 1986. By the end of the decade, the average length of stay had begun to increase, however.
>
> Reductions in beds, admissions, and length of stay reduced the rate of cost growth, but their cost-restraining impact was mitigated by other changes in the hospital environment. Reductions in admissions and other factors coincided with a shift of services to an outpatient setting. Outpatient visits were increasing at an annual rate of 1.1 percent in the years 1980–83, but the rate increased to 5.1 percent per year for the period 1983–89. This shift was one source of the rising inpatient case complexity experienced in the 1980s—the simpler cases were treated on an outpatient basis while the more complex cases were treated in the hospital. (U.S. General Accounting Office 1992, 13)

The DRGs had the effect of encouraging physicians and hospitals to shift inpatient costs to less stringently regulated outpatient care, giving the illusion that total health care costs had been cut because hospital costs had been cut. In fact, the costs had been shifted rather than cut. Even the DRG success in cutting the annual rise in the cost of hospital care was short-lived. Labor costs rose because the DRGs encouraged hospitalization of a higher proportion of sicker patients, requiring more and better-trained staff. Finally, the rush to expensive high technology and the additional costs it imposes on hospitals was untouched by DRGs.

High Technology

High-tech innovations in medical care frequently have the opposite effect of high-tech innovations in other industries. In automobile manufacturing or structural engineering, high-tech innovations are usually incorporated in order to save money. In medical care, technological innovation frequently requires the purchase of expensive equipment, a new place to put it, and an enlarged staff to operate it. In addition, it requires a steady stream of patients to use it in order to generate adequate cash flow to pay it off and to compensate investors. Since most high-tech equipment is rushed into widespread distribution and use before its effectiveness has been adequately researched, it may or may not increase the length or quality of life when used appropriately. Last, self-referrals, fee-for-service medicine, and other financial incentives often mitigate against the judicious and appropriate use of such equipment. The use of high technology in health care is one of the principal causes of the increase in hospital costs.

Administration

Nearly 25 percent of all hospital costs in the United States can be attributed to all aspects of hospital administration, and well over 22 percent of all hospital costs are just administrative salaries, according to a study of 6,400 Medicare Cost Reports representing virtually every hospital in the United States (Woolhandler, Himmelstein, and Lewontin 1993). These costs do not include the additional billions of dollars wasted in advertising by hospitals competing among each other for market share. Furthermore, hospital administration costs have shot up dramatically even as the patient load has been dropping over the years.

Compare the 25 percent administrative costs in U.S. hospitals with comparable Canadian costs, which average 9 to 11 percent of hospital revenues (Woolhandler, Himmelstein, and Lewontin 1993, 402). These savings accrue in large part because the Canadian health care system is a public single-payer system. Instead of 1,500 private insurance companies, the Canadians have one public health insurance program in each province. This type of medical-cost-reimbursement system saves Canada tens of billions of dollars annually by streamlining billing and accounting procedures. Whereas a typical U.S. hospital has a huge billing and accounting staff, the typical Canadian hospital has a room with a few people in it, most of them serving the more complicated insurance needs of foreigners. Woolhandler and colleagues estimate that a Canadian-style public single-payer system in the United States would cut a very impressive $50 billion off the cost of hospital administration services and would save another $50 billion by the elimination of unnecessary private health insurance overhead and billing-related physician's paperwork (Woolhandler, Himmelstein, and Lewontin 1993, 403; Lampert and Bjork 1992).

Public Hospital Emergency Rooms

There are about 5,700 emergency rooms across the nation; they are staffed by 110,000 physicians and nurses and a myriad of technicians, social workers, paramedics, and other emergency medical staff. In 1989 these ERs saw a total of 90 million patients. The busiest of these ERs were flooded with an average of two hundred visits in a frenzied twelve-hour shift. Emergency medicine as a specialty was established in the 1970s; however, regional trauma centers got a big boost in the early 1980s when hospital administrators had visions of an endless stream of seriously injured but well-insured patients coming their way. It didn't work out that way. A large proportion of ER patients are uninsured; consequently, hospitals claim to lose thousands of dollars on the average ER patient. As a result, for-profit hospitals and increasingly some private nonprofit hospitals discourage ER patients, either through a variety of tactics preventing them from coming to the hospital in the first place or by diverting them when possible to public hospitals (Gibbs 1990).

As mentioned earlier in this chapter, newer for-profit hospitals are sometimes built without emergency rooms in order to avoid having to care for uninsured or underinsured patients. Other hospitals have downgraded or eliminated beds in their intensive-care units in order to avoid having to provide money-losing intensive-care services. Since the intensive-care unit is where many serious ER patients would be headed next, cuts in the intensive-care unit result in backups and delays in the ER. For-profit hospitals in particular are apt to simply close down existing emergency rooms in order to avoid treating indigents because a 1986 law requires that every ER patient must be seen. Chicago had ten trauma centers in the 1980s; by 1990 it had only six. Dade County, Florida, with 2 million residents, had several trauma centers, but now the county has only one. These tactics mean that ever rising numbers of ER patients are funneled into ever fewer remaining emergency rooms and that the burgeoning ranks of the uninsured are increasingly diverted to underfunded, overwhelmed public-sector hospital ERs (Gibbs 1990). Another researcher notes bluntly that "when neighborhood clinics are inadequate, overburdened, or nonexistent, the flood of inappropriate visitors to hospital emergency departments should come as no surprise" (Kellermann 1991, 1124).

Big-city ERs—and increasingly rural ERs—are incapable of delivering the needed care. Some physicians working in these ERs reluctantly admit people are dying due to their inability to properly care for all the patients. Injured and ill patients on cots and gurneys line the hallways and are sometimes jammed into closets. Ambulances scream into ER patient-unloading areas only to experience "medical gridlock." All the gurneys and cots are full. All the staff are tending to patients already there. There is no one to receive the new arrival, and there is nowhere in the ER for the new patient to go. Hospitals in this situation often go on "bypass"; that is, they request that no more ambulances drop patients off for some period of time while the staff deals with existing patients. Bypass, however, once a rare event, has become a way of life. Los Angeles County–University of Southern California Medical Center, for example, requested bypass for a total of nine hours in March 1989. In the same month two years later, the hospital's ER required bypass

status for 236 hours. Nearby for-profit hospitals with perhaps 50 percent oc-
cupancy rates and relatively quiet emergency rooms are very reluctant to
take the Medical Center ER spillover because of the high proportion of
uninsured patients (Spiegel and Wielawski 1991).

A GAO study found clear evidence that certain classes of patients are more
likely to be showing up in ERs:

> The most commonly cited factors contributing to the increase in visits, from
> 1985 to 1991, were the number of people without health insurance, especially
> those seeking nonurgent care; the elderly's growing use of emergency services;
> and the increasing prevalence of more serious illnesses. The majority of hospitals
> reported these three factors increased their [ER] caseloads. . . . During this
> same time period, the number of visits by uninsured [ER] patients grew almost
> 15 percent and by Medicare recipients, almost 29 percent. (U.S. General Ac-
> counting Office 1993, 19)

During this same period, however, the increase in ER visits by the privately insured was only 11 percent. The national growth of the "doc-in-the-
box" urgent care drop-in clinics has siphoned off many of the privately insured patients who might otherwise have gone to the ER for nonurgent or
less-urgent care. On the other hand, this type of for-profit clinic typically will
not see patients who do not have cash or who are not fully insured by a private company. The result is that emergency rooms end up seeing a higher
proportion of the uninsured and the government-assisted insured but a
lower proportion of the privately insured. Since higher reimbursements from
the privately insured partially compensate for the uninsured and underinsured, the declining proportion of the privately insured plunges ERs deeper
into debt (U.S. General Accounting Office 1993, 5, 25–26).

In 1990 an average of 43 percent of all ER visits were nonurgent; in other
words, 38 million ER patients theoretically could have been treated in a
clinic or a health care provider's office. Under ideal circumstances, these options would have been preferable, since patients so treated would not have
clogged ERs and treatment in a clinic or office would have been far less expensive than treatment in an ER. However, circumstances are considerably
less than ideal for tens of millions of people. Fifteen million of these nonurgent patients did not have a regular primary health care provider for nonurgent care for one reason or another, and 6 million were unable to find a primary care provider willing to see them because they were uninsured or
because they had Medicaid or some other government-assisted health insurance program. Nearly 14 million of these nonurgent ER patients went to the
ER because their regular source of health care was closed, they had transportation problems or work schedule conflicts, or other reasons. Rural hospitals had a higher proportion of after-hours use of ERs for nonurgent care,
in large part because alternative sources of nonurgent care, particularly after

hours, are far more difficult to find in rural areas than in urban areas (U.S. General Accounting Office 1993, 19–22).

Resolving the ER Crisis

Glamour magazine recommends to its readers who require medical attention that they should avoid the ER if their condition is not serious. If they do end up in an ER, however, *Glamour* makes recommendations such as: "Present most ominous problem first," "If you are in pain, show it," and "Ask the admissions clerk your status regularly. Don't just sit quietly." Such tactics may help an individual bully his or her way to the head of the queue, but they contribute nothing to the resolution of a nationwide problem ("Emergency Room Tactics" 1992).

It is widely recognized among health care providers who specialize in emergency medicine that there are no viable shortcuts to solving the emergency room crisis that is paralyzing big city public hospitals and increasingly affecting other urban and rural ERs. The College of Emergency Physicians (Kellermann 1991), for example, proposes the following five strategy plan:

1. Increase the capacity of hospitals, particularly overburdened larger urban public hospitals, to provide adequate inpatient beds, critical care facilities, and home health care services.
2. Since emergency care is more expensive than other forms of health care, adjust payment mechanisms to reflect that fact, particularly for those hospitals providing a disproportionate amount of emergency care.
3. Because nursing shortages chronically plague most of the busiest emergency rooms in the nation, attract more nurses by improving working conditions and benefits.
4. Since a large proportion of the flood of emergency room users results from lack of access to primary care due to financial and other restrictions, vastly expand access to primary care. In addition, expand programs to prevent illness and injuries.
5. Provide an adequate level of health insurance for every citizen, since high-quality emergency medicine cannot be assured until everyone has access to necessary health care.

Emergency Room Crisis in the Suburbs

Private hospitals in the well-heeled suburbs, particularly private for-profit facilities, are having an emergency room crisis as well. Their ERs are languishing for want of more patients. For-profit hospitals tend to locate in parts of the country, such as the sunbelt region, where people are more likely to be well-insured. Moreover, within any region, they tend to locate in suburbs, targeting a well-insured population in order to maximize reimbursement for treatment and ultimately maximize profits. Since nearly all for-profit health care facilities have the same strategy, there tends to be some congestion of facilities in these suburban areas.

Not only are there often other hospitals competing for well-insured patients in the catchment area, but there are about 4,000 urgent care centers congregating in the same neighborhoods ("Clinics Alter Brisk Emergency-Room Style" 1993). These facilities are sometimes derisively called "doc-in-the-box" clinics because of a marketing strategy reminiscent of fast food outlets. The clinics are commonly located in or near popular malls, do not require appointments, are open on weekends, and feature extended hours of operation. They are far less expensive than fully equipped and staffed emergency rooms; and unlike emergency rooms, they are not required to treat everyone who walks in the door. In fact, they typically refuse to treat anyone without cash or private insurance. The entire system of urgent care centers and fast-track emergency room programs has been criticized by some physicians as an unacceptable substitute for the continuity of care offered by a regularly seen primary care provider ("Clinics Alter Brisk Emergency-Room Style" 1993).

Hospitals Can Be Dangerous Places

The Joint Commission on Accreditation of Health Care Organizations (JCAHO) is one of the main bodies regulating the safety and appropriateness of hospitals and hospital-based care. It is not a government agency, and in fact it was established by the AHA, whose members the JCAHO is supposed to be regulating. Dr. Sidney Wolfe, a long time health consumer advocate, characterizes the JCAHO as a "partly owned subsidiary of the AHA and its member hospitals" (Wolfe 1992). Despite these inherent conflicts of interest, JCAHO investigations in the latter half of the 1980s found

- 1,700 hospitals failed to meet important minimum standards;
- 51 percent of hospitals did not have adequate monitoring to determine if unnecessary surgery was being done . . . [or] whether the operation was done safely;
- 50 percent did not adequately monitor the care of patients in intensive care and coronary care units. . . .
- 35 percent did not routinely monitor all blood transfusions to see if they were necessary and, if they were, whether the right kind of blood components were used. (Wolfe 1992)

Anyone interested in knowing whether his or her local hospital suffers any of the deficits noted above is out of luck. The JCAHO does not typically release that kind of specific information because it is their belief that the media and the public are not responsible in the way they use it. On the other hand, despite that fact that 1,700 hospitals failed one or more of the standards noted above, fewer than a hundred lost their accreditation, although some have been given conditional accreditation. By the way, JCAHO will reveal the names of hospitals that have lost their accreditation, but they will not say why. These facts call into question the concept of self-regulation versus regulation by a socially accountable public agency.

Summary and Discussion

Private hospital chains are enjoying horizontal growth; that is, they are adding more hospitals to the centrally owned networks. Private hospitals are also integrating vertically; that is, they are incorporating services that formerly were performed by other, unrelated corporations before and after hospitalization of the patient. The resulting tendency is concentration of ownership, with more hospitals (and other health care services) owned by fewer corporations. Profit-maximizing strategies among the for-profit hospitals have resulted in the absorption of a portion of the private nonprofit sector, on the one hand, and the increasing conversion of the remaining nonprofit sector into a mirror image of the for-profit sector on the other. The social consequences of these trends has been the growing exclusion of the uninsured and the inadequately insured from private health care services and their abandonment to the inadequate and disintegrating public health care sector. This has had a disproportional adverse impact on low-income minorities and single female heads of households.

As the private for-profit sector grows and engulfs the private nonprofit sector, the waste and inefficiency of the private for-profit sector spreads throughout the health care system. Overpaid administrators and swollen bureaucracies eat up health care money, as do profits, fraud, marketing, advertising, the building of unnecessary facilities, the purchase of lavish interior furnishing, subsidies to physician practices, and the establishment of duplicative and unnecessary medical services. All of these wasteful practices, employed in the name of market share and financial gain, divert vast sums of money from the actual delivery of needed health care, particularly among those excluded from private-sector services. The concentration of wealth and political power among the corporate leaders of the hospital industry means that it becomes easier for them to rein in support for and growth of public-sector "competition" such as community health centers. At the same time, this political influence is wielded to use government powers to the best advantage of the industry and to blunt government actions, such as effective cost containment, that threaten industry profits.

References

"Clinics Alter Brisk Emergency-Room Style." 1993. *New York Times* (February 11):A20(N).

"Emergency Room Tactics to Get the Fastest Care." 1992. *Glamour* (January):33.

Freudenheim, Milt. 1990. "Hospitals Battling Specialists over Revenues from Testing." *New York Times* (July 6):A1(L), D15.

———. 1993. "Hospitals Begin Streamlining for a New World in Health Care." *New York Times* (June 26):F12(N).

Gibbs, Nancy. 1990. "Do You Want to Die?" *Time* (May 28):58–65.

Iglehart, John K. 1993. "The American Health Care System: Community Hospitals." *The New England Journal of Medicine* 329(5):372–76.

Kellermann, Arthur L. 1991. "Too Sick to Wait." *Journal of the American Medical Association* 266(8):1123–25.

Lampert, Joan, and David Bjork. 1992. "Annual Survey: Executive Compensation Under Fire." *Hospitals* (September 5):24–32.

Lindorff, Dave. 1992. *Marketplace Medicine: The Rise of the For-Profit Hospital Chains*. New York: Bantam.

Lutz, Sandy. 1991. "Inpatient Bias Keeps Ambulatory Growth Modest; Rehabilitation, Sports Medicine Increase Their Pace." *Modern Healthcare* (May 20):103–6.

———. 1993. "Not-for-Profits Lure Investors." *Modern Healthcare* (July 26):49–54.

Pear, Robert. 1990. "Tax Exemptions of Nonprofit Hospitals Scrutinized." *New York Times* (December 18):A1(L), B17.

Spiegel, Claire, and Irene Wielawski. 1991. "Care Rationed at Overcrowded County-USC." *Los Angeles Times* (December 16):A1, A38–40.

Starr, Paul. 1982. *The Social Transformation of American Medicine*. New York: Basic Books.

U.S. General Accounting Office. 1992. *Hospital Costs: Adoption of Technologies Drives Cost Growth*. Report to Congressional Requesters. Washington, D.C. September.

———. 1993. *Emergency Departments Unevenly Affected by Growth and Change in Patient Use*. Report to the chairman, Subcommittee on Health for Families and the Uninsured, Committee on Finance, U.S. Senate. Washington, D.C. January.

Wolfe, Sidney M. 1992. "When Our Hospitals Get Sick." *Washington Post,* January 19.

Woolhandler, Steffie, David U. Himmelstein, and James P. Lewontin. 1993. "Administrative Costs in U.S. Hospitals." *The New England Journal of Medicine* 329(6):400–403.

Zellner, Wendy, Mike McNamee, and David Greising. 1993. "And Now, Monolith Hospital." *Business Week* (June 28):33–34.

6
Managed Care

The concept of managed care, often typified by HMOs, was given federal support to blunt the political initiative for a unified, equitable national health care system. HMOs were hailed as the solution to greedy fee-for-service physicians and rapacious health insurance corporations. Now most HMOs are owned by health insurance companies, the very institutions HMOs were established to counter. For-profit managed care commonly limits the choice of health care providers, may not save money compared to other social forms of health care delivery, establishes wasteful practices and bureaucracies, and may encourage undertreatment by health care providers. Moreover, the elderly and those with serious and chronic health care problems tend to be excluded from HMOs. The same social forces that have shaped a two-track hospital system are influencing the development of managed care—with similar consequences.

Until the 1940s most physicians and hospitals dealt directly with a patient on a fee-for-service basis. During the next few decades traditional indemnity health insurance grew to cover tens of millions of Americans. This kind of health insurance provides coverage regardless of which physician or hospital the patient goes to. Since the 1970s, however, and particularly in the 1980s managed care has begun to displace indemnity health insurance because of managed care's reputed ability to reduce the cost of health care. Managed care organizations (MCOs) come in all sizes and flavors, but John Iglehart (1992) has developed a generic definition that seems to capture the central similarities among them. Managed care organizations combine health care financing and delivery functions via

> contracts with selected physicians and hospitals that furnish a comprehensive set of health care services to enrolled members, usually for a predetermined monthly premium; utilization and quality controls that contracting providers agree to accept; financial incentives for patients to use the providers and facilities associated with the plan; and the assumption of some financial risk by doctors. (Iglehart 1992, 742)

It should be clear that managed care is fundamentally different than traditional indemnity health insurance. Under managed care there are financial incentives pushing the patient to use certain health care providers or to go to certain health care facilities. There are no such pressures under indemnity health insurance. Further, under managed care there is a standing relationship between the managed care organization and the health care providers, a relationship that covers financial questions of reimbursement as well as various aspects of the practice of medicine. No such relationship exists between an indemnity health insurer and the health care provider that an insured person chooses to visit.

HMOs are a significant form of managed care. There are two major types of HMOs: group and staff models, and independent practice associations (IPAs). A staff model HMO hires physicians and other health care workers as staff in the HMO's facilities. In 1992 staff model HMOs enrolled nearly 12 percent of all HMO members, up nearly 3 percentage points from the previous year. In a group model HMO, health care providers are members of independent medical groups but provide services exclusively to HMO members. This type of HMO enrolled about 30 percent of all HMO members. In both cases a member of the HMO must use the health care providers and facilities in the HMO network in order to receive full benefits.

Typically, HMOs provide a more complete range of services than are covered under the average indemnity insurance plan, and once the premiums are paid there are few if any copayments or deductibles to be made by a patient. An IPA is a type of HMO in which physicians stay in their own offices and are also able to treat patients who are not members of the IPA. During most of the 1980s and the early 1990s the IPA form of HMO was the fastest growing, in large part because it requires less initial investment and is less risky for investors than other types of HMOs. In 1992 nearly 45 percent of all HMO members were enrolled in IPAs ("An HMO Balance Sheet" 1993).

Brief History of HMOs

Prepaid health plans similar to HMOs have had a curious zigzag history in the United States. In the early decades of the twentieth century hundreds of industries, employing a couple of million workers by the 1930s, established for their employees forms of industrial medicine that had some of the elements of modern HMOs. In many of these health plans, workers, employers, or both would pay fixed monthly sums of money to contracted clinics or physicians for medical care.

In the late 1920s the medical cooperative movement in the United States began in rural areas among farmers with populist and socialist political leanings. The cooperative movement differed from the industrial-based prepaid medical care programs in that it stressed consumer control by elected boards, even to the extent of hiring physicians and controlling their salaries and working conditions. During the 1930s and early 1940s rural health cooperatives appeared in various locations across the nation, eventually covering hundreds of thousands of low-income people. However, from the very beginning the AMA and state medical societies did everything in their power to discredit participating physicians and to sabotage the cooperatives, which they viewed as unfair competition. Despite a 1943 ruling by the Supreme Court upholding a conviction of antitrust violations by a lower court against the AMA, the association's efforts paid off. The medical cooperative movement was strangled in its infancy, and just a handful of such cooperatives are operating today (Starr 1982, 300–305).

Meanwhile, in the 1930s Blue Cross and Blue Shield health insurance programs were initiated under the control, respectively, of hospitals and physicians. Commercial health insurance took off after World War II, and together these forms of health insurance controlled by corporate and professional interests squeezed out cooperatives and prepaid plans operated by business. By the 1960s, however, it was clear that private health insurance was not capable of providing benefits to large numbers of people and that it was not capable of containing costs. At the same time, nationwide pressure was building for national health insurance. In response the Nixon administration adopted the idea of the health maintenance organization in the early 1970s to contain costs, to increase access, and, most importantly, to act as a foil against the prospect of government-sponsored national health insurance. The idea was similar to that of the early cooperatives but with one very important exception: HMOs would be controlled by profit-making corporations rather than by service-oriented consumers (Starr 1982, 405–408).

In 1973 the HMO Act was passed. The act laid out numerous requirements for HMOs but provided few incentives. The emasculation of the legislation was the result of extremely heavy lobbying and numerous suits by the AMA and other like-minded constituencies. Meanwhile, the onset of a serious recession in the mid-1970s put to rest all talk of national health insurance, and the Carter administration did not decisively act on the health care issue. Additional legislation was passed in 1976 and 1978 to provide more federal assistance to the development of HMOs and to reduce government regulation over them. By 1979, 217 HMOs covered nearly 8 million people, double the number covered in 1970 but still only 4 percent of the U.S. population. However, by 1987, 650 HMOs covered over 29 million persons, nearly 12 percent of the population (Starr 1982, 405–408, 415; Knickman and Thorpe 1990, 255).

Current Overview of HMOs

In 1992, 550 HMOs enrolled 41.4 million people. While the number of enrolled members had climbed steadily since 1987, the number of HMOs had declined precipitously by over 15 percent as a result of bankruptcies, mergers, and buyouts. The HMO business is growing in absolute terms while ownership of the industry is concentrating in fewer and fewer hands. In addition, former competitors are forging deals to work together in order to keep costs down and to create regional, vertically integrated networks to prepare for the anticipated economic realities of health care reform. As a result, the largest HMOs, which have annual revenues exceeding $150 million, account for 70 percent of all HMO enrollments and control two-thirds of all HMO plans. Ironically, the health insurance industry has been furiously acquiring HMOs in recent years and by 1992 owned three hundred such plans, well over half of all HMOs in existence (Kenkel 1993b). Recall that Nixon established special legislation to create HMOs as an alternative to expensive and wasteful traditional health insurance. The insurance industry simply bought out the nominal competition. Now the health insurance industry is focusing attention on hospital-based HMOs. This, too, is ironic, in that the health insurance industry claims to save money by negotiating discounts with certain hospitals for savings. This will not be possible when the insurers own those hospitals as well as the associated HMOs. These tendencies toward vertical integration and regional monopolies mean that both financial and political power are being increasingly concentrated in the health care industry—a tendency that does not bode well for consumers.

HMOs have not all grown equally. During a one-year period ending July 1, 1992, 42 percent of all HMOs experienced a growth rate of 10 percent or more, and another 19 percent experienced a growth rate of less than 10 percent. On the other hand, 38 percent of all HMOs experienced declines in enrollments, with nearly half of those experiencing declines of 10 percent or more. The largest HMOs were more likely to be experiencing growth than the smaller and medium-size plans. This pattern of growth and decline is consistent with the tendency toward regional monopolization of health care. Meanwhile, as the hundreds of HMOs continue to fight it out across the nation for dominance, they are offering alternatives to traditional HMO forms of organization to attract bigger enrollments. The trend of adding these various options to replace standard HMO plans dilutes the possible cost containment features of HMOs because all these options allow people to use services not directly controlled by the HMO. Between 23 percent and 35 percent of all HMOs offer one or more "managed care products" such as:

A point-of-service (POS) plan, in which a member of an HMO has some insurance coverage if he or she uses hospitals and physicians outside the network but must pay relatively high out-of-pocket expenses to do so.

A managed fee-for-service plan, which is essentially a traditional health insurance policy with some attempts at cost savings, such as the requirement that the patient call for preapproval of elective surgery (Woolsey 1993; "An HMO Balance Sheet" 1993).

Managed Care Does Not Appear to Reduce Health Care Costs

Despite the fact that tens of millions of Americans are enrolled in various managed care programs, and despite the fact that the managed care industry generated about $7 billion in revenues annually in the early 1990s, managed care may not be lowering the cost of health care in the United States. Physicians for a National Health Program (PNHP), an organization of several thousand physicians who support a Canadian-style single-payer health care system, has released findings indicating that HMO premiums increased at the same rate as rates for traditional health insurance between 1982 and 1991. They also point out that administrative costs, overhead, and profits divert a larger percentage of money from health care in HMOs than among traditional health insurance plans (Day 1993). Representative Pete Stark (D–Calif.) blasted several HMOs by name in a 1993 issue of the *Congressional Record*, questioning whether HMOs could solve the health care problems since they tend to recruit only the healthiest people, they spend on average 18 percent of their income on expenses unrelated to health care, and their premiums still go up by about 10 percent per year (Brostoff 1993).

Benefits consultants working with employers frequently report that managed care plans have a significant one-time reduction in costs of perhaps 15–20 percent, but after that the rates rise just as rapidly as they did with the traditional insurance plans that were replaced. This is particularly true for preferred provider organization (PPO) and POS plans, which are somewhere in between a traditional HMO and an indemnity health insurance plan. Kenneth E. Thorpe, an expert in health care financing from the University of North Carolina School of Public Health, observed that "if employers hope to keep health care cost increases in line with other payroll costs . . . there's no possible way that I see that managed care could ever do that" (quoted in Crenshaw 1992).

Managed care has had limited success for a variety of important reasons, and its future successes are likely to be even more limited. The first and most obvious reason is that managed care simply does not address the problem of nearly 40 million uninsured people in the United States. Second, the massive bureaucracies created by utilization-review staff and the associated levels of management eat up most if not all of the savings. Third, since managed care is implemented by an anarchic mass of hundreds of insurers, costs are easily shifted by providers to those on other plans and to those paying cash. Fourth, health care costs that originate outside the managed care plan obviously cannot be controlled by managed care. Finally, even if 80 percent of the population, instead of the current 50 percent, were enrolled in managed care plans, significant savings would still not materialize for the reasons noted above (Finkel 1993, 109–10).

When HMOs Go Belly-Up

From 1980 through 1986 the total number of HMOs grew from 211 to 550, a net increase of 339. However, during this same period 180 additional HMOs disappeared. Mergers or acquisitions finished off 119 HMOs, and 61 went bankrupt. In all probability, a large percentage of those that merged or were acquired would have failed had they not been "rescued" by corporate wheeler-dealers. In other words, of 730 HMOs existing during this period, nearly 25 percent failed, merged, or were taken over. At least 8 percent of all HMOs in existence during this period went bankrupt. The late 1980s were far worse for financial instability among HMOs. In the three-year period from 1987 through 1989 there was a decline in the total number of HMOs from 633 to 564, but that is only a small part of the story. During this three-year period 232 HMOs disappeared: 108 went bankrupt, and 124 merged or were acquired. In other words, of a total of 865 HMOs that existed during this period, 12.5 percent went bankrupt and in all probability a great many more would have if they had not merged or been acquired. HMOs failed in forty-five states between 1976 and 1990, and twenty states experienced five or more failures during the period (Christianson, Wholey, and Sanchez 1991, 87).

Acquisitions, mergers, and failures of HMOs are not esoteric financial abstractions of interest only to bankers, investors, and stockbrokers. People who purchased an HMO membership in good faith may all of a sudden find that a merger or acquisition has drastically altered the terms of their health care or has changed who they may and may not see for health care. A bankruptcy can leave people overnight with no health care coverage and can strand families in a situation where finding alternative health care coverage may be too expensive or impossible under any circumstances. Moreover, health care providers are owed huge outstanding bills when an HMO fails.

Since 1990 bankruptcies seem to have tapered off somewhat, although mergers and acquisitions may not have. Nevertheless, serious researchers of the subject do not seem to think HMOs have put all their financial difficulties behind them. As HMOs get bigger and try to serve more enrollees with more plans, as they try price cutting to expand market share, as they prepare for health care reform while not really knowing what it will finally look like, many more will probably fail (Coyne and Hansen 1992, 38).

The federal government regulated HMOs fairly stringently in the original HMO Act of 1973. However, subsequent amendments, regulations, and budget cuts weakened regulatory oversight by the federal government. As a result of the decline of federal regulation of HMOs, and in response particularly to the hundreds of bankruptcies and near-failures of HMOs in the last twenty-some years, individual states have increasingly developed a regulatory stance toward HMOs; typically, states' regulatory powers have resided in the state department of insurance. While nearly all states regulate HMOs to some extent, the regulatory authority and the effectiveness of regulators varies considerably, in part as a consequence of the relative strength of industry lobbyists at the state level. For example, as of 1990 only slightly more than half the states had the authority "to require prior approval of construction or acquisition of new medical facility." This type of regulatory authority is important to contain costs of overbuilding. Only sixteen states required HMOs to file a plan outlining an orderly, fair process in the event of financial failure, and nearly two-fifths of the states failed to require hold-harmless clauses, which, in the event of financial failures, protect HMO enrollees from financial claims by providers who were not reimbursed by the failed HMO (Christianson, Wholey, and Sanchez 1991, 88–90).

Quality of Care and Consumer Protection Issues

Despite the phenomenal growth of HMOs since the mid-1970s, not all that much is known about the quality of the health care they provide. Much of what has passed for knowledge about quality of care by HMOs is anecdotal, based on pilot studies, or has resulted from self-serving studies generated by the industry itself. The few large scale research projects funded by the government have not returned very positive reports. For example:

> A federally financed study of 17,671 patients in a variety of medical settings found that HMO patients were more likely to complain of more difficulty contacting the physician by phone, longer waits, and shorter periods of time with the physician. Similar complaints were found in a federally financed study of el-

derly Medicare patients in HMOs and other medical settings. (Freudenheim 1993)

A study by the HMO Quality of Care Consortium, an organization in large part funded by the HMO industry, looked at 642 hysterectomies selected at random from medical records at seven HMOs. Researchers found that over 16 percent of the hysterectomies were inappropriate, and 25 percent were of uncertain necessity. (Winslow 1993)

ChoiceCare is the largest HMO in Cincinnati, with 2,400 physicians and 180,000 enrollees. The corporation exercises extraordinary control over the medical community, with over 80 percent of the local physicians on contract to the HMO. In a move designed to suppress information about quality-of-care issues from the public, the standard ChoiceCare contract with a physician "forbids physicians from doing or saying anything that 'undermines or could undermine the confidence of enrollees, potential enrollees, their employers, plan sponsors or the public in ChoiceCare or in the quality of care which ChoiceCare enrollees receive'" (Kenkel 1993a).

Apparently the local medical society has made no public protest as of early 1993 about this important abridgment of a physician's relationship with patients, not to mention the apparent restriction of free speech. Only 2 percent of all physicians under contract with ChoiceCare refused to sign a contract renewal that included the new clause restricting speech.

There is a fair amount of research that raises the question of the relationship between how a physician is paid and the quality of care. *Consumer Reports*, not known to beat around the bush on controversial issues, says simply that "in most HMOs, the kind and amount of medical care you receive is directly linked to the way your primary-care doctor is paid" ("Are HMOs the Answer?" 1992). Most HMOs have payment schemes aimed at reducing the amount of medical care given. For example, many HMOs pay physicians bonuses at the end of the year if the HMO makes money or if the physicians do not refer too many people to expensive specialists outside the HMO network. These financial incentives may influence physicians to avoid overtreatment, but at the same time they may promote undertreatment. Another common payment scheme is to offer the primary care provider a capitation payment, a fixed amount of money for each patient who signs up with that provider. This type of payment also has the tendency to promote undertreatment. Finally, some HMOs pay physicians on a fee-for-service basis, which research suggests has a strong tendency to promote overtreatment.

In 1986 nearly three-quarters of all HMOs were federally qualified; however, the number of qualified HMOs has dropped precipitously since then so that by the end of the decade fewer than half of all HMOs were so qualified. HMOs that are federally qualified receive some relatively minor competitive advantages from the federal government, but of more importance to the health care consumer are some protections required by the federal government in return:

- At least one-third of the board of directors of federally qualified HMOs must be consumer-members with no financial ties to the corporation.
- If the HMO serves a medically underserved area, members of the community must also serve on the board.
- The HMO must make available financial and utilization data to members so that they can determine if the organization is using their monthly payments wisely.

Dr. Sidney Wolfe, editor of *Health Letter,* the epistle of the Ralph Nader spin-off group Public Citizen Health Research Group, points to the non-profit Group Health Cooperative of Puget Sound (GHCPS) as a model HMO (Wolfe 1991). The cooperative has been in the Seattle area since the late 1940s. As of 1990 it was the twelfth largest HMO in the nation, with nearly half a million enrollees, $660 million in revenues, and more than nine hundred physicians on staff. Physicians are paid a straight salary, so they have no financial incentives to under- or overtreat. Consumers have meaningful, structural input throughout the cooperative from the consumer-dominated board of trustees, who are elected by enrollees to membership referendums on important policy and plan issues.

HMOs and Advertising

HMOs advertise for business using the full gamut of media: radio to billboards, newspapers to television. Humana, for example—a big player among HMOs—spent $18.6 million dollars advertising its managed care products during the two year span 1990–1991. However, according to the Health Care Financing Administration (HCFA), which oversees Medicare, Humana was not entirely forthright with the public in its marketing and advertising campaigns. The organization was investigated by the HCFA, which found abusive sales practices widespread. Humana agreed to change the way it trains its agents and agreed to get approval from HCFA for all Medicare sales literature before it is distributed. Other HMOs have been found to be equally deceptive (Kenkel 1992).

Summary and Discussion

The managed care industry, largely but not exclusively embodied in the HMO sector of that industry, has captured the health care delivery of tens of millions of U.S. residents. Meanwhile, the health insurance industry has captured the managed care industry. The extraordinary irony of this event cannot be missed. HMOs were supported by federal legislation nominally intended to break the hold of the insurance industry and fee-for-service physicians on health care delivery. Seeing both a potential threat and an economic opportunity, the insurance industry simply purchased the competition, and it now owns the lion's share of HMOs. All the weaknesses of for-profit corporate ownership of health care services and all the weaknesses of private health insurance and the health insurance industry have been transferred to HMOs. They are financially unstable, wasteful, and inefficient, and they provide health care of questionable quality. They discriminate against the elderly and the chronically ill, and there is little indication that they can reduce the nation's health bill. Furthermore, they cannot solve the problem of the uninsured. In short, HMOs appear to be a diversion from the real problems of providing health care to tens of millions of Americans who cannot afford it and of containing health care costs so that additional millions will not lose the access they currently have.

References

"Are HMOs the Answer?" 1992. *Consumer Reports* (August):519–27.

Brostoff, Steven. 1993. "Stark Makes HMO Investors Jittery." *National Underwriter, Property, and Casualty* (March 15):6.

Christianson, Jon B., Douglas R. Wholey, and Susan M. Sanchez. 1991. "State Responses to HMO Failures." *Health Affairs* 10(4):78–92.

Coyne, Joseph S., and Dennis J. Hansen. 1992. "HMO Financial Solvency: Should Hospitals Be Concerned?" *Health Systems Review* 24(1):38–43, 49.

Crenshaw, Albert B. 1992. "'Managed' Care Not Always Managing Costs." *Washington Post* (June 28):H1, H4.

Day, Kathleen. 1993. "HMO Cost-Saving Claims Challenged." *Washington Post* (July 9):C11.

Finkel, Madelon L. 1993. "Managed Care Is Not the Answer." *Journal of Health Politics, Policy, and Law* 18(1):105–12.

Freudenheim, Milt. 1993. "Many Patients Unhappy with H.M.O.'s." *New York Times* (August 18):A14(N).

"An HMO Balance Sheet." 1993. *Business and Health* (May 1993):18–19.

Iglehart, John K. 1992. "The American Health Care System: Managed Care." *The New England Journal of Medicine* 327(10):742–47.

Kenkel, Paul J. 1992. "Managed-Care Units on Hot Seat." *Advertising Age* (August 3):20.

———. 1993a. "Cincinnati HMO Imposing 'Gag Clause' in Effort to Mute Criticisms by Physicians." *Modern Healthcare* (February 1):24.

———. 1993b. "Provider-Based Managed-Care Plans Continue Growth Trend." *Modern Healthcare* (May 10):26–34.

Knickman, James R., and Kenneth E. Thorpe. 1990. "Financing for Health Care." In Anthony R. Kovner, ed. *Health Care Delivery in the United States*, 4th ed. New York: Springer.

Starr, Paul. 1982. *The Social Transformation of American Medicine*. New York: Basic Books.

Winslow, Ron. 1993. "HMOs Perform Inappropriate Hysterectomies." *Wall Street Journal* (May 14):B1(W).

Wolfe, Sidney M., ed. 1991. "How You Can Make HMOs More Accountable." *Health Letter* (November):1–4.

Woolsey, Christine. 1993. "HMO Competition Escalates." *Business Insurance* (March 15):3, 17.

7

Alternative Health Care Industry

The reasons people turn to alternative forms of medical treatments have remained remarkably unchanged at least since the mid-1800s:

> Today's medical counter-culture mirrors the nineteenth-century experience. At that time, as now, advocates worked for what they termed the democratization of medical knowledge, with "every man his own doctor," and for a "holistic," self-care alternative to a disease-oriented, impersonal medical system. The nineteenth-century movement arose in response to the development of modern clinical methods with the then-new emphasis on localized pathology. The contemporary version stems at least in part from an analogous reaction to today's technologic, heroic medicine, against which the public attempts to protect itself through living wills, court battles to achieve the "right to die," and demands for "humane" alternatives. (Cassileth 1989, 1248)

Brief History of Alternative Practitioners

Alternative health care, or perhaps a variety of health care options, has characterized North America since the time of the founding of the colonies. In the 1700s and during the first half of the 1800s health care was commonly delivered in the home by the women who lived there. Simple herbs and potions formed the basis of medicine. In the 1700s and well into the 1800s the world of medicine in North America was pluralistic, freewheeling, and unregulated. Frequently medicine was practiced as a sideline by the clergy. Women combined midwifery with the curing of ringworm and piles. Merchants sold dried fruit and tea side by side with medical concoctions. By the time of the American Revolution there were perhaps 4,000 physicians in the colonies, but only about 5 percent of them actually held medical degrees. Lay therapists abounded: "Botanic practitioners and midwives were probably the most numerous of the lay therapists, but there were also uncounted cancer doctors, bonesetters, inoculators, abortionists, and sellers of nostrums. Many were itinerant and moved freely into and out of various trades" (Starr 1982, 48).

In the early 1830s a number of states introduced licensure of regular physicians (that is, the forebears of the kind of medicine taught in most medical schools today). The main purpose of this was to capture the market from the irregulars (that is, practitioners of alternative medicine) by preventing them from practicing. The regulars argued that they were scientific practitioners whereas the irregulars were quacks. The irregulars argued that the freedom to practice medicine and to choose any kind of health care one wanted was as irrevocable as religious freedom. Moreover, they argued that licensure was simply a monopolistic power grab. Regular physicians were outnumbered, and in fact, at that point in history, they did not have science on their side. Bowing to the popular antimonopoly sentiments of the time, during the 1820s through the 1850s a number of states repealed the laws licensing physicians, again opening up the market for all forms of medicine (Starr 1982, 47–59).

During the latter half of the nineteenth century medical sects multiplied, but the main ones were the Eclectics and the homeopaths. The beliefs and principles of the Eclectics were closely related to those of the regular physicians, except that the Eclectics shunned the bleeding and harsh drugging characteristic of the regulars. The Eclectics had numerous medical colleges and for the most part accepted women practitioners, in sharp contrast to the regulars, who increasingly squeezed women out of practice (Starr 1982, 96). Homeopaths believed that diseases could be cured by minute doses of drugs that, at a higher strength, would create the same symptoms in healthy persons that the disease did in sick persons. These beliefs originated with immigrant German physicians in the United States and took their strongest hold among the urban upper class.

> Homeopathy stressed the need for sympathetic attention by the physician and individualized diagnosis and treatment of patients. (The parallel with certain schools of modern psychiatry will be obvious.) Moreover, because homeopathy called for reduced dosages, it provided an alternative to the pharmacological excesses of orthodox physicians. Homeopathic treatment was probably more pleasant than were the ministrations of the conventional doctor of the epoch. (Starr 1982, 97)

The AMA, founded in midcentury by regular physicians, waged war against homeopaths during much of the latter half of the 1800s. The homeopaths had garnered a large portion of the market and were constantly disparaging the regulars. Homeopaths and regular physicians who sympathized with them were kicked out of the AMA and related medical societies and discriminated against in a variety of ways. During this period a count of the various types of medical schools and physicians indicates that regulars composed about 80 percent of the health care providers and that irregulars constituted the balance (Starr 1982, 97–99).

Despite the intense campaign by the regulars to oust the irregulars from the marketplace, they were not particularly successful. State legislatures and the press generally sided against the grab for monopoly control of health care, and popular sentiment sided with the oppressed irregulars. In the late 1870s and 1880s regular physicians apparently decided it was time to try another tactic: peaceful coexistence. Homeopathic faculty began to be accepted in a few medical schools, and the AMA relaxed its stance against homeopaths. On the other side, many homeopaths adopted beliefs and practices closer to those of the regular doctors.

During this period, the late 1800s, regular physicians needed maximum political strength and, consequently, unification with the irregulars to push for a new round of state licensing standards. This proved to be the key to co-optation. The strategy worked. States began to develop boards of medical examiners. Some of these were multiple boards, one each for the regulars, homeopaths, and Eclectics. Other states simply combined them all into one board (Starr 1982, 99–106). Ironically, this was the beginning of the end for the irregulars:

> Both the homeopaths and Eclectics won a share in the legal privileges of the profession. Only afterward did they lose their popularity. . . . The turn of the century was both the point of acceptance and the moment of incipient disintegration. . . . Homeopathy had one foot in modern science, and the other in prescientific mysticism; this became an increasingly untenable position. . . . The Eclectics also succumbed to quiet co-optation; they were only too glad to be welcomed into the fold. (Starr 1982, 107–8)

Near the end of the century, just as the Eclectics were sputtering out of history and the homeopaths were sliding into relative obscurity, a new crop of medical sects arose to replace them. Dr. Andrew Still started his school of osteopathy in rural Missouri. His idea was that the body had to be mechanically in the proper relationship in order to have structural and functional balance. Chiropractic was founded about the same time on similar principles. Christian Science was founded by Mary Baker Eddy, who treated her sect as a business and became wealthy preaching that disease was a function of spiritual matters (Starr 1982, 108).

During the first three decades of the twentieth century regular physicians fully consolidated their near monopoly via state licensing legislation. They had no need to be tolerant of or to co-opt chiropractors or osteopaths because they did not need their political power. Regular physicians and their professional organizations fought to oust these relatives of the irregulars out of the medical marketplace, but they failed because of popular support of the alternative practitioners. Chiropractors and osteopaths won licensing privileges in most states, but they were typically barred from access to hospitals and from prescribing drugs. "According to a survey of nine thousand families carried out over the years 1928 to 1931, all the non-M.D. practitioners combined—osteopaths, chiropractors, Christian Scientists and other faith healers, midwives, and chiropodists—took care of only 5.1 percent of all attended cases of illness. Physicians finally had medical practice pretty much to themselves" (Starr 1982, 127).

AMA Stung by Chiropractors

Chiropractic relies on spinal manipulation to treat back problems and other medical conditions. The guiding theory is that the relationship between the spinal column and the nervous system is crucial to the maintenance of good health. Chiropractic is by far the largest organized alternative to allopathic medicine (that is, the kind taught in the typical medical school) in the United States. There are 55,000 chiropractors currently in practice, annually earning approximately $2.5 billion for their services. At least one study in recent years, published in the *British Medical Journal,* found that those suffering severe and chronic back pain were more likely to improve as a result of chiropractic treatment than as a result of hospital outpatient care. On the other hand, there is a great deal of controversy among chiropractors and between chiropractors and physicians regarding the use of chiropractic to cure medical problems such as inner ear infections, to replace children's vaccinations, or to treat infants and young children at all (Beresford 1991, 51; "Ruling May Spur Some Medical Arm-Twisting" 1991; Smith 1993).

Perhaps because chiropractic is the major competitor to allopathic medicine in the medical marketplace, the AMA launched all-out war against chiropractors in the mid-1960s. Chiropractic was branded as an "unscientific cult" by the association, and members of the AMA were banned from associating professionally with chiropractors on the authority of a specially adopted section of the AMA Principles of Medical Ethics. Specifically, this section was developed in order

> to prevent medical physicians from referring patients to chiropractors and from accepting referrals of patients from chiropractors, to prevent chiropractors from obtaining access to hospital diagnostic services and membership on hospital medical staffs, to prevent medical physicians from teaching at chiropractic colleges, and to prevent any cooperation between medical physicians and chiropractors [in order] to eliminate the practice of chiropractic. (Berg 1990)

As a result of this nationwide conspiracy to eliminate the profession of chiropractic, in 1976 four chiropractors brought an antitrust suit against the AMA, the American College of Physicians, and the Joint Commission of Accreditation of Hospitals. The AMA ceased actively conspiring against chiropractic by 1980, but the court case dragged on through two trials and two appeals until the end of 1990. The chiropractors won the case, and the AMA was enjoined by the court from pursuing an unlawful boycott against chiropractors. Moreover, the AMA was ordered to mail a copy of the court's order to every AMA member, to publish the court's opinion in the widely read *Journal of the American Medical Association*, and to revise the AMA ethics statement to clarify the position on chiropractic ("Ruling May Spur Some Medical Arm-Twisting" 1991; Berg 1990).

Alternative Health Care in the United States Today

Evidently wresting control from the irregulars did not result in a final victory for regular physicians over alternative forms of health care. In fact, quite the contrary is true: Alternative medicine appears to be more popular now than it was fifty or a hundred years ago. In a recent study, researchers interviewed a national sample of over 1,500 adults about their use of "unconventional therapies," defined as "medical interventions not taught widely at U.S. medical schools or generally available at U.S. medical schools or generally available at U.S. hospitals" (Eisenberg et al. 1993). These unconventional therapies include, for example, acupuncture, massage, chiropractic, homeopathy, folk remedies, herbal medicine, commercial weight-loss programs, and spiritual healing.

Remarkably, one-third of the population sampled reported using at least one unconventional therapy during 1990. Two-thirds of these alternative health care users did not visit a provider during 1990, but the remaining one-third visited a provider of alternative health care an average of nineteen times that year. This pattern of extensive use of alternative health care was more or less pervasive among all socioeconomic groups and did not differ by sex or insurance status. As a group, African-Americans tended to use less alternative health care than others. Alternative health care use was significantly more common among the college educated, people twenty-five to forty-nine years of age, those with annual incomes of more than $35,000, and those living in the West. In these groups, from 39 to 44 percent of the people surveyed used an alternative health care. National projections of the use of alternative health care services and products are astounding:

[I]n 1990 an estimated 61 million Americans used at least 1 of the 16 unconventional therapies we studied and approximately 22 million Americans saw providers of unconventional therapy for a principal medical condition. . . .

The estimated number of ambulatory visits to providers of unconventional therapy in 1990 was 425 million. . . . This number exceeds the estimated 388 million visits in 1990 to all primary care physicians . . . combined. (Eisenberg et al. 1993, 250)

Despite the heavy usage of unconventional therapy, respondents with serious medical problems rarely visited an alternative health care provider without also visiting a physician. In fact, users of alternative health care were more likely to visit a regular physician than a provider of alternative health care. The authors estimated that the cost of the 425 million visits to alternative health care providers totaled $11.7 billion in 1990. National cost projections for consumption of megavitamins and commercial diet supplements in 1990 totaled $2 billion. Most of these costs were out-of-pocket, that is, not covered by insurance. These out-of-pocket costs, totaling $10.3 billion, were nearly equal to the out-of-pocket expenditures for all hospital care in the United States in 1990.

Physicians Heavily Involved in Alternative Medicine

Not too long ago the American Cancer Society commissioned a national random survey that interviewed 5,000 individuals (Lerner and Kennedy 1992). The purpose of the survey was to determine various aspects about the prevalence, users, and purveyors of "questionable cancer treatments." Dr. Irving Lerner, the principal investigator of the Cancer Society study, defined questionable cancer treatments as "treatment methods which are promoted for use, but which have not met the safety and efficacy requirements of the United States Food, Drug and Cosmetic Act. Safety and efficacy are established by providing reproducible scientific data according to well-recognized methodologies. In contrast to questionable treatments, legitimate investigational treatments . . . are not promoted for general use" (Lerner 1993, 96).

Lerner found that 9 percent of all cancer patients in his study used questionable cancer cures. Projecting this percentage to the 8 million American patients with a history of cancer, an estimated 720,000 nationwide have used alternative cancer treatments. Paralleling the findings of other studies, white, higher-income, better-educated cancer patients were more likely to use alternative cancer treatments.

Some of the extraordinary findings in Lerner's research involve the role of the physician. Patients reported that about a third of the time alternative cancer treatment methods had been recommended by the patient's primary physician—making the physician the leading source of information about alternative cancer treatments! In an additional 15 percent of cases, the patient's physician had approved the alternative treatment. Even more interesting is the finding that fully 60 percent of those actually administering alternative cancer treatments were physicians. Of these physicians, 83 percent received their medical training in the United States, and 18 percent were board certified in a specialty. The 40 percent of alternative cancer treatment practitioners who were not physicians were homeopaths, chiropractors, osteopaths, naturopaths, or nutritionists.

Huckstering, Fraud, Deception, Misrepresentation, and Unproven Alternatives

Perceptions of Alternative Medicine

Allegations of fraud, misrepresentation, and questionable medical practices are widespread both in mainstream medicine and in alternative medicine (Kottow 1992; Pietroni 1992; Campion 1993). Some allopathic physicians argue that, in general, mainstream medicine is scientifically based whereas alternative medicine is not. The problem with this argument is that some types of alternative medicine have been subjected to scientific investigation, and some of these have, indeed, been found to be effective. Others have been found to be ineffective. Furthermore, the same process of scientific investigation—with similarly mixed results—has been applied to mainstream medicine.

Mainstream medicine has come to accept, embrace, and use some alternative medicines that it once scorned, such as stress–reduction techniques, acupuncture, and to some extent chiropractic. Alternative medicine is typically used as an adjunct to allopathic medicine, not a replacement for it. Some practitioners of alternative medicine know the limits of their practice and refer patients to medical doctors under certain circumstances. Others do not. Ultimately, it is probably more useful to evaluate what is known about a particular treatment than to determine if the treatment fits into the social categories of "mainstream" or "alternative."

The Food and Drug Administration

The Food and Drug Administration (FDA) enforces the federal law mandating that drugs cannot be sold unless the FDA has found them to be safe and effective for their intended use. The FDA has established a special Health Fraud Unit that works closely with the National Association of Attorneys General and the Association of Food and Drug Officials. The purpose of the unit is to achieve better coordination among states and local enforcement agencies to target specific health frauds. In addition to enforcement, the unit holds educational conferences and disseminates health fraud information that can be used locally for education and press releases (Henney 1993).

In 1992 the FDA seized more than seventy fraudulent substances, such as anabolic steroids, a serum alleged to cure cancer and AIDS, and "perpetual youth drugs." The fraudulent antiaging potion market around the world is immense, with $2 billion worth of annual sales in the United States alone. In addition to seizures, the FDA sent hundreds of warning letters to promoters of products of unproven therapeutic value. Despite this enforcement activity, the market for fraudulent and unproven medical products is so huge that these enforcement actions are hopelessly inadequate.

Issues in Alternative AIDS Treatment

Both medical and social factors have shaped the environment in which alternative treatments flourish for human immunodeficiency virus (HIV) and acquired immunodeficiency syndrome (AIDS). The disease is deadly and has no known cure. Initially, the government reacted with glacial slowness to the epidemic, and to this day there is considerable criticism of the speed and magnitude of government support of HIV/AIDS research. The combination of pervasive homophobia plus misinformation about HIV/AIDS added an inhibiting moral element to public and government responses to the disease when it was thought to be limited primarily to the male homosexual population. Discrimination against HIV/AIDS patients by some health care providers and facilities exacerbated fears among many HIV/AIDS patients about the usefulness of the institutions of mainstream medicine. Finally, the limited, formal, years-long process of FDA approval of drugs can be extremely frustrating to people who believe they do not have time to wait for results (Sampson 1993, 92). Because of all these factors, the emergence of HIV/AIDS has simultaneously spawned a large and active alternative health network.

> From early in the epidemic, many infected gay men used other systems such as physical exercises, homeopathy, meditation, and naturopathy. They also looked to nutritional supplements and investigational drugs obtained through black and gray markets, hoping to strengthen their immunity. Buyers' clubs sprang up nationwide to sell chemicals and drugs obtained from manufacturers and renegade secret laboratories. (Sampson 1993, 92)

Because of the proliferation of black and gray markets for experimental and outright fraudulent HIV/AIDS treatments, FDA enforcement officials were entirely inadequate for the task. In addition intense political pressure was brought to bear on the FDA to speed up the HIV/AIDS drug testing and release process. As a result the FDA hurriedly approved a number of new drugs and devices for "investigational" use. Meanwhile, in the broader alternative health care market, over two hundred allegedly effective HIV/AIDS drugs, supplements, and curative methods have been identified.

One of these is promoted by the people who sold the FDA-exposed cancer fraud, Laetrile. They have a hospital in Tijuana, Mexico, with inpatient and outpatient treatment programs for AIDS patients. A wide variety of treatments are administered, including herbal teas and enemas, chelation therapy, a strict vegetarian diet, antibiotics, vitamin and fatty acid supplements, amino acids, and much more. An initial two-week inpatient treatment costs $6,600, and treatment costs $400 per month after that. The treatments are widely considered "scientifically unproven, highly unlikely to work, or fraudulent" (Sampson 1993, 93; Guzley 1992).

In order to ferret out a sample of alternative HIV/AIDS treatments, an interesting survey was conducted in forty-one health food stores in Houston, Texas. The "wife" of a fictional husband with HIV infection requested information about materials she might obtain to protect her from becoming infected. All the sales people she encountered assured her that they did have products that would protect her. These products ranged from numerous vitamin supplements and lecithin to raw glandular extracts and hydrogen peroxide. "None of these is active against AIDS. No store clerk recommended use of a condom" (Sampson, 1993, 93).

The Bizarre Story of Laetrile

Without doubt the best known quack cancer cure of the twentieth century is Laetrile (Guzley 1992). In the 1920s Dr. Ernest Krebs, Sr., was working away at his home laboratory, dedicated to improving the lot of humanity by finding a flavor enhancer for bootleg whiskey. Instead he synthesized amygdalin, a bitter substance derived from almond and apricot pits and some other seeds. Later in his career Krebs mentioned that an extract of apricot seeds could reduce cancerous tumors in rodents but that the chemical was too dangerous for human use because of its high cyanide content. Twenty years later his son, Ernest Krebs, Jr., announced to the world the synthesis of Laetrile, allegedly a safer version of amygdalin, for the treatment of cancer in humans. Clinics were soon opened in Mexico and on the West Coast.

Meanwhile, the National Cancer Institute (NCI) conducted animal trials with Laetrile for a twenty-year period beginning in the late 1950s without finding any benefit in the substance. In 1972 a vocal and well-financed right-wing fringe group, the John Birch Society, adopted the cause of Laetrile, giving it a big boost in the media. In the late 1970s NCI capped its two decades of animal studies with a retrospective study of ninety-three patients treated with Laetrile. The researchers found two complete remissions and four partial remissions, but could not attribute these to Laetrile. Later, NCI sponsored its own clinical trials with 175 patients, but only one had a partial remission. Researchers analyzed Mexican-made Laetrile and found it contained 6 percent cyanide by weight. The oral doses recommended by the clinic were potentially lethal. Oral and injectable forms of the drug were "chemically subpotent, mislabeled, and of poor manufacture" (Guzley 1992, 521). In addition a number of the samples were contaminated with microbes and other substances.

Vitamins and Amino Acids

The FDA considers over-the-counter (OTC) vitamins, minerals, and amino acids to be not drugs but, rather, "food supplements." The meaning of this distinction appears to be historically evolving in a bubbling social ferment of large and small private-sector business interests, national and grassroots politics, tumultuous emotional zeal, a pinch of scientific evaluation, and 150 years of American traditions of self-help and distrust of mainstream medical institutions.

For nearly ninety years food or food supplements sold in the United States were banned from making health claims linking consumption of the item with specific disease or health conditions.

> But in 1984 Kellogg's took a chance. The company printed on its All-Bran cereal boxes "preventive health tips from the National Cancer Institute," including advice that Americans make a point of eating foods high in fiber (like All-Bran). . . .
> [T]he FDA backed away from its "no health claims" rule. In 1987 federal officials gave the go ahead for health messages on foods as long as the claims were truthful, not misleading, and supported by well-designed medical studies. These good intentions quickly went awry. (Long 1993, 46)

Manufacturers added to their labels all manner of unproven overt and covert claims for health benefits. The claims were far more outlandish for food supplements than for foods themselves. Some companies labeled their products "energy formulas" or "PMS formulas," while others, slightly more discreetly, implied health benefits in the names of their products, names like "Mental Wisdom Tab" or the name of the supplement presumably for sagging libidos, "Ultra Male." One company sold an entire line of products with names like "Runner's Edge" and "Extra Energy Enzymes," all of which had a single identical ingredient: wheat sprouts. Within a couple of years the FDA saw what was happening, and tried to close Pandora's box. Meanwhile, Congress passed the Nutrition Labeling and Education Act of 1990 making health claims on foods and supplements legal as long as the FDA preapproved such claims for accuracy. In 1991 the FDA proposed its new labeling rules, unleashing an avalanche of 50,000 letters, mostly from protesting manufacturers, retailers, and consumers.

The FDA's position was that a claim on a label is like a guarantee and therefore has to be backed up with rigorous proof. The industry's response was that such proof often included quarter-billion dollar clinical trials, which were unnecessary and unaffordable for most manufacturers. The supplement industry countered by offering to provide lesser levels of proof, an offer that the FDA has so far rejected. Another proposal by the FDA was to regulate dietary supplements in the same way that foods are regulated; this proposal led to some controversial results:

> Specifically, the FDA has proposed to allow health claims only on supplement containers in which the pills each deliver about what you'd ideally get in a day's meals (doses near the recommended dietary allowances, or RDAs, in other words). Bigger doses would *not* be made illegal, nor would they be reclassified as prescription drugs. But bottles containing high-dose pills could not carry any kind of health claims. Nor could herbal formulas or concentrated plant extracts, such as garlic oil capsules. (Long 1993, 46–47; emphasis in the original)

Vitamins

In the United States nearly half the population takes vitamins, minerals, or both, from daily to every now and then. Many do so at the suggestion of their physician for specific conditions—for example, taking calcium for osteoporosis or niacin for cholesterol—but most do so as a form of self-medication to achieve a nearly endless list of alleged benefits. Scientific evidence for the benefits of vitamins and minerals at high doses beyond the recommended daily allowance (RDA) is scarce, but numerous adverse or harmful consequences of vitamin and mineral overdoses are documented. As a result, in a strategy somewhat similar to current proposals, the FDA in the 1970s tried to limit the dose of each vitamin pill to less than 150 percent of the RDA. The health food industry organized a letter-writing campaign deluging Congress with an astounding 2 million pieces of mail. Consequently, Congress felt obliged to pass the Proxmire Amendment in 1976 preventing the FDA from yanking supplements off the shelves because the agency views the dose as too high or the substance as worthless. Nevertheless, the FDA can regulate health claims, but so far the only approved claim that can appear on supplements is that getting enough calcium can reduce the risk of osteoporosis. This does not make for a happy industry. Proposed regulations would also allow claims about sodium and hypertension, fat and cancer, and fat and cardiovascular disease. (Long 1993; Williams 1992, A34).

Apart from anecdotal reports in the medical literature, there is very little systematic information about the harmful effects of megadoses of dietary supplements. The major reason is that, in contrast to prescription drugs, manufacturers of supplements are not required to report adverse reactions to any government agency. Some information about acute effects can be gleaned from the 56,000 calls about vitamin and mineral supplements that were received by U.S. poison control centers in 1991. Of these inquiries,

1,191 involved adverse reactions, including forty-seven life-threatening reactions and eighteen deaths (Long 1993, 47). Most of those who died were infants who had managed to swallow some of Mom's iron supplements.

The toxic effects of vitamin and mineral megadoses taken over long periods of time are harder to document, but there are a growing number of cases. For example, until the early 1980s megadoses of vitamin B-6 were often recommended by physicians to treat premenstrual bloating or carpaltunnel syndrome. However, in some people the treatment caused difficulty walking, numb feet, and other neurological problems. More recently, niacin pills taken to reduce cholesterol are known to have caused at least two dozen cases of serious liver disease. Many of the long-term adverse medical effects of taking megadose supplements are never picked up by health care providers because they do not link patient medical problems to consumption of dietary supplements.

In contrast to prescription drugs, supplements are not required to meet any government-enforced standards. They may be contaminated with impurities, substantially above or below stated potency, or highly variable from pill to pill. They may be poorly manufactured so they pass through the body without fully dissolving. Supplement labels may carry no warnings of side effects and may have no expiration date related to duration of potency, and the container may not be tamper resistant or child proof. As the spokesperson for an FDA task force of dietary supplements recently was quoted as saying, "It is really 'buyer beware'" (quoted in Long 1993, 50).

Amino Acids

Dozens of amino acids are available in health food stores as dietary supplements with all sorts of alleged benefits to the user. Amino acids are the building blocks of protein and are normally consumed as part of food. Straight amino acids taken as a supplement can have very different, and perhaps very potent, effects on the human body. In 1977 amino acids were accidentally included in a "generally recognized as safe" list due to a clerical error. The courts ruled that the FDA's attempt to correct the error would not be allowed to proceed. The 1976 Proxmire Amendment weakened the FDA's regulatory authority over dietary supplements, so the FDA just backed off. In recent years, at the request of the FDA, a panel of scientists conducted a literature review to evaluate the safety of all amino acids taken as supplements. While the review found few human studies, in laboratory research utilizing animals

> amino acid supplements were found to cause decreased growth changes in brain chemistry, and offspring with abnormally small brains. Some kinds, such as lysine, appear in animal studies to be fairly harmless; others seem quite toxic. Methionine can damage the spleen, pancreas, and kidneys.

The panel saw the highest danger for pregnant women (whose infants' brains could be harmed), for diabetics or people with chronic liver disease, and for those with a genetic inability to metabolize particular amino acids. (Long 1993, 54)

Summary and Discussion

Alternative health practitioners and potions have existed in North America since the Colonial era, and they exist today for many of the same reasons that they existed 150 years ago. Mainstream medicine is expensive, alienating, technological; it often provides only minimal relief; and sometimes it offers no hope. Alternative health care is typically cheaper, warmer and fuzzier, low-tech and "natural"; it may offer relief; and it nearly always offers hope. Despite a long history of efforts by regular medicine and the AMA first to destroy alternative medicine and then to co-opt it, alternative health care devotees today number in the tens of millions and are widespread across all sectors of society. Many physicians practice alternative medicine, and others tolerate it to a greater or lesser extent.

References

Beresford, Larry. 1991. "Is It Time to Back Chiropractic?" *Business and Health* (December):50–56.

Berg, Robert N. 1990. "AMA Enjoined from Boycotting Chiropractors." *Journal of the Medical Association of Georgia* 79:391–93.

Campion, Edward. 1993. "Why Unconventional Medicine?" *The New England Journal of Medicine* 328:282–83.

Cassileth, Barrie R. 1989. "The Social Implications of Questionable Cancer Therapies." *Cancer* 63:1247–50.

Eisenberg, David M., Ronald C. Kessler, Cindy Foster, Frances E. Norlock, David R. Calkins, and Thomas L. Delbanco. 1993. "Unconventional Medicine in the United States." *The New England Journal of Medicine* 328:246–52.

Guzley, Gregory J. 1992. "Alternative Cancer Treatments: Impact of Unorthodox Therapy on the Patient with Cancer." *Southern Medical Journal* 85(5):519–23.

Henney, Jane E. 1993. "Combatting Medical Fraud." *New York State Journal of Medicine* 93(2):86-87.

Kottow, Michael H. 1992. "Classical Medicine v. Alternative Medical Practices." *Journal of Medical Ethics* 18:18–22.

Lerner, Irving. 1993. "The Physician and Cancer Quackery." *New York State Journal of Medicine* 98(2):96–100.

Lerner, Irving J., and B. J. Kennedy. 1992. "The Prevalence of Questionable Methods of Cancer Treatment in the United States." *CA: A Cancer Journal for Clinicians* 42(3):181–91.

Long, Patricia. 1993. "The Vitamin Wars." *Health* (May–June):45–54.

Pietroni, Patrick C. 1992. "Alternative Medicine: Methinks the Doctor Protests Too Much and Incidentally Befuddles the Debate." *Journal of Medical Ethics* 18:23–25.
"Ruling May Spur Some Medical Arm-Twisting." 1991. *Wall Street Journal* (January 18):B1(W).
Sampson, Wallace I. 1993. "AIDS Fraud, Finances, and Fringes." *New York State Journal of Medicine* 93(2):92–96.
Smith, Timothy K. 1993. "Chiropractors Seeking to Expand Practices Take Aim at Children." *Wall Street Journal* (March 18):A1(W).
Starr, Paul. 1982. *The Social Transformation of American Medicine*. New York: Basic Books.
Williams, Lena. 1992. "F.D.A. Steps Up Effort to Control Vitamin Claims." *New York Times* (August 9):A1(L), A10.

8

The Drug Industry

In 1993 total sales by the member companies of the Pharmaceutical Manufacturers Association (PMA) were $85 billion, with about two-thirds of that being domestic sales and the balance exports. Of the total figure, about $5.5 billion were generic drugs, and (in 1991) $13 billion were nonprescription, over-the-counter drugs. The balance, nearly 80 percent of all pharmaceuticals sold by U.S.-based drug manufacturers, were name-brand prescription drugs (Shon 1993, 3–4). Roughly one-eleventh of the nation's health care costs are for prescription drugs.

Prescription Drug Prices

Drug manufacturers are under no obligation to reveal how and why they price drugs the way they do since they consider pricing strategies proprietary information and as such, the information is legally protected (Flanagan 1993, 11). During the 1980s the average prescription drug price increased at nearly three times the general inflation rate. As a result, Representatives Byron L. Dorgan and Pete Stark asked the GAO to examine price increases for twenty-nine widely used drugs that are commonly purchased by the Department of Veterans Affairs (VA) as well as by the general public. GAO investigators found in general that

> prices for nearly all 29 drug products increased more than the percentage changes for all three consumer price indexes for the 6-year period ending December 31, 1991. The maximum price increase for each product during this period generally exceeded 100 percent, with some prices increasing by 200 to 300 percent. . . . During this same period, the CPI [Consumer Price Index] for all items increased by 26.2 percent, the CPI for medical care by 56.3 percent, and the CPI for prescription drugs by 67 percent. (U.S. General Accounting Office 1992b, 3)

The GAO report demonstrated another extremely interesting fact about drug sales: Wholesale prices of identical prescription drugs vary tremendously depending upon who they are sold to. The difference between low and high wholesale prices is yet another indication of how overpriced many prescription drugs are. Big institutional buyers such as hospitals, HMOs, and Medicaid programs can negotiate deep discounts, so the drug manufacturers shift high prices to the community pharmacies that are unable to command substantial discounts. Presumably the manufacturer is making a profit at the lower wholesale price as well as the higher. If so, the profit margin in the higher price must be astronomical.

An example is Tylenol with codeine, sold by McNeil Pharmaceutical as a pain killer. In 1991 wholesalers paid an average of $26.57 for 100 tablets of number 3 Tylenol with codeine; however, the identical bottle of pills was sold to the VA for $2.50. Wholesalers paid more than ten times as much as did the VA for this drug. The implication is that consumers shopping at pharmacies also paid ten times as much as was necessary for Tylenol with codeine. The inequity of this situation has not escaped the chain and independent pharmacies. Late in 1993 representatives of about 5,000 retail drugstores sued seven major pharmaceutical companies for putting the retailers at a competitive disadvantage by giving such deep discounts to other institutional buyers but not to the pharmacies or their wholesalers (Tanouye 1993b).

Price Gouging

Attempting to blunt government threats to contain prescription drug costs by legislation and trying to divert a growing popular animosity toward the drug giants, 13 of the 112 members of the PMA promised to restrain the pricing of new drugs and to keep price increases for older drugs at or below the general rate of inflation in the 1990s. Congressional leaders of a Senate panel on aging had less than flattering comments about the pharmaceutical industry's high-profile voluntary cost containment efforts. Panel members presented a study of two hundred of the top-selling prescription drugs; this study indicated that price hikes for these drugs averaged 6.4 percent in 1992 whereas the Producer Price Index for all finished goods rose only 1.5 percent. Senators David Pryor and William Cohen accused the industry of "price gouging" and of blithely conducting business as usual despite their promises ("Drug Makers Broke Promise" 1993).

The congressmen noted that drug manufacturers may have shown greater restraint in price hikes to major institutional buyers such as hospitals and Medicaid programs (institutional buying power in the market left the manufacturers little choice); however, most elderly people are outpatients who buy their drugs at pharmacies, where drug prices have suffered the biggest increases. They also noted that the makers of the top twenty prescription drugs have long averaged 15-percent profit margins; the average profit margin for the Fortune 500 companies is 3.2 percent.

Separating Ideology from Facts

In pursuing research into price changes of twenty-nine common drugs mentioned above, the GAO

> asked each company to explain why each drug product increased in price. To verify the information they gave us, we asked five companies to provide more specific explanations. However, none of them did so because they considered the information proprietary. As agreed with your offices [that is, the congressional representatives who requested the research], we made no further effort to verify the information they gave us because it appeared likely that the other 13 companies would give us similar answers. (U.S. General Accounting Office 1992b, 3)

The explanations for drug price increases given the GAO were "general" and "provided few details," and they could not be independently evaluated since the drug manufacturers would not release the necessary information. A few of the most common responses received by GAO researchers along with a brief explanation include the following:

"Increased research and development (R&D) or operating costs." The PMA estimates that the pharmaceutical industry spent about $8 billion for research in 1992; however, analysts of the drug industry estimate that up to 25 percent of that figure is fluff—marketing expenses that pad alleged R&D expenses. In addition, an industry study shows that between 1975 and 1989 about 60 percent of drug industry research was invested in copycat drugs, that is, known drugs that are slightly reformulated or recombined in order to find a niche in the market but that offer no new therapeutic benefits to the consumer. In all likelihood, less than half the $8 billion allegedly spent on research is actually spent developing new drugs with new medical benefits. Compare this figure to the approximately $10 billion spent in 1991 by the drug industry on advertising and promotion (Rock 1993, 133; Wolfe 1993, 11).

"Prices for comparable therapies." In other words, drug manufacturers raise their prices because other therapies for the same condition are also expensive—and the market will sustain it.

"Increased product value due to new indications or uses." Costs to produce the drug have not risen, but new markets have been discovered that will pay the increased price.

"Physician and patient education programs." Advertising.

The Struggle to Maintain Profits

Pharmaceutical manufacturers have real concerns about protecting their uniquely remunerative position among American industries. The drug companies are increasingly squeezed by institutional buyers who demand and get deep discounts. Mail-order prescription drug firms are another emerging group of institutional buyers that are increasingly threatening to the drug manufacturers. Finally, government proposals to slash tax breaks for drug manufacturers or to limit or cap drug prices are bandied about with increasing frequency. Consequently, the drug companies are fighting back.

In its heyday the pharmaceutical industry had a 50,000-strong "detail force" of sales persons who banged on doctors' doors and "educated" them about the home company's drugs, gave physicians gifts, took them out to dinner, and more. With an increasing proportion of the sales effort now aimed at buyers for large institutions rather than individual doctors, the army of detail agents has become somewhat redundant. For example, Merck, the world's largest pharmaceutical company, gave pink slips to 8 percent of its detail agents between fall 1991 and spring 1993. In 1993 Bristol-Myers cut its workforce by 2,200 employees, about 6 percent of the total. In the foreseeable future, downsizing to preserve profit margins will be the name of the corporate game among pharmaceutical manufacturers (Cutaia 1993; Weber and Bhargava 1993, 105).

Corporate mergers, joint operations, buyouts, and reorganizations are a major part of the strategy to preserve profit margins. Like a growing number of other drug companies, Merck started its own captive generic drug manufacturing operation, West Point Pharma, to produce generic versions of its own products when they lose patent protection. Some drug manufacturers are selling off less-profitable subsidiaries, and others are purchasing specialized operations in order to focus on a market. American Cyanamid Co., for example, bought 54 percent of the biotech company Immunex for $740 million in cash, which made American Cyanamid the second biggest maker of cancer drugs in the United States. In a precedent-setting example of vertical integration, Merck paid $6 billion for Medco Containment Services, the nation's largest mail-order drug company. Mail-order companies are the fastest growing institutional buyer of prescription drugs, often at deep discounts. However, a mail-order company is much less of a threat to the bottom line of a pharmaceutical manufacturer if the mail-order business is wholly owned by the manufacturer. One corporate marriage joins Merck, with $10 billion in annual sales, to Medco, with annual sales of $1.8 billion worth of drugs to employer health plans covering 33 million members (Freudenheim 1993, D5; Cutaia 1993).

Cheaper Drugs in Canada and Mexico

Representative Henry A. Waxman (D.–Calif.), chairman of the Subcommittee on Health and the Environment of the Committee on Energy and Commerce, requested that the GAO produce a report comparing factory prices of popular prescription drugs in Canada and the United States. The GAO compared 121 of the 200 most popular drugs sold in the United States, matching them by dosage forms, strength, and package size to sales of identical drugs in Canada. The researchers found that

> for the prescription drugs we examined, drug manufacturers charge wholesalers significantly more in the United States than the same manufacturers do in Canada. If a common U.S. prescription of each drug included in our study was purchased at factory price in both countries, the entire basket of 121 prescriptions would cost 32 percent more in the United States than in Canada. Alternatively, when price differentials are computed drug by drug, the median price differential per package between the United States and Canada was 43 percent.
>
> U.S.-Canadian price differentials at the factory level vary widely for particular drugs. Price differences ranged from the U.S. price being 44 percent lower to 967 percent higher than the Canadian price. . . . Despite this wide range, most drugs we studied were more expensive in the United States. . . . Of the drugs we compared, 98 were priced higher in the United States than in Canada. Almost half the 121 drugs studied were priced over 50 percent more in the United States than in Canada. (U.S. General Accounting Office 1992c, 12)

In contrast to assertions by some drug manufacturers, GAO researchers found that differences in drug manufacturers' costs do not account for the differences in prices charged in the two countries. There are two key factors that do keep prices of drugs lower in Canada than in the United States: The first is Canadian federal regulations designed to restrain price increases during the market life of a prescription drug, and the second is the regulatory and market control by centralized provincial drug-benefit plans.

The Canadian federal role in the control of drug prices was substantially altered by a 1987 revision of the Patent Act in Canada. On the one hand, that act increased the number of years during which drug manufacturers are protected from competition in the market by generic products (the extended period is still only a fraction of the time the drug companies are protected from competition in the United States). On the other hand, in order to guard against pricing abuses by pharmaceutical manufacturers with monopoly control over the market for seven to ten years, the Canadian Parliament established the Patented Medicine Prices Review Board (PMPRB). The review board is an independent, quasi-judicial body with five board members and a staff of about thirty-five employees. Its principal mandate is to ensure that the prices charged for patented prescription drugs are not excessive. It has no jurisdiction over drugs whose patents have expired or over generic drugs. Here's how it works:

> The Board periodically publishes guidelines that it uses to determine if a manufacturer's introductory price on a new drug or price increase on an older patented drug is excessive. The Board generally considers an introductory price to be excessive if the product's cost per day or per treatment exceeds the maximum cost per day or per treatment for therapeutically comparable medicines. If there are no therapeutically comparable medicines; that is, if the drug is a breakthrough product or judged to be a substantial improvement over existing therapies, the introductory price is excessive if it is higher than the median price charged for the product in seven other industrialized countries. The price of an existing patented drug is excessive if its cumulative price increase—either since its introduction or since the Board's inception, whichever is more recent—exceeds the growth in Canada's consumer price index (CPI) for the same period.
> . . .
> If a manufacturer sets a price considered to be excessive, the Board can order the manufacturer to lower the drug's price, but has no authority to enforce that order. It can also take away a drug's market exclusivity, after a public hearing. When removing market exclusivity, the Board can choose to do so for the drug in question, another drug produced by the same manufacturer, or both drugs. (U.S. General Accounting Office 1993, 5–6)

The board enforces its mandate largely with the club of bad publicity and the threat of exposing drug ingredients at public hearings. The initial prices of most drugs and subsequent increases in the price of older drugs usually fall within the board's guidelines. Private negotiations resolve the balance of the pricing problems, usually within a few months. As of the end of 1992 the board had come close to holding a hearing only once. The "gentle persuasion" techniques of the board appear to work. Since the review board's inception in 1987 the prices of patented drugs have risen more slowly than the Canadian CPI and more slowly than the prices of drugs without patents, which are not regulated by the board. Interestingly enough, during the same period that drug prices have been successfully contained in Canada, R&D has doubled. This fact refutes a major argument of U.S. drug manufacturers that price controls would result in reduced funds for R&D.

Although the GAO has not researched drug prices in Mexico, some studies and anecdotal information indicate that drugs there may be even cheaper than in Canada and far more accessible to Americans. The *Wall Street Journal* reports that "thousands" of drug stores just across the border cater to a huge number of Americans, some of whom travel long distances to purchase an entire year's supply. The prices of prescription drugs have been controlled in Mexico since the 1940s. A Mexican study reportedly shows that prescription drug prices in Mexico average one-fifth the prices of their U.S. counterparts. Studies by the University of Texas School of Public Health and the consumer group Families USA both indicate that large numbers of U.S. residents regularly cross the border for cheap prescription drugs and health care. Physicians on the U.S. side, even the county hospital, routinely refer low-income patients to the Mexican side of the border to purchase cheaper drugs (Solis 1993).

Prescription Drug Marketing

Marketing Directly to Consumers

During the end of the 1980s and the beginning of the new decade, things were not looking up for the drug manufacturers. They were being dragged to congressional hearings, assailed by an FDA that had recently awoken from a long Reagan-induced slumber, and attacked in the press for excessive pricing. Sensing that their public image might be tarnished, Searle Pharmaceuticals hired a public opinion polling organization to produce a nationwide snapshot of attitudes about drug manufacturers. It was not a pretty picture, as recalled by Jack Doneischel, vice president of Searle's corporate communications:

"'It was bad enough that more than half those interviewed thought pharmaceutical companies were greedy,' Doneischel said. 'The worst part was that only 11% thought they were getting value for the prices they were paying'" ("Pharmaceutical Giants Tell Their Story" 1993).

As a result, Searle developed a damage-control plan by the name of "Rx Partners," a multifaceted industry-wide plan to bolster a seriously damaged image. Rx Partners was quickly joined by a number of other drug industry giants, all of whom were suffering the same problem, according to public opinion polling—a collective look in the mirror, so to speak. Rx Partners initiated a program to get pharmaceutical industry CEOs in front of the news media to tell their side of the story. The chairman of Hoffmann-La Roche, for example, found himself on CNN and the *Larry King* radio show preaching the corporate gospel to millions. The PMA reinvigorated a "feel good" national printed media blitz focusing on the message that drugs help people live better and longer. The PMA gave a higher profile to the Indigent Patient Program, in which drug companies give free drugs or discounts to low-income patients, usually through their physicians. The media loved it. Did Rx Partners work? A quick and dirty analysis done a couple of months after the start of the campaigns indicated that "only 31% of the articles were judged unfavorable, down from 77% two months earlier. The number of favorable stories grew from 20% to 53%; the balance of the stories were neutral" ("Pharmaceutical Giants Tell Their Story" 1993).

As a result of grumbling among FDA officials and some very unfavorable public exposure, in 1990 both the AMA and the PMA adopted ethical guidelines regarding gift-giving. The PMA agreed that it was unethical for member drug companies to offer substantial gifts to physicians, and the AMA agreed that it was unethical for physicians to accept them. The issue, of course, is that such gifts could be perceived as bribes to physicians by the manufacturers to push certain drugs, thereby converting the physician into an agent of the drug company rather than an unambiguous advocate for the patient. The drug companies changed their errant ways. They started giving substantial gifts directly to the consumers of drugs.

One of the first major advertising efforts of this sort involved a two-page spread in *Parade* magazine in summer 1991 by the manufacturer of Tenormin, a blood-pressure drug. The ad offered free and discounted merchandise—gifts that ranged from decaffeinated coffee to camera film and music CDs—to anyone taking Tenormin. Now nearly every major drug company offers patients incentives of one kind or another to encourage them to pressure their physician to prescribe some ballyhooed drug, to switch to it from another, or to keep taking it.

The stakes are high for drug manufacturers. Industry representatives cite data indicating that the vast majority of physicians will consider prescribing a drug requested by a patient. In addition pharmacists and drug manufacturers estimate that they lose $2.8 billion annually because patients either forget to refill their prescriptions or simply stop taking the drug. Among patients who do continue to take their medications, the manufacturers want to foster "brand loyalty." Tenormin, for example, sells for about $25 per month, but a generic substitute costs only about $10. In such a case buying brand loyalty for the price of a few trinkets and a discount or two makes very good sense for the financial standing of the manufacturer.

The new pharmaceutical initiative of direct advertising to consumers retains something of the old tradition of offering incentives to physicians and pharmacists: Often the coupons or forms that patients require to receive the giveaways are provided to physicians and pharmacists to give directly to patients, and the pot may be sweetened to encourage them to do it. For example, Marion Merrell Dow, makers of the blood-pressure medication Cardizem CD, offers pharmacists $5 to successfully switch their clients, with physician approval, to Cardizem CD from an earlier form of the medication (Podolsky and Newman 1993, 58).

A significant proportion of the drug company pitch to consumers obscures the connection between the purpose of the advertising and the vested interests of the drug company. For example, the National Mental Health Association is a nonprofit "educational" organization that launched a $3 million to $4 million advertising blitz in 1993 urging people who suspect they are depressed to see their physician (Tanouye 1993a). The high-profile campaign included ads in *Parade* magazine, the *New York Times,* and on the television show *60 Minutes,* among other places. It was estimated that the three-week media saturation extravaganza reached 93 percent of all adult Americans. The ads were presented as public service announcements.

Although its name, "National Mental Health Association," suggests that this is a large nonprofit organization, it is not. In fact, the millions of dollars spent by this organization for the media blitz on the symptoms of depression actually came from one private source: the pharmaceutical manufacturers Eli Lilly and Company. It is no coincidence that Lilly sells Prozac, the world's best-selling antidepressant drug, with annual sales of about $1.2 billion. The entire ad campaign was strongly criticized by the American Psychological Association, which noted that the campaign's emphasis was to encourage people to see primary care providers, who are likely to treat clinical depression exclusively with drugs (Prozac, in particular) rather than with counseling or psychotherapy. In a parallel effort Lilly gave the National Mental Health Association another half-million dollars to work with four hundred local mental health organizations for a period of nine months to identify depressed but untreated people in the communities and to encourage them to obtain treatment.

Public relations firms note that these kinds of campaigns "condition the marketplace" by laying a firm foundation among the public, pharmacists, physicians, and other health care providers for a subsequent more direct, targeted sales approach. In 1991 pharmaceutical companies spent $91 million advertising prescription drugs directly to consumers. In 1992 the amount spent on advertising to consumers more than doubled. About $100 million in 1992 alone was spent advertising prescription nicotine patches, and we can expect to see a growing trend by the pharmaceutical companies to pressure consumers to pressure their physicians to prescribe something that is profitable (Winters 1993, 10).

Marketing to Physicians and Other Health Care Providers

It is estimated that in the late 1980s about 175,000 physicians annually took part in dinners sponsored by drug companies, dinners at which they were typically handed $100 for attending and listening to a promotional spiel about the company's drugs. Since the critical congressional hearings of the early 1990s, the $100 cash payment has been largely replaced with a $100 "educational" gift, such as a textbook. The pharmaceutical industry estimates it makes $5 in increased sales for every $1 invested in promotional dinners. A typical physician can still expect to be visited by detail agents two or three times a week throughout the year (Randall 1991; Drake and Uhlman 1993; Paul 1993, 95).

In 1990, just a few weeks before congressional hearings on the pharmaceutical industry, both the AMA and the PMA adopted nearly identical ethical codes regarding gift giving by the drug manufacturers to physicians. Key points in the guidelines include these:

Cash payments should be avoided, but textbooks and meals are acceptable if they serve an "educational" function.

Grants cannot be given to individual physicians for travel or lodging to attend meetings. Subsidies for meals and social events are acceptable as long as they are part of the conference.

Scholarships and related funds to allow medical students and residents to attend conferences are acceptable as long as the recipients are chosen by their institution. (Conlan 1991, 44).

Critics point out that the creation of "ethical codes of conduct" may be good public relations, but they may not be very useful in getting the drug manufacturers to change their behavior. Codes of ethical behavior are not legally binding on anyone. Such codes are not laws; they are simply guidelines that the respective trade organizations recommend members follow. The history of the PMA and the AMA shows a lack of willingness to effectively police their own ethical standards to any significant degree. Second, this particular set of guidelines appears to have a number of loopholes: Gifts of various kinds are allowed just as before, but they are supposed to be "modest" or "educational." Just what that means is anyone's guess; such vague language is always debatable. Finally, only drug manufacturers who are members of the PMA are even theoretically supposed to follow these ethical guidelines. Many drug manufacturers are not members of the PMA, and for them the code of ethics is even less binding.

Corporate Influence in Continuing Medical Education

Albert Einstein College of Medicine in New York, a fairly typical medical school, offers an array of continuing medical education (CME) classes to help physicians earn enough CME hours to retain specialty certifications and hospital privileges and to keep their medical licenses current. Physicians have to take CME courses on a regular basis. At Albert Einstein nearly half of all costs for CME courses are paid for by pharmaceutical companies and related industries. In some cases the corporations sponsor real education, but in other cases their offerings degenerate into simple product promotion. "Industry support for CME can take many forms, ranging from subsidies for travel money and speakers' fees to the creation of entire courses complete with faculty, syllabus, slides, and handouts" ("Pushing Drugs to Doctors" 1992, 90).

Corporations are ready to take advantage of the information superhighway: Consider the Whittle organization's Medical News Network (MNN) is a system intended to replace a significant chunk of the pharmaceutical industry sales force and to place CME more directly into the hands of the drug companies. Here's how it works: A physician is given a TV-VCR unit, complete with the capability to receive and send satellite transmissions, and an interactive keypad similar to one used to control a video game. Five days a week an electronic signal beamed from a satellite activates the machine and records fourteen to twenty-four minutes of programming on the VCR, to be watched at the physician's leisure sometime during the day. The first four-teen minutes contains ten minutes of medical news plus two two-minute drug commercials. The last ten minutes contains more medical news. The interactive pad allows the physician to provide information, ask questions, and request product information from the sponsors. CME presentations are also planned as part of the MNN system, with credit automatically electroni-cally beamed to the American Academy of Family Physicians if the physician passes the course. The exam is given over the television, and the answers are entered through the interactive pad. Network owners anticipated the system would be in the offices of 50,000 physicians by 1995. There was no trouble raising cash for the MNN startup. Seven pharmaceutical giants handed over $100 million to get in on the ground floor (Castagnoli 1993). By 1994, however, MNN had gone bankrupt—a victim of the emergence of HMOs and pharmacy benefit management corporations, which are replacing indi-vidual physicians as the main purchasers of drugs (Schwartz 1995).

Corporate Influence in Medical Journals

Physicians consider peer-reviewed medical journals to be one of their pri-mary sources for unbiased medical information. Prior to being published, submitted articles must be reviewed by several experts in the field, experts who are chosen by the editors of the journal. No such process, however, oc-curs with the $350 million worth of drug advertisements that appear in medical journals each year. Lack of journal oversight combined with a histor-ical lack of regulatory enforcement by the FDA, which has jurisdiction over drug advertisements, has led to fast and loose advertising by many of the pharmaceutical advertisers.

A consumer organization, the Public Citizen Health Research Group, sent a sample of over one hundred pharmaceutical advertisements found in sev-eral medical journals to a panel of drug experts for evaluation. The panel found that about 60 percent of the drug advertisements were in violation of federal regulations and required substantial revision or outright rejection (Steinbrook 1992). This is particularly noteworthy since a study by Harvard researchers demonstrated that physicians retain information from drug ads but often erroneously recall that they got it from objective articles ("Pushing Drugs to Doctors" 1992, 88).

The purchase of supplements is an even more insidious method by which the drug companies subvert the peer-reviewed "objective" information that physicians expect to find in medical journals. Typically, supplements are bundled with the regular journal and are designed and typeset to look just like the accompanying medical journal. However, that is where the similarity stops. Often the supplements are wholly paid for and produced by a drug manufacturer. Commonly they include a series of articles originally presented at a company-sponsored symposium. As an FDA enforcement officer candidly commented, "Repeatedly, we have found these publications not to be balanced, objective sources of information regarding current drug research or drug treatment" (quoted in "Pushing Drugs to Doctors" 1992, 93).

Prescription Drug Research

Corporate Research

During the 1980s consumer groups and Congress were becoming increasingly critical of the rapidly rising cost of prescription drugs. In 1988 Congressman Henry A. Waxman requested the Office of Technology Assessment (OTA) to investigate the relationship between the cost of drug company research and the price of prescription drugs. A draft of the OTA's definitive 741-page report on the subject emerged three years later. It found that previous cost-of-research figures released by the drug industry were arbitrary and insupportable. OTA researchers found no evidence of longer, more complex clinical trials, and they discovered that the financial stability of the drug manufacturers was so solid that they were exposed to little financial risk resulting from drug R&D. During the mid-1980s the average new drug released on the market brought in at least $40 million in the first year. Finally, the drug companies had their federal taxes reduced by nearly 60 percent in 1987 because they benefited from special tax credits equal to $2.4 billion (Freudenheim 1991).

Early in 1993 an updated version of this study was released. This study found that the full cost of R&D for the average drug in the 1980s was $194 million (in 1990 dollars). This sounds like a lot, but the OTA also found that "new drugs introduced in the 1980s generated higher revenues for the pharmaceutical industry than ever before" (Office of Technology Assessment 1993b, 1). The average drug earned at least $36 million more than was needed to pay off all R&D costs. From 1976 through 1987, OTA researchers found that drug industry profits were 2 or 3 percentage points higher than profits in other industries with equal risk burdens. In summary, the OTA noted that "pharmaceutical research and development (R&D) is a costly and risky business, but in recent years the financial rewards from R&D have more than offset its costs and risks" (Office of Technology Assessment, 1993b, 1).

Most scientific research in the United States is funded by the federal government, and nearly 50 percent of all the most promising cancer and AIDS drugs have been developed in university or government laboratories. Taxol is one such drug. It is derived from the bark of the relatively scarce Pacific yew tree. It has been approved for treating ovarian cancer and may also be effective for lung and breast cancers. The drug was discovered in the early 1970s and was developed and brought through much of the FDA approval process by the National Institutes of Health (NIH) at a cost of $32 million to taxpayers. In 1991 the government authorized Bristol-Myers Squibb to market Taxol under a cooperative R&D agreement. Bristol-Myers charges $4,000–6,000 for a four-month treatment for a typical patient. During congressional hearings early in 1993, consumer advocate James P. Love of the Ralph Nader spin-off Taxpayer Assets Project of the Center for Study of Responsive Law accused Bristol-Myers of price gouging and pointed out that the NIH had commissioned subcontractors to produce Taxol at one-eighth the wholesale cost charged by Bristol-Myers. The company responded with the standard industry assertion that Taxol was fairly priced compared to other cancer treatments, but that response evades the whole issue of the relationship of drug cost to drug price. The company did assert that it had spent more than $114 million for development and planning but gave no details about what that was spent on. The company also noted that the cost of producing the drug accounts for as little as one-quarter of the price charged to consumers. Meanwhile, industry analysts claimed that worldwide annual sales of Taxol could easily total $800 million (Leary 1993; Vernaci 1993; Carey 1993; Hilts 1993).

Influencing Academic Research

All new drugs are required by the FDA to undergo extensive testing to demonstrate that they are safe and effective. Drug manufacturers pay physicians and other researchers at academic medical centers to conduct a large portion of these investigations. A 1990 survey of members of the American Federation for Clinical Research, for example, revealed that over one-third of the respondents received corporate grants averaging $31,000 a year. They also discovered that these corporate research grants were "profit centers" for the researchers since they often received thousands of dollars more for the grant than they actually spent on the research. Ultimately, corporate control is significant:

> These manipulations do have a measurable effect. In a review of 107 published studies comparing a new drug against traditional therapy, Dr. Richard Davidson of the University of Florida found that drug company–supported studies of new drugs were far more likely to favor those drugs than were studies supported by noncommercial entities. ("Pushing Drugs to Doctors" 1992, 93)

Politics of Drug Manufacturing

The drug industry lobbying enterprise is an awesome, well-oiled machine. At the center of it is the PMA, with an annual budget of $31 million. That kind of money can grease a lot of wheels in Washington. In addition, the lobbying effort can draw on the resources of the thirty-three drug companies with lobbyists based in Washington, and on the PACs. In 1992 drug company PACs funneled $4 million to their favorite congressional candidates, 27 percent more than in 1990. "Top recipients Sens. Dan Coats (R–Ind.) and Orrin Hatch (R–Utah), both conservatives, can be counted on to make the industry's arguments in Congress" (Novak 1993, 59). Finally, there is Rx Partners, the $2-million face-lifting and lobbying effort that was started by Searle Pharmaceuticals, joined by half a dozen other huge pharmaceutical manufacturers, and implemented by Powell Tate, a high-powered public relations firm (Levine and Silverstein 1993).

Jody Powell, press secretary to Jimmy Carter, headed the Powell Tate effort. Its principal stated goal was to cast doubt on the Clintons' attack on drug industry prices and to undermine any effective threat to drug industry profits that might surface in proposals for health care reform in the Clinton administration. One of Rx Partners first campaigns was to send out a letter signed by the chief scientific officer of Eli Lilly and Company. It contained a form letter bashing proposed drug industry price controls that the recipients were to send to their congressional representatives:

> These efforts generated more than 50,000 letters and messages to Congress, though it's difficult to measure their true impact. An aide to one Democratic Congressman said that nearly one in five of the form letters his office received had been altered by the senders to favor price reforms, and contained such messages as "Regulate these bastards" and "Screw them to the wall." (Levine and Silverstein 1993, 731)

PMA Plays the Race Card

Another prong of the Rx Partners campaign was the utilization of allegedly grassroots organizations with no apparent ties to the drug companies. Politically these supposedly independent organizations are quite influential in Washington circles; however, many of them have been supported over the years with low-profile drug company money and in-kind contributions. Despite the presumed sincerity of the leadership and constituencies of these organizations, they have been cultivated to support corporate interests at key political moments. These organizations include the National Multiple Sclerosis Society and the Cystic Fibrosis Foundation, but a disproportional number of organizations convinced to back the pharmaceutical industry are minority organizations such as the NMA, representing African-American physicians, and the National Coalition of Hispanic Health and Human Services Organizations. At least one critic of the PMA says it "played the race card" in orchestrating a lobbying campaign against a bill sponsored by Senator David Pryor (D–Ark.) that would use the $5.5 billion (in 1991) annual drug buying power of Medicaid to force price concessions from the drug companies:

> The trade group [PMA] hired civil rights veteran Vernon E. Jordan, former president of the National Urban League and partner with the law and lobbying firm Akin Gump Hauer & Feld, to help make its case. (Jordan recently served as chairman of the transition team for President Bill Clinton.) Jordan urged minority groups to oppose the proposal; they did, saying its provisions would mean "second-class medicine" for poor blacks. One letter from the National Black Caucus of State Legislators to another group characterized the Medicaid proposals as coming from "mean-spirited bigots [who] want to strike at the black underclass"—Pryor's strong civil rights record notwithstanding.
>
> PMA even persuaded Jesse Jackson and other minority leaders to write participants in the 1990 budget summit and voice their opposition to the Medicaid measures, according to the *National Journal.* The National Black Nurses Association, the League of United Latin American Citizens, and others amplified the "second-class medicine" argument with a press conference, maintaining that provisions favoring the use of less expensive medications would limit Medicaid recipients' access to drugs.
>
> But Pryor's aides point out that the bill contained an override allowing doctors to prescribe any drug they deemed "medically necessary." Many third-party payers and hospitals nationwide use rules similar to those the bill would have imposed, they maintain. (Novak 1993, 62)

Ultimately, despite the cynical and perhaps racist tactics of the PMA, a weakened version of the bill did pass. Some minority organizations, such as the Center on the Black Aged, were not persuaded by the PMA lobbying effort. Other organizations supported the bill unwaveringly, organizations such as the American Association of Retired Persons (AARP), the National Governors Association, the National Caucus, and the American Public Welfare Association. The gutted version of the law requires drug manufacturers to bill Medicaid at the same rate that they give other bulk purchasers. The industry's response was to immediately raise the prices for all bulk buyers. Within one year, for example, the Department of Veterans Affairs was hit with an average drug-price increase of 21 percent, resulting in an annual drug bill increase of $90 million.

Dinner Time!

The PMA has more direct ways of influencing our elected officials other than the orchestration of "grassroots" organizations. They seem to lean heavily on dinners and parties. In spring 1992, for example, an organization by the name of the "Alliance for Aging Research" sponsored an elaborate dinner to "hand out awards" to Louis Sullivan, secretary of Health and Human Services and well-placed Senators Pete Domenici and Jay Rockefeller. Sumptuous cuts of filet mignon and salmon provided the ambiance for political influence. A closer look reveals that half the members of the event-organizing committee were drug industry lobbyists and that the bash was funded by fourteen major drug manufacturers. In addition, "the industry sponsored parties and [was] a big presence at the 1992 Democratic and Republican presidential conventions" (Novak 1993, 59).

Dinners are nice, but high-powered lobbyists are better. The classic "revolving door" is nowhere in better evidence. Former top-level congressional aides, legislators, and other well-placed persons are hired at opulent salaries to return to their former political haunts and convince legislators to do the drug industry's bidding. "Senate staffers say the industry has at least one lobbyist covering each member of the Senate Labor and Human Resources Committee" (Novak 1993, 63). One of the lobbyists keeping the Labor and Human Resources Committee in line is former committee member Paula Hawkins, who was a senator from Florida. Genentech pays her $120,000 annually as a lobbyist to cruise around Washington in a limo and bend the ear of former colleagues.

A prized drug industry possession, jealously guarded by Hawkins and other lobbyists, is the corporate tax break in Puerto Rico. Puerto Rico is manufacturing heaven for the pharmaceutical industry. Twenty-six of the largest drug manufacturers in the United States have facilities in Puerto Rico, and among other commodities they produce seventeen of the twenty-one most prescribed drugs in the nation (U.S. General Accounting Office, 1992a, 1–5). Section 936 of the federal tax code was designed to help create jobs in Puerto Rico by waiving corporate taxes under certain conditions. Although it has largely failed to create jobs, it has created excessive profits for the drug industry by dismissing a big chunk of their tax obligations. Other taxpayers, of course, have had to make up the difference.

Drug Misadventuring

The term "drug misadventuring" is a curious phrase. Perhaps it connotes to the lay person an "adventure" with recreational drugs that goes awry. However, this is actually a common phrase used among pharmacists, physicians, and others in health care to refer to the unexpected consequences of taking a prescription drug, unexpected consequences that can range from mild discomfort to death. Drug misadventures can result from a wide variety of causes. Virtually all prescription drugs have known risks of some kind. In a small number of people, the drugs may increase the risk of cancer or birth defects or cause ulcers or bleeding, or they may be particularly dangerous for children or older patients. Drugs can be prepared or used improperly. They may dangerously interact with other drugs being taken by a patient. Drug misadventures can also be caused by social phenomena. The pressure to rush potentially profitable drugs to market may lead to the falsification of data, the bribing of officials at the FDA to release drugs to the market more quickly, the establishment of a black market in prescription drugs, and the establishment of political barriers to effective controls over the manufacture, distribution, and adverse consequences of consuming prescription drugs. All these social phenomena may contribute to the collective experience of drug misadventuring in America.

The first patent for medicine was awarded in 1796 to Samuel Lee, Jr., for "billious pills" made of gamboge (tree resin), aloe, soap, and potassium nitrate. There were probably unanticipated consequences for some of Lee's customers, and from that day to this, drug misadventuring has been a very significant part of the American drug experience. Between 1969 and 1987 the FDA collected records on about 400,000 drug misadventures voluntarily reported by physicians and others. In 1987 alone over 54,000 drug misadventures were reported to the FDA. About 3,400 of these cases involved biologics such as vaccines, while the rest involved drugs. Fifteen percent of the cases involving biologics resulted in the hospitalization or death of the patients, while 20 percent of the cases involving drugs resulted in similar adverse consequences. Several studies indicate that one of every ten hospital admissions in the United States is the result of a drug misadventure. The American Society of Hospital Pharmacists estimates that medication errors occurring inside the hospital range from 1 percent to 20 percent. A major study finds that nearly 5 of every 2,000 hospital patients die as a result of drug misadventures (Manasse 1989, 929, 931, 936). Most disturbing of all, however, is that the best available evidence indicates that drug misadventures are vastly underreported:

> Although some may derive comfort from the "remarkable safety of drugs" statements of [some] investigators . . . , the truth is that we have little information to support such beliefs. Drug misadventures are substantially underreported. In England, for example, where a reasonable approach has been taken to systematically collecting such data, only about 10 percent of such incidents are reported. (Manasse 1989, 942)

Interestingly, the principal obstacle to establishing an adequate reporting system for the United States is that "a substantial political will is needed to undergird the establishment and evolution of a more statistically refined system for drug misadventure reporting in the United States" (Manasse 1989, 943).

Drug Labeling

American drug manufacturers produce, finish, and market drugs in foreign countries through wholly-owned subsidiaries as well as via other corporate arrangements. The OTA studied a random sample of 241 drugs sold by U.S.-based multinational pharmaceutical companies in Brazil, Kenya, Panama, and Thailand between 1988 and 1990. OTA researchers found that fully two-thirds of these drugs "failed to provide the kind of complete information a physician needs to use the drugs safely and effectively." Moreover, "reliance on this labeling information alone could lead to serious or life-threatening medical problems or, at best, ineffective treatment" (Office of Technology Assessment 1993a).

Tailgate Medicine

Tailgate medicine was inevitable. The cost of prescription drugs in the United States has skyrocketed since the late 1970s, the cost of getting in to see a physician is prohibitive for millions of families, and the ranks of the uninsured and the underinsured number in the scores of millions and keep growing. Health services for low-income communities are overcrowded, hard to get to, have limited hours, or are nonexistent. Immigrants without legal papers are frequently afraid to use existing health care facilities. Given these conditions, a black market in medicines was inevitable. "Tailgate medicine" is the name informally given to the illegal sale of prescription, banned, or unapproved drugs. According to those responsible for policing tailgate medicine, the problem is national in scope but seems to be worse (or perhaps more visible) in low-income ethnic communities in the Southwest, and particularly in southern California.

The drugs involved include the full range of prescription drugs found in the United States plus many drugs from Mexico, Southeast Asia, and other places around the world. Some of the imported drugs are legally available without prescriptions in the countries of origin but must be purchased from a pharmacist who, at least theoretically, doles out advice along with the drugs. Some of the drugs are outdated, and some are homemade folk remedies concocted locally or imported from abroad. These may be contaminated with high levels of dangerous heavy metals or formulated utilizing mixtures of regulated or banned drugs. Tailgate medicines are widely available in community convenience stores, at swap meets, at open-air markets, and sometimes from a vehicle parked at the side of a busy intersection. Often desperate low-income parents will purchase these drugs to administer to their children.

There is a curious lack of enforcement of tailgate drugs. For example the California Department of Health Services' food and drug branch in Los Angeles only has between one and three enforcement officers at any given time battling the black market drug trade in all of southern California. While they commonly confiscate black market drugs, they rarely arrest vendors. In March of 1991 a multiagency Los Angeles County task force was established to deal with the problem. Major drug manufacturers pledged $70,000 to fund a community education project recommended by the task force. However, within a relatively short period of time the drug manufacturers had backed away from the whole effort, without explaining why, and they took their pledge with them. About that time the task force fell apart. A similar set of circumstances befell the Hispanic Pharmaceutical Education Committee in Orange County.

According to California Assemblyman Richard Katz from Sylmar, who served on the erstwhile task force, the drug companies suddenly backed out of the community education effort because they feared their participation could be construed to imply that they were responsible for adverse medical consequences caused by any of their prescription drugs that might have been purchased on the black market. In other words, they did not want to be liable. Katz also divulged that employees at the California Department of Health Services told him they had little incentive to crack down on the tailgate medicine trade since the state saves money when low-income people treat themselves rather than seeing a physician and leaving the state with the bill. Apparently, in the eyes of some officials, illegal, contaminated, outdated, dangerous, and ineffective "medicines" are perfectly acceptable for low-income, disproportionately minority families.

Summary and Discussion

The prescription drug industry in the United States is a huge industry with an obvious, direct impact on the lives of tens of millions of Americans and an indirect impact on nearly everyone else. Although it is easy to get lost in the discussion of mergers, downsizing, and tax breaks, all of these seemingly abstract economic machinations of the industry deeply affect the lives of many U.S. residents. Perhaps pricing policies have the pharmaceutical industry's most obvious impact on low- and middle-income Americans. Unlike in many industrialized countries throughout the world, the cost of prescription drugs in the United States is virtually unregulated. The uninsured and the underinsured are those hardest hit by the lack of regulation, and these groups are more likely to be single female heads of households, the unemployed, the self-employed, minorities, and employees of small businesses.

Effective government regulation of pharmaceutical industry pricing policies has been deliberately thwarted by industry lobbyists, massive public relations campaigns, manufactured "grassroots" protest, and hundreds of millions of dollars in PAC money and other contributions. This same political influence has, through the patent system, bought the drug industry some of the strongest government monopoly protection in the world and has resulted in government-sponsored giveaways to the industry of drugs whose development was funded publicly. The irony is that this super-profitable industry has been able to purchase a vast array of government influence with money extorted by monopoly conditions from the very public victimized by the industry.

The ideology of the "free market" as it applies to the drug industry is something of an oxymoron. The lack of effective government regulation simply results in the drug companies buying up the competition and concentrating more and more financial strength in fewer and larger multinational drug companies. Mail-order discount drug companies challenged drug industry pricing, so the drug companies are buying them up. Generic drug manufacturers were undercutting profits of the major drug manufacturers, so the biggest manufacturers simply bought out the generic producers and now make their own generic drugs. Free-market ideology, together with the lack of government regulation, has led to the creation of monopoly. This means that fewer people have access to increasingly overpriced drugs. In those cases where there appeared to be effective, market constraints on drug prices, negotiated, for example, by the VA or by larger private managed care organizations, drug prices have been climbing steeply anyway, and higher prices are shifted to weaker segments of the market, such as community pharmacies. Once again, the elderly, the uninsured, and the underinsured are hardest hit by cost shifting since they have the least amount of organized market clout and tend to buy their drugs from high-priced community pharmacies.

Industry marketing of drugs involves the wholesale manipulation of physicians, pharmacists, and other health care providers by inundating them with a sales force of tens of thousands of agents who endlessly drop in to regale them with trinkets, samples, literature, promotional offers, dinner invitations, and the occasional cruise. The integrity of professional journals has been undermined by the uncritical acceptance of often misleading drug advertisements and the solicitation of deceptive drug company supplements masquerading both in style and content as peer-reviewed journal articles. The credibility of professional conferences has been breached by the purchase of entire sessions by drug companies. The believability of scientific research has been compromised by the corporate purchase and control of research carried out across the country in the most prestigious universities and medical schools. The total of this marketing effort is the manipulation of the thoughts and actions of hundreds of thousands of health care providers throughout the land, the undermining of cost consciousness and alternative approaches to health care, and the betrayal of trust among tens of millions of patients who are dependent upon health care providers who have become, to some extent, agents of the drug industry.

References

Carey, John. 1993. "How Many Times Must a Patient Pay?" *Business Week* (February 1):30–31.

Castagnoli, William G. 1993. "Whittle's Medical News Network: Making Waves in Rx Marketing." *Medical Marketing and Media* (June):14–18.

Conlan, Michael F. 1991. "Drug Firms Spend $165 Million a Year to Influence Prescribers." *Drug Topics* (January 7):44–48.

Cutaia, Jane H. 1993. "Swallowing a Bitter Pill." *Business Week* (January 11):82.

Drake, Donald C., and Marian Uhlman. 1993. "Bought and Paid For: America's Pharmaceutical Industry." *Anchorage Daily News* (Knight-Ridder Newspapers) (January 13):C1, C4–5.

"Drug Makers Broke Promise to Restrain Prices, Panel Says. 1993." *Anchorage Daily News* (Associated Press) (May 13):D1, D6.

Flanagan, Patrick. 1993. "Drug Prices: What's the Rationale?" *Management Review* (July):10–15).

Freudenheim, Milt. 1991. "Costs of Drug Research Seen as Overestimated." *New York Times* (April 30):D5(L).

———. 1993. "Merck Will Pay $6 Billion for Giant Drug Discounter." *New York Times* (July 29):D1(L), D5.

Hilts, Philip J. 1993. "U.S. Seeks to Protect Fruits of Tax-Supported Research." *New York Times* (June 17):A12(N).

Leary, Warren E. 1993. "Companies Accused of Overcharging for Drugs Developed with U.S. Aid." *New York Times* (January 26):C6(L).

Levine, Art, and Ken Silverstein. 1993. "How the Drug Lobby Cut Cost Controls." *The Nation* (December 13):713, 730–32.

Manasse, Henri R. 1989. "Medication Use in an Imperfect World: Drug Misadventuring as an Issue of Public Policy, Part 1." *American Journal of Hospital Pharmacy* 46(May):929–44.

Novak, Viveca. 1993. "How Drug Companies Operate on the Body Politic." *Business and Society Review* 84(Winter):58–64.

Office of Technology Assessment. 1993a. *OTA Examines Labeling Practices for Drugs Sold in Developing Countries.* Press Advisory. May 20.

———. 1993b. *Pharmaceutical R&D: Costs, Risks, and Rewards.* February. Washington, D.C.: U.S. Government Printing Office.

Paul, C. Marshall. 1993. "Solving the Media Puzzle: Time to Cut Back on Detailing." *Medical Marketing and Media* (October):94–98.

"Pharmaceutical Giants Tell Their Story." 1993. *Public Relations Journal* (October):20.

Podolsky, Doug, and Richard J. Newman. 1993. "Prescription Prizes." *U.S. News and World Report* (March 29):56–60.

"Pushing Drugs to Doctors." 1992. *Consumer Reports* (February):87–94.

Randall, Teri. 1991. "AMA, Pharmaceutical Association Form 'Solid Front' on Gift-Giving Guidelines." *Journal of the American Medical Association* 265(18):2304–5.

Rock, Andrea. 1993. "Cut Your Spiraling Drug Costs 70%." *Money* (June):131–34.

Schwartz, Harry. 1995. "Shifting Sands of Time." *Pharmaceutical Executive* 15(2) (February):20–22.

Shon, Melissa. 1993. "Holding Back the Tide." *Chemical Marketing Reporter* (March 8):SR3–8.

Solis, Dianne. 1993. "To Avoid Cost of U.S. Prescription Drugs, More Americans Shop South of the Border." *Wall Street Journal* (June 29):B1(W), B5.

Steinbrook, Robert. 1992. "Doctors Dangerously Misled by Drug Ads, Consumer Group Says." *Los Angeles Times* (July 31):A3.

Tanouye, Elyse. 1993a. "Critics See Self-Interest in Lilly's Funding of Ads Telling the Depressed to Get Help." *Wall Street Journal* (April 15):B1(W), B4.

———. 1993b. "Drug Makers Sued by Stores over Pricing." *Wall Street Journal* (October 15):A2(E).

U.S. General Accounting Office. 1992a. *Pharmaceutical Industry: Tax Benefits of Operating in Puerto Rico.* Washington, D.C. May.

———. 1992b. *Prescription Drugs: Changes in Prices for Selected Drugs.* Washington, D.C. August.

———. 1992c. *Prescription Drugs: Companies Typically Charge More in the United States Than in Canada.* Washington, D.C. September.

———. 1993. *Prescription Drug Prices: Analysis of Canada's Patented Medicine Prices Review Board.* Washington, D.C. February.

Vernaci, Richard L. 1993. "Drug Firms Threaten to Back Off Research." *Anchorage Daily News* (Associated Press) (January 26):C1, C6.

Weber, Joseph, and Sunita Wadekar Bhargava. 1993. "Drugmakers Get a Taste of Their Own Medicine." *Business Week* (April 26):104–5.

Winters, Patricia. 1993. "Prescription Drug Ads Up." *Advertising Age* 64(3):10, 50.

Wolfe, Sidney M., ed. 1993. "Drug Prices." *Health Letter* (April):11–12.

9

Medical Services

In the last twenty years most of the medical services industries have been dramatically transformed from poky, independent enterprises into monolithic corporate entities wielding billions of dollars in physical assets and political influence. Small, local operators of home health care and long-term-care services were bought out or trampled into oblivion by huge corporate chains employing armies of minimum-wage, minority, female workers. Once-arcane science fiction technologies like magnetic resonance imaging (MRI) and positron emission tomography (PET) emerged as standard medical techniques, with equipment scattered about the United States at thousands of sites. Miniature clinical laboratories sporting the latest in high-tech "profit centers" sprouted up by the hundreds of thousands in back rooms and broom closets of physicians across America. These were joined by nascent chains of freestanding clinical labs jostling one another in the heady environment of mergers, buyouts, expansions, and monopolies in a market with nearly unlimited potential. For-profit plasma centers, nonprofit community blood banks, the Red Cross, and hospitals of all stripes fought it out for donors in the multibillion-dollar blood products market.

Until very recently there was no moderation in sight to the burgeoning health services industry. However, has this growth actually improved the health care of Americans? Has access improved? Have new technologies kept costs down? Have the emerging corporate and investor-driven health care enterprises improved the quality of patient care? In this chapter we consider these and related issues as we take a closer look at a few of these health services industries.

Dialysis Industry

The most unusual health care program under Medicare's purview is the End Stage Renal Disease (ESRD) Program. Dialysis treatment for ESRD is the only health care expense reimbursed by Medicare that people of all ages are entitled to. This has put the federal government in the role of single payer, giving Medicare a virtual monopsony in terms of purchasing dialysis treatments for people with diseased kidneys. Furthermore, taking inflation into account, this single-payer clout has actually reduced by over half the real treatment cost per patient during the last two decades. This is a remarkable achievement indeed during a period of frequent double-digit annual increases in the total cost of health care. Nevertheless, the ESRD Program is perennially engulfed in controversy.

Chronic or end-stage renal disease is a condition caused by kidneys no longer capable of purging toxins from the blood. There are two treatment options: (1) renal dialysis, in which the blood is cleansed by filtering out toxins through a membrane, or (2) a kidney transplant. The technology for both treatments was initially developed in the 1950s and 1960s; however, due in large part to the tremendous expense, few people were treated for ESRD. In 1965 a mere three hundred patients were receiving hemodialysis, the most common form of dialysis, in which the blood is cleansed by a membrane in an external piece of medical equipment. By 1972, 3,700 patients were receiving dialysis, but about 10,000 persons were eligible for the treatment. Thousands died because they could not afford dialysis or a kidney transplant. Dialysis cost $40,000 per year in 1972, a time when the average wage was a small fraction of that figure (Daniels 1991, 223–27). In that same year President Nixon signed Public Law 92-603. Buried in the maze of Social Security amendments was authorization for the federal government to pay dialysis expenses via Medicare for about 93 percent of all patients with ESRD (Iglehart 1993, 367). Coverage became effective summer of the following year.

Currently, 165,000 Medicare patients are being treated for ESRD, and the numbers continue to climb year after year (Iglehart 1993, 368). About one-quarter of these patients ultimately receive a new kidney, and most of the rest receive some form of dialysis (Port 1992, 5). Although there is consensus among physicians that a kidney transplant is usually the far better choice of treatment, a severe shortage of donor kidneys and the expense of the procedure prevent most victims of ESRD from receiving this preferred treatment (Iglehart 1993, 367).

Discrimination and Economic Obstacles to Treatment

Prior to 1973 overt racism and sexism as well as economic barriers greatly restricted treatment of women and minorities for ESRD. Table 9.1 contrasts a number of important demographic characteristics for those receiving treatment for ESRD at a point several years prior to the 1973 enactment of the

TABLE 9.1 Demographic Characteristics of the Hemodialysis Patient Population (1967 and 1978)

	Percentage of Population	
Characteristic	*1967*	*1978*
Male	75.0	49.2
Female	25.0	50.8
White	91.0	63.7
Black	7.0	34.9
Less than high school education	10.0	28.7
Postgraduate education	13.0	1.8
55+ years of age	7.0	45.7

Source: Daniels, Rudolph. 1991. "Legislation and the American Dialysis Industry: Some Considerations About Monopoly Power in Renal Care." *American Journal of Economics and Sociology* 50(2):229.

legislation and again several years after enactment. Before the legislation the demographic profile of those being treated for ESRD was reminiscent of an elite country club—an overwhelming predominance of well educated, well-off white men in the middle of their careers. The exclusion of women and minorities in need of treatment resulted in unnecessary death among them.

The incidence rate of kidney failure among African-Americans is nearly four times the rate among whites (Feldman et al. 1992, 398), which explains why nearly 35 percent of those on dialysis after the ESRD legislation (see Table 9.1) are African-Americans despite the fact that they make up only about 12 percent of the U.S. population. On the other hand, the fact that only 7 percent of the hemodialysis population were African-Americans prior to the legislation provides an approximate social measure of the depth of racist and economic exclusion during that period. Moreover, substantial discrimination against African-Americans with ESRD appears to persist. African-Americans constituted about 30 percent of the patients with ESRD in 1989 but received only 20 percent of the transplants in that year. In addition African-Americans had to wait on average nearly twice as long as whites for their kidney transplant (Levinsky and Rettig 1991, 1145).

Despite the fact that Medicare reimburses about $29,000 per ESRD patient per year to cover treatment, Medicare cost sharing requirements leave an annual average of $4,000 to be paid by the patient. For low-income patients this sum can be a serious obstacle to treatment in the absence of state or private charity programs to help cover these onerous out-of-pocket expenses (Iglehart 1993, 367). In addition, low income African-Americans who are receiving dialysis treatment are at a higher risk of death than higher income African-Americans or whites (Port et al. 1990). Finally, the legislation itself excludes important sectors of minorities, low-income families, and women because eligibility for coverage of ESRD treatment is tied to Social Security. This excludes "some state and federal employees; some domestic, farm and other workers in covered occupations who may not have applied for benefits; and those who have never worked, such as young, unwed, nonworking mothers and their children" (Levinsky and Rettig 1991)."

In recent years a new form of alleged discrimination in the dialysis industry has caused an avalanche of controversy: discrimination against HIV-positive ESRD patients.

A New Industry Is Born

In 1969, a few years before the ESRD legislation was enacted, there were about 250 dialysis centers across the United States (Daniels 1991, 231). Nearly all of these were special units inside nonprofit hospitals. As can be seen in Table 9.2, by 1991 there were 2,082 dialysis centers, but well over half of these were freestanding (that is, they were not a unit inside a hospital) for-profit facilities.

Several factors account for the dramatic increase in the number of outpatient dialysis facilities since the mid-1970s, particularly the explosive proliferation of for-profit freestanding clinics. Some of these factors include:

- *Medicare Financing of Dialysis.* Overnight, federal legislation gave financial support for dialysis treatment to scores of thousands with ESRD who otherwise would not have constituted an "effective market" for treatment. Health care entrepreneurs saw the writing on the wall.
- *Expanded Patient Base for Dialysis.* (1) The 1972 legislation establishing Medicare financing for the ESRD Program also prohibited discrimination based on skin color, ethnicity, and so on. Although not perfectly implemented, this civil rights feature of the legislation opened the doors for treatment to minority and women ESRD patients who might otherwise have been excluded. (2) Note on Table 9.1 the tremendous increase in the number of older people receiving dialysis treatments since the legislation. This reflects in part the emerging medical acceptability of placing older people with ESRD on treatment rather than considering such treatment appropriate primarily for younger persons. (3) People are living longer now than previously, and older persons are at far greater risk for ESRD. (4) It is possible that increasing environmental toxins attack the kidney (Port 1992, 4). (5) Sicker patients are now considered eligible for

TABLE 9.2   Outpatient Dialysis Providers

| | Hospital-Based | | Freestanding | | |
Year	Nonprofit	For-Profit	Nonprofit	For-Profit	Combined
1980	583	17	79	325	1004
1991	687	19	217	1159	2082
Percent change	18	12	175	257	107

Source: Adapted from Iglehart, John K. 1993. "The American Health Care System: The End Stage Renal Disease Program. *The New England Journal of Medicine* 328(5):368.

dialysis than was the case in the past. These patients might have illnesses such as cancer, AIDS, hypertension, or diabetes (Port 1992, 4–5).

- *A Severe Shortage of Kidneys for Transplanting.* Only about 10,000 donor kidneys become available each year for kidney transplants. This figure has remained stable for a number of years (Iglehart 1993, 367).
- *Publicly Granted Monopolies for Dialysis Facilities.* Federal legislation has encouraged locally determined, federally supported regional monopolies of dialysis facilities. The process has resulted in the establishment of stable, profit-generating facilities by investors who are assured of a steady stream of revenue-generating patients from the facility's catchment area.

Since its inception, the annual cost of the ESRD Program has escalated from approximately $250 million to $6.6 billion in 1991 (Daniels 1991, 224; Iglehart 1993, 367). By any measure this is a very large sum of money and a juicy plum for any investor, particularly if the cash is reimbursed directly by the federal government (and therefore guaranteed), there is virtually no competition, and the patient catchment area is guaranteed. One corporation, National Medical Care (NMC), has aggressively cashed in on this bonanza by dominating the freestanding for-profit dialysis clinic business. By the mid-1980s this company's clinics were treating nearly half of all dialysis patients in the United States. During the same period it is estimated that they captured over 75 percent of Medicare ESRD payments. At that time NMC had two hundred facilities in thirty-one states, 68 percent more facilities than the combined total of all other for-profit dialysis clinics (Daniels

1991, 236). In the early 1990s NMC owned 380 dialysis facilities and several collateral businesses and held contracts with 350 physicians to direct the corporation's facilities (Iglehart 1993, 369).

At the same time that the for-profit freestanding dialysis clinic rose to undisputed dominance of the dialysis market, the HCFA, which administers the ESRD Program, drove per-patient costs of dialysis down. The market power of this virtual single-payer federal agency has been a unique achievement during a period characterized by massive inflation of nearly all other health care costs:

> The program has been remarkably successful at controlling its cost per patient. The initial reimbursement rates for outpatient dialysis were arbitrary and not based on cost. They were established in 1973 and remained unchanged until 1983. The rates were lowered in 1983 and again in 1986; no adjustments for inflation were allowed. The reimbursement rate for outpatient dialysis was $138 in 1974 and $125 in 1989. After adjustment for inflation, the 1989 rate was less than $54 in 1974 dollars, a reduction of 61 percent over this period. (Iglehart 1993, 366–67)

The Quality Issue

On the other hand, it appears that HCFA has done a remarkably poor job assuring the maintenance of high-quality health services during the period when reimbursements have steadily declined. In fact, none of the responsible federal agencies nor the providers have systematically monitored or measured quality of health care in the dialysis industry. Nevertheless, on the basis of independent audits that confirm the profitability of stand-alone clinics, the HCFA continues to hold reimbursement levels down (Iglehart 1993, 367). Stable profit margins may keep investors happy; however, profit does not necessarily translate into high-quality medical services. The literature is replete with warnings like these:

> Research indicates that "lower rates of reimbursement for dialysis were associated with higher frequency of hospitalization." . . . Pressures to reduce cost have led to shorter dialysis treatment times in the United States. Studies show a relationship between decreased reimbursement and decreased treatment time, and shorter treatment time and higher mortality. (Levinsky and Rettig 1991, 1147)

> Twenty years ago most dialyzers were used once and discarded. Now, in a highly controversial attempt to save money, about 70 percent of all dialyzers

are disinfected and reused. For-profit clinics are twice as likely to reuse dialyzers as nonprofit clinics. The Food and Drug Administration (FDA) has research evidence that suggest "an association between one or more disinfectants or disinfection methods and increased mortality among patients undergoing dialysis." (Iglehart 1993, 328)

Finally, there is the crucial question of conflict of interest between quality of care and physician financial interest in a dialysis clinic:

A substantial portion of dialysis clinics are owned by the physicians that run them. These physicians/owners control patients' running times through the treatment prescriptions they write. And in writing these prescriptions, they are likely to consider *both* the clinic's profitability and quality of care. . . . [G]iven the negative relationship that exists between profitability and quality of care . . . the trade-off between profits and quality must be confronted in making decisions concerning treatment duration. That is, for a fixed reimbursement rate set by HCFA, the physician/owner is placed in the position of having to select some profit/quality combination where higher quality will necessarily yield lower profits. (Kaserman 1992, 84–85)

Laboratories

In the early 1970s the vast majority of medical testing was conducted in centralized laboratories located in hospitals. Twenty years later there were 202,050 medical labs of all kinds in the United States, but nearly 92 percent of them were small physician office labs (POLs). Despite the proliferation of POLs, the hospital-based laboratory segment still performed the bulk of the medical testing, conducting $19.5 billion worth of business in 1992 of a $31.7 billion medical laboratory market. The POLs conducted a total of $2.4 billion worth of business in 1992, and independent commercial labs accounted for most of the rest of the medical laboratory market. It is estimated that by 1997 the clinical laboratory services market will climb to $42 billion ("Clinical Laboratory Services Seen Growing to $42 Billion" 1993). Until 1992, only about 12,000 of the laboratories in the United States were regulated by the federal government as a result of legislation passed in the mid-1960s (Pear 1991, A24).

Physician Office Labs

Thanks to the invention of microprocessor computer chips, medical testing equipment that was formerly huge, expensive, and found only in large laboratories is now sold in "bench top" sizes at bargain prices. For as little as $6,000 or $7,000, a physician can purchase a clinical chemistry analyzer that can process "27 routines tests" and comes equipped with "electrolyte and special chemistry modules" (Hook and Fernandes 1991, 881). Just about anyone can operate one of these units with a few hours training. The physician can often recoup the cost of the equipment in only one or two years because of the ample profits typically generated by clinical testing lab equipment (Pear 1991, A24).

For nascent entrepreneurs, the $26-billion-a-year blood chemistry business might be just the ticket. According to *Forbes* magazine, stocks in the top four or five companies that manufacture this kind of testing equipment are expected to grow 15–20 percent in value in the foreseeable future. Despite the fact that the top five companies control only 14 percent of the market, there will be less and less competition as time goes by because the bigger firms are rapidly buying up the smaller ones. What if there were a federal cost containment effort to reduce reimbursements for blood chemistry tests? *Forbes* says not to worry: "While this would create some short-term concerns, the need for testing will not be diminished. More important, a reduced amount of government funds would most probably put pressure on the least efficient, smallest firms, thereby speeding up the consolidation process that is already under way in this business" (Salomon 1992, 300).

In short, the market for physician's office-based clinical chemistry testers, immunochemistry analyzers, and cell-counting equipment is booming. Investors are happy because manufacturers are selling plenty of equipment. Physicians are happy because they have a quick turnaround time for results and their office-based lab is typically an excellent "profit center." Patients who get wrong test results from unreliable office-based labs, however, are not especially happy, particularly if the results of those tests are a life-or-death matter. Some government agencies have not been happy with office-based labs since the federal government is the single biggest reimburser of health care costs. For many government economists and regulators, fundamental questions of quality and cost of care have relegated the glitter of this profitable new technology to the distant background.

Within the federal government, serious questions about the cost and accuracy of large medical testing labs arose in conjunction with Medicare legislation passed in 1965. Federal concern paralleled the release of considerable amounts of federal Medicare funds for health care reimbursements, including reimbursements for medical testing. The first Clinical Laboratory Improvement Amendments (CLIA) legislation passed in 1967. It regulated Medicare labs and labs that operated across state lines. During the following years tens of thousands of physicians established labs in their offices; however, these labs were entirely unregulated by federal agencies. Regulation by the states ranged from nonexistent to inadequate. The Commission on Office Laboratory Accreditation (COLA) is the principal voluntary private credentialing program to become established specifically for physician's office-based labs. Since its establishment in 1988, however, only about 1 percent of all physicians with office-based labs have applied for accreditation with the body (Loschen 1992, 1274). Clearly, the voluntary approach to establishing standardized, minimal quality assurance in office-based labs has not worked. Meanwhile, a growing body of evidence has accumulated indicating "rather conclusively that testing done in the [physician office laboratory] environment by individuals without formal laboratory training is less well-controlled, and the data from this testing are thought to be less accurate and reproducible, than from similar testing in regulated hospital or independent laboratories" (Loschen 1992, 1273).

There is, in addition, very good evidence that physicians typically use untrained personnel to do their lab work. For example, a survey of a 4,400-member sample of the American Academy of Family Physicians discovered that nearly 65 percent of those physicians with office-based laboratories employed lab personnel with no formal laboratory training (Loschen 1992, 1274).

The Saga of CLIA '88

The Clinical Laboratory Improvement Amendments of 1988 (CLIA '88) included provisions for regulating every medical laboratory in the United States—large and small, public and private, office based and hospital based. But despite the fact that Congress mandated this law and President Reagan signed it, CLIA '88 and related legislation under the Reagan administration languished in the Department of Health and Human Services. In 1986 Congress directed the department to develop standards by the following year to regulate labs in physician's offices. Five years later the report still had not been received by Congress. CLIA '88 had numerous provisions that were to be enacted within the first few months of 1990, but most were ignored by the administration. Performance and consumer data was to have been published, but it was not. Procedures for civil and criminal penalties were to have been established, but they were not. The Public Health Service (PHS) was to have sent Congress five major research reports, but PHS had barely begun planning them by May 1990.

Something very suspicious was going on with CLIA '88. Little glitches occur now and then in the great machinery of government to slow it down a bit, but the massive failure of a federal agency to come even close to statutory deadlines is highly unusual. The cause, however, was not bureaucratic incompetence or inertia—it was politics. The AMA in particular, and perhaps other similar interests content with unregulated labs, exerted overwhelming influence on a friendly Republican administration. Representative

Ron Wyden of Oregon, one of the bill's sponsors, noted that the HHS was deathly afraid of offending the "medical establishment" by sending federal regulators into the offices of physicians (Pear 1991, A24).

It appears that the AMA devoted more energy fighting CLIA '88 than did hospitals and larger independent laboratories. The reasons have to do with market share in the emerging clinical laboratory industry:

> There has been the festering concern of laboratorians that POLs have an unfair competitive advantage in their unregulated utopian state. The fact that POLs have been largely free to perform whatever tests they desire, without the necessity of proficiency testing, unannounced inspections, and quality assurance and documentation requirements, etc., and can still charge the full amount for laboratory tests that they perform has not gone unnoticed by hospital and independent laboratories. (Loschen 1992, 1273)

Finally, the administration submitted the Proposed Rule for implementation of CLIA '88 to public comment for a period ending in September 1990 (well beyond the deadline when the legislation was supposed to be implemented, not merely opened for comment). The HCFA received an astounding 60,000 letters protesting that CLIA '88 was either too harsh or too lenient. The feds withdrew the rules, weakened many of the provisions considerably, and resubmitted them for public comment ending April 1992. Predictably, the same forces were at work influencing HCFA's latest rewrite. An additional 16,000 letters were received by the end of the 1992 comment period, but CLIA '88 finally took effect in September 1992 (Lumsdon 1993, 51).

Laboratory Staff Issues

The implementation of CLIA '88 has exacerbated a chronic shortage of trained laboratory personnel. Of course the political value of a trumped-up claim that there is a shortage of trained lab personnel cannot be dismissed in a situation where the industry is trying to temper legislation requiring a modicum of trained personnel in a high percentage of labs. Be that as it may, it appears that there has been something of a shortage of trained lab staff, but it has been most acute in rural areas and low-income neighborhoods. The initial shortage resulted in part from growth restrictions on training programs and in part from the explosion of office-based and independent laboratories in the last two decades. The lack of federal and effective state regulation over most laboratories has allowed them to operate without formally trained personnel or with a minimum of trained staff. With the advent of CLIA '88, trained laboratorians will be taking jobs with government regulatory agencies and private accreditation organizations, diverting trained personnel from working labs. The lab staff shortage has pitted physicians against the larger labs for scarce lab personnel and has created pressure in all labs to find alternatives to the use of staff (Loschen 1992, 1276–77). As one analyst noted:

> Laboratory administrators are trying a number of approaches to replace higher paid trained staff with lower paid lesser trained personnel, or to reduce staff numbers altogether. Lobbying at the federal and state levels for reduced regulatory requirements has been a long-standing strategy. Some hospitals across the country are following the lead of the automotive manufacturers and are exploring the use of robots in laboratory operations to replace trained staff. (Hard 1991)

By the time CLIA '88 had repeatedly run the political gauntlet before finally being implemented, it had been gutted of many of the original staffing regulations. The final version allows 60–70 percent of all lab work to be conducted by "medical lab technicians" with no more than on-the-job training, military training, or trade school training. Staff with no more than high school diplomas can perform "highly complex tests" as long as they have qualified supervision. Traditionally, hospital labs have used a fairly high proportion of "lab technologists," who typically have a bachelors degree and are often paid $3–$6 more per hour than a medical lab technician (Lumsdon 1993). The new CLIA '88 may actually allow hospital labs to reduce their proportion of highly trained lab technologists and replace them with lesser-trained lab technicians.

This has placed medical technologist professional organizations in direct opposition to the cost-cutting measures of the AHA and the AMA and in opposition to the marketing strategy of the Health Industry Manufacturers Association (HIMA). In the face of a weakened CLIA '88, medical technologist associations have pursued the tactic of seeking state legislation requiring more stringent licensing and training requirements for laboratory personnel. Their effectiveness has been blunted, however, by a coordinated state-by-state lobbying response by the AHA, the AMA, and the HIMA. Some medical technologists have abandoned their associations altogether to become entrepreneurial consultants to smaller laboratories with no formally trained staff. The federal government, in conjunction with laboratory owners and administrators, has established programs to train lab staff in apprenticeship programs, ultimately leading to cheaper trained staff. In addition public schools, colleges, and universities are being encouraged to develop additional laboratory-staff training programs. This will relieve lab administrators of the cost of on-the-job training and move the expense to the public sector (Lumsdon 1993).

Diagnostic Imaging Equipment

Diagnostic imaging equipment creates pictures, shadows, or other visual representations to assist diagnosis. In this field the old standby for many decades has been the X-ray. Ultrasound has been around for a while too, but in recent years there has been a proliferation of new imaging technologies. Computerized axial tomography (CAT)–scan technology has been in use since the 1970s. It was a tremendous improvement in X-ray technology. MRI technology was a leap forward compared to CAT scans, and it rapidly proliferated in clinical usage beginning in the early 1980s. Finally, PET has been used in research for over twenty years but is coming into its own as a clinical diagnostic tool in the 1990s (Pollack 1991). MRIs and PETs are particularly interesting because of the tremendous expense involved in purchasing and operating these pieces of equipment and because they are still being aggressively marketed to first-time buyers and users as well as repeat customers.

MRI Equipment

Overhearing a discussion about MRI equipment is like listening to a conversation about the inner workings of the Starship Enterprise. The technology is very esoteric. The heart of an MRI scanner is a ten-ton magnet the size of pickup truck. The magnet exerts a force 30,000 times stronger than the magnetic field around the earth. The patient is slid into an MRI scanner like a pizza into an oven. The magnet surrounding the patient makes all the protons in the body's hydrogen atoms spin in one direction. Radio waves are transmitted into the body, where they collide with wobbly hydrogen atoms and reflect a pattern of signals to receivers hooked up to computers. The computers produce crystal clear images of the soft tissue in the body based on the reflected radio signals. The picture is so clear that individual arteries can be identified and the blood flowing in them can be seen. Even the lenses in a patient's eyes make a clear image on the computer screen. MRI equipment is particularly good for diagnosing soft-tissue disease such as tumors, spinal problems, knee and extremity ailments, and other maladies of particular interest to cardiologists, gynecologists, and urologists (Moffat 1992a).

Despite the fact that an MRI scanner initially costs $1 million to $2 million, they have sprouted up across America. There are well over 2,000 of them in the United States—proportionally four times as many as in Germany and eight times as many as in Canada. More than 70 percent of all large hospitals in the United State have at least one MRI scanner in-house, as do about 40 percent of all medium-sized hospitals. MRI manufacturers are grossing half a billion dollars a year in sales. Hospitals and physician-entrepreneurs have been collecting $800 to $1,200 for each MRI procedure. In 1991 5 million MRI scans were performed in the United States for an estimated total cost of 6 billion to 10 billion dollars. Finally, an extraordinary fact is that it has taken a mere eight or nine years for MRI scanners to become this entrenched in the health care industry (Moffat 1992a; Wagner 1991).

Marketing the MRI

The marketing and proliferation of MRI equipment is a remarkable story in and of itself. More importantly, as a case study this story exposes the major social, political, and economic forces that propel the American medical-industrial complex. A good place to start is on the Wisconsin prairie, site of the General Electric (GE) Medical Systems "campus." GE sells $3 billion worth of medical equipment a year in the U.S. and abroad and annually sinks a quarter-billion dollars of that into research. The site in Wisconsin is the center of their operations to research, manufacture, and market MRI scanners as well as CAT scanners, X-ray equipment, and PET imaging equipment. GE is one of the pillars of the HIMA, the industry trade group (Moffat 1992b).

Through the HIMA, GE and other manufacturers tell anyone who will listen that voluntary efforts such as practice guidelines and outcomes data must be used by physicians to curb overutilization of the equipment. Manufacturers are keenly aware that federal and state regulators are closing in on the overuse of this equipment, and the manufacturers do not want to have their market limited by regulations on capital outlays for medical equipment or on insurance reimbursements for its use. In addition manufacturers are showing purchasers how to use the equipment more efficiently in order to bring the per-procedure cost down, although there is growing research evidence that more efficient use leads not to costs coming down but to profits going up. Another strategy to fend off government regulation affecting the market is GE's funding of studies intended to show that MRI use saves money by replacing other, more-expensive diagnostic procedures. Presumably this research will find its way into medical journals and be presented at conferences to "educate" physicians and legislators (Moffat 1992b; Pollack 1991).

Southern California is home to a glut of hundreds of MRI machines. While California and Canada have roughly the same population, California has twenty-five times as many MRI scanners. The concentration of MRIs in California is largely the result of a concentration of well-insured potential patients, a concentration of physician-entrepreneurs, and the historic lack of effective state regulatory control over health-related capital investments. "Free-market competition" in the MRI industry in southern California has not dropped prices substantially, but it has given rise to widespread practices to increase usage of the equipment. After all, an underutilized immensely expensive piece of equipment will not make a profit for the hospital or investor-physicians. Once purchased, diagnostic imaging equipment must be used because it must be paid for (Moffat 1992a).

A highly questionable spin-off industry, MRI telemarketing, has developed in California. Rooms full of callers solicit the general public to undergo

MRI procedures, despite the fact that there is no reason to believe such a procedure would be medically useful for them. Some MRI facilities hire brokers to drag in patients on workers' compensation in order to keep the machines operating at a profitable capacity. One study found that California Medicare recipients receive 50 percent more MRI scans than the national average. Among physician-entrepreneurs who own MRI facilities, this leads to an annual excess of 270,000 to 450,000 MRI procedures. If the average cost per procedure was $1,000, these unnecessary procedures diverted up to half a billion dollars each year in California—money that might otherwise have been used for medical care for those who desperately need it (Moffat 1992a).

MRI as Cash Cow

Growth of the MRI industry is related in large part to the decision by Medicare in the mid-1980s to reimburse for MRI procedures and to the private insurance industry's decision to follow suit. Once third-party reimbursement was assured, investors in MRI facilities needed only one more missing ingredient: physician referrals. It is illegal to offer kickbacks to physicians for referring a patient to another physician or medical facility; however, in many cases it is not illegal for a physician to make self-referrals to a facility that he or she invests in. Physicians, typically specialists who would normally refer the bulk of the patients to such facilities, were quick to realize the profit potential of an investment in an MRI facility, particularly if they were contacted by a group of investors.

The fact is that physician-investors often do make a return of 50 percent or more per year on their MRI investments. The high returns reflect not risk but, rather, the need to financially tie in physicians to a particular MRI facility for referrals. The key to profitability of an investor-owned MRI facility is high use, and high use can best be accomplished with a steady stream of physician self-referrals. Physician-entrepreneurs have investments in MRI facilities in freestanding centers, private hospitals, and even in contracted operations in public hospitals. At the DeKalb Medical Center in Atlanta, for example, a partnership of fifty-nine physicians leases the MRI to the hospital. The physician-investors receive a base rent and 15 percent of all revenues if at least 1,200 procedures are performed in the year. However, if more than 1,700 procedures are performed, the self-referring physician-investors receive 30 percent of all MRI revenues (Pear and Eckholm 1991).

These kinds of incentives lead to some very tangible results for the physician-investor who self-refers. One study of self-referring physicians who had an ownership interest in diagnostic imaging equipment found that their charges per episode of care were 440 percent to 750 percent higher than the charges of physicians who did not self-refer (Swedlow et al. 1992). Finally, in

1990 the GAO conducted a massive study of 1.3 million imaging procedures in freestanding facilities in Florida (Shikles 1993). These procedures represented over 55 percent of all Florida Medicare referrals for diagnostic imaging that year and involved thirty-nine facilities and 3,000 investor-physicians. The findings represent a stunning indictment against the practice of self-referral:

> GAO found that physician owners of Florida diagnostic imaging facilities had higher referral rates for all types of imaging services than nonowners. The differences in referral rates were greatest for costly, high technology imaging services: Physician owners had 54 percent higher referral rates for MRI scans, 28 percent higher referral rates for computed tomography (CT) scans, and 25 percent higher referral rates for ultrasound and echocardiography. (Shikles 1993, Summary [n.p.])

Summary and Discussion

At the center of some of the medical services we have reviewed are large, expensive pieces of equipment and accompanying facilities, such as diagnostic imaging centers. Because these centers exist in a political-economic framework, their establishment, use, and social consequences are frequently driven by financial or political issues rather than by the medical needs of the population. In fact, these social forces may result in the advanced technology having an adverse impact on the equitable delivery of high-quality health care. The following discussion summarizes the general relationship between some of the political-economic driving forces behind capital-intensive medical equipment and the social consequences of those forces.

Hospitals want the latest diagnostic imaging equipment because in and of itself it may be highly profitable; because it attracts secondary use by other hospital facilities; because it enhances the image of the hospital as a center of excellence, attracting investors, who bring money, and physicians, who bring additional patients; and because in-house equipment may be more convenient to use for physicians and patients. Investors in freestanding diagnostic imaging centers want to make a profit.

In either case, in order to make a profit or just to break even, this expensive equipment must have a high rate of use. Initially there does not have to be much demonstrable medical need for the equipment because need can be generated. Investors locate the facility in an area with a well-insured population that will pay higher fees than Medicare. This leads to the systematic avoidance of low-income and minority neighborhoods. Physician-investors divert their patients from other facilities to the one in which they have a financial interest, charge more, and typically utilize the medical procedure much more often than do non-investor-physicians.

Extensive public relations campaigns may be launched to attract non-investor-physicians to use the facility and to directly attract the public to use the medical services as well. Demand for the services must be drummed up, but these expensive public relations efforts divert money from needed health care and ultimately lead to overutilization of the medical procedure, additional risk to the patients, and the development of immense unnecessary medical costs charged to both public and private payers. A hospital spreads the cost of equipment purchase and underutilized equipment time to other patients, thereby raising the general cost of health care. Facilities that lose out in the competition for patient referrals close, having wasted huge amounts of health care money on the bumpy ride to investment returns rather than having spent it wisely on the provision of needed services. Predominantly nonprofit facilities serving a significant indigent, minority, and low-income population lose revenue from higher-paying private insured patients who have been lured to for-profit facilities by physician-investors. As a result, the low-income population finds access increasingly difficult.

The development of a health care sector built around the demand for, utilization of, and profits from expensive pieces of medical equipment results in the growth and coalition of related political interests. The bigger the sector becomes, the stronger the political influence locally and nationally. PAC money flows freely, and lobbyists pour into the offices of legislators to fight against joint venture restrictions, restrictive Medicare regulations, effective cost-containment measures, and so forth. All of this lobbying for maximum economic return distorts public policy for a rational health care plan and funnels health industry funds into arenas that have nothing to do with the delivery of health care to those who need it.

References

"Clinical Laboratory Services Seen Growing to $42 Billion." 1993. *Chemical Marketing Reporter* (February 22):9.

Daniels, Rudolph. 1991. "Legislation and the American Dialysis Industry: Some Considerations About Monopoly Power in Renal Care." *American Journal of Economics and Sociology* 50(2):223–42.

Feldman, Harold I., Michael J. Klag, Anne Page Chiapella, and Paul K. Whelton. 1992. "End-Stage Renal Disease in US Minority Groups." *American Journal of Kidney Diseases* 29:397–410.

Hard, Rob. 1991. "Robots: Can They Help Solve the Technologist Shortage?" *Hospitals* (June 20):56–58.

Hook, Walter C., and John J. Fernandes. 1991. "Laboratory Instruments for the Physician's Office Laboratory: Technology and Cost-Benefits." *Journal of the American Osteopathic Association* 91:880–88.

Iglehart, John K. 1993. "The American Health Care System: The End State Renal Disease Program." *The New England Journal of Medicine* 328:366–71.

Kaserman, David L. 1992. "Reimbursement Rates and Quality of Care in the Dialysis Industry: A Policy Discussion." *Issues in Law and Medicine* 8 (1):81–102.

Levinsky, Norman G., and Richard A. Rettig. 1991. "The Medicare End-Stage Renal Disease Program." *The New England Journal of Medicine* 324:1143–48.

Loschen, D. J. 1992. "The Impact of New Regulations on Laboratory Testing in Physicians' Offices." *Clinical Chemistry* 38:1273–79.

Lumsdon, Kevin. 1993. "The CLIA Maze." *Hospitals* (January 20):50–52.

Moffat, Susan. 1992a. "Body Scanner Boom." *Los Angeles Times* (May 10):D1, D8.

———. 1992b. "Tomorrow's Technology Gets the Put-Off." *Los Angeles Times* (May 10):D8–D9.

Pear, Robert. 1991. "1988 Standards for Medical Labs Go Unenforced by Administration." *New York Times* (March 20):A1, A24.

Pear, Robert, and Erik Eckholm. 1991. "When Healers Are Entrepreneurs: A Debate over Costs and Ethics." *New York Times* (June 2):A1(L), A30(L).

Pollack, Andrew. 1991. "Medical Technology 'Arms Race' Adds Billions to the Nation's Bills." *New York Times* (April 29):A1(L), B8(L).

Port, Friedrich K. 1992. "The End-Stage Renal Disease Program: Trends over the Past Eighteen Years." *American Journal of Kidney Diseases* 20(1) Suppl. 1:3–7.

Port, Friedrich K., Robert A. Wolfe, Nathan W. Levin, Kenneth E. Guire, and C. William Ferguson. 1990. "Income and Survival in Chronic Dialysis Patients." *ASAIO Transactions* 36(3):154–57.

Salomon, R. S., Jr. 1992. "Testing, Testing . . . " *Forbes* (October 26):300.

Shikles, Janet L. 1993. "Physicians Who Invest in Imaging Centers Refer More Patients for More Costly Services." Statement of Janet L. Shikles, director, Health Financing and Policy Issues, Human Resources Division, General Accounting Office. GAO/T-HRD-93-14.

Swedlow, Alex, Gregory Johnson, Neil Smithline, and Arnold Milstein. 1992. "Increased Costs and Rates of Use in the California Workers' Compensation System as a Result of Self-Referral by Physicians." *The New England Journal of Medicine* 327:1502–6.

Wagner, Mary. 1991. "Report Views Imaging Equipment Trends." *Modern Healthcare* (December 2):44.

10

Federal Government

The federal government plays a massive role in health care in the United States. This chapter discusses a few examples of the major federal institutions involved with health care. Some of these institutions, such as the Indian Health Service (IHS), deliver health care directly through government-owned facilities by health professionals who are government employees. Other federal programs, such as Medicare, simply fund health care delivered by the private sector. Another extremely important role played by federal institutions is the provision of public health services and enforcement. The FDA has the responsibility of safeguarding the public by regulating food, drugs, and medical devices. The Environmental Protection Agency (EPA) has the tasks of protecting air and water and of dealing with most aspects of hazardous waste. OSHA is mandated to ensure a safe and healthful workplace for scores of millions of American workers.

It would be comforting to believe that each of these federal agencies is staffed by personnel driven entirely by the quest to do good for humanity. It would be reassuring to know that they are insulated in their mission from ignoble values such as bureaucratic territoriality, political meddling influenced by private interests, and the quest for profit maximization. However, the federal government is a major social institution in the midst of a modern advanced capitalist nation. It is not above the social forces that dominate the larger society or that drive the struggle to achieve social power. In other words, the resources of the federal government are not outside political struggle and class conflict in its variety of forms; rather, these resources are fully enmeshed within these social forces. The federal government, its programs, its missions, and its budget are at the center of political struggle because the power of the state to funnel immense sums of money and valuable resources for use by private interests is unparalleled. As a consequence, none of the health care programs delivered or funded by the federal government can be understood without also knowing something of the nature of the social struggle and social influences that continually rage around them.

148

CHAMPUS

The Civilian Health and Medical Program of the Uniformed Services (CHAMPUS) is a health insurance program run by the Department of Defense (DoD) for military dependents who cannot or will not use military hospitals. CHAMPUS is one piece of a vast international health care network operated by the military:

> The Military Health Services System (MHSS) [has] an active workforce of 200,000 military and civilian personnel and over 200,000 reserve personnel. . . . Comprised of 148 hospitals, 554 medical clinics, more than 300 dental clinics . . . and the Civilian Health and Medical Program of the Uniformed Services (CHAMPUS), the system serves nearly 9 million beneficiaries . . . and will exceed $15 billion in fiscal year 1993. (Lanier and Boone 1993, 122)

The policy of providing varying levels of health care to military dependents was formalized in the 1884 Appropriation Bill for the War Department by a single sentence that allowed the military to provide medical services to military dependents free of charge. Through World War II this policy in practice delivered primarily emergency services and obstetrical care. Until World War II the standing army was quite small, and when larger numbers of recruits were mobilized families were typically left behind. Providing minimal health care for dependents was not a difficult task for military medical services until the massive mobilization for World War II. The depression had impoverished many of the families of the men who were drafted, so their families followed because they had no other recourse. Military medical services were suddenly overwhelmed with young military dependents giving birth.

The mobilization that took place in the early 1950s around the Korean War had the same consequences for military medical services. By the end of the war, however, it became clear that a better policy for military dependent health care was needed. The military had settled on the policy of a large standing armed forces even in peacetime. A health care policy for dependents was seen as an effective means to attract and retain recruits and to attract and retain physicians, whose families would also be covered, to treat them. In 1956 an act of Congress firmly established a health care program with funding for military dependents, which, within a few years, evolved into CHAMPUS (Potter 1990).

CHAMPUS is one of the fastest growing components of the DoD budget—so much so that DoD budget planners have not been able to keep up with it. In fiscal year (FY) 1989, for example, CHAMPUS spent $100 million more than the $2.8 billion that Congress had appropriated for the program, and the following year CHAMPUS spent $700 million more than Congress's $3.1-billion appropriation. By 1993 the CHAMPUS budget had climbed to nearly $4 billion, exclusive of overruns. The DoD estimated that the 1993 unfunded health benefit liability for current and future military retirees and their dependents was a quarter of a trillion dollars (Starr 1993, 80). Military analysts are particularly upset about these excessive costs because Congress has consistently told the DoD to take CHAMPUS overruns out of other funds already appropriated to DoD. The Pentagon has responded to the rising costs of CHAMPUS by experimenting with several internal and external program initiatives. Internally, the armed services have been experimenting by giving local control over CHAMPUS funds to base commanders, along with the authority to negotiate a private health care network in communities adjacent to the base hospital, that is, the catchment area. The various military services like this well enough, but what they do not like is Pentagon experimentation with private managed care firms because that siphons large amounts of money away from use by the health bureaucracies of the three military services:

> Foundation Health . . . was tapped as manager of the CHAMPUS Reform Initiative, a five year program that will funnel $3 billion in revenues to the company. The contract for the program, which began operating at 26 military bases in California and Hawaii in August 1988, vaulted Foundation Health into the ranks of the nation's top 50 defense contractors. (Kenkel 1990b)

It was no accident that Foundation Health landed this juicy $3-billion contract with the Pentagon. The corporation had done its homework and had kept the revolving door wide open: "Retired Vice Adm. Earl B. Fowler was the company's acting CEO during the start-up phase of the project; retired Rear Adm. Stuart Platt and retired Army Col. Charles Upton managed Foundation Health's government division" (Kenkel 1990a).

Ironically, shortly after Foundation Health landed the huge DoD managed care contract, the company experienced severe administrative problems. A new administrative team was brought in to take care of the mess, and the brass were kicked out. Meanwhile, at the end of the initial three-year contract, it was not clear that the DoD's managed care contract had saved any money. Despite the fact that the Pentagon is eager to expand the program to four more states, two studies by major national firms funded by the Pentagon raised serious questions about its value. One study noted that there had been extremely high increases in the utilization of medical services and estimates that an expanded managed care program would raise CHAMPUS costs by $400 million to $600 million per year. Another study noted that the managed care program was not the lowest-cost alternative available (Weissenstein 1993).

It also now looks as if CHAMPUS costs will increase rapidly as an unexpected consequence of base closings. As of early 1993 six bases with major hospitals have been closed down as part of an effort to downsize the military and save money. Thousands of retired military and their dependents who once utilized less-expensive on-base hospitals will now be forced to use more-expensive CHAMPUS facilities. As more bases with hospitals are closed, an increasing number of retirees and their dependents will use private-sector medical facilities and bill CHAMPUS (Palmer 1993).

Indian Health Service

The IHS is located in the Public Health Service, which is part of the Department of Health and Human Services. The IHS is a unique institution in the United States. It provides a wide range of health care at no cost to a group of people based on their tribal affiliation. The government obligation to provide health care for Native Americans is rooted in the genocidal land-grab that fueled America's growth for several hundred years at the expense of the Native peoples who originally occupied the land. Based on treaties, on the historical "ward status" of Native peoples under the federal government because of conquest and displacement, on various court rulings, and finally on the Snyder Act of 1921, the federal government assumes the responsibility to provide Native Americans with health care services. Given the very low economic status of most Native communities across the United States–due in large part to the historical theft of resources–and given the correspondingly poor health status of Native Americans as a people, services provided by the IHS have been extremely important for those Native Americans who have been able to use them.

According to the 1987 Survey of American Indians and Alaska Natives (Cunningham 1993), about 40 percent of the adults did not work at all during 1987, and most of the rest had only seasonal or part-time work. Fully one-third of those surveyed lived below the poverty line, and nearly an additional third lived in households with very low incomes. Almost 60 percent of those surveyed had no private or public health insurance or medical services other than IHS for at least some part of 1987, but the unemployed and underemployed were much more likely to rely on IHS services. Extremely high rates of unemployment and poverty play a major role in the injuries and illnesses that plague Native peoples across the country:

> Of all American Indian and Alaska Native people who died during 1986–1988, one-third were under 45 years of age, compared to one-tenth of the general population.
> They are much more likely than the general population to die of certain causes . . . : alcoholism, 438 percent greater; tuberculosis, 400 percent greater; diabetes, 155 percent greater; accidents, 131 percent greater. (Ambler 1994, 11)

In FY 1991 the IHS spent $1.4 billion to provide health care services at no charge to 1.1 million eligible Native Americans. The IHS employed about 14,000 people to accomplish this task, scattered across twelve IHS Service Areas and IHS Service Unit subdivisions in thirty-two states. Services are delivered through thirty-three urban Indian health organizations partly funded by the IHS, fifty hospitals, and 452 IHS outpatient clinics. In 1975 the Indian Self-Determination and Education Assistance Act was established, allowing the IHS to fund willing and able Native organizations to directly take over and operate IHS facilities with grants from IHS. As a result, 16 percent of the IHS hospitals and nearly 75 percent of the clinics are operated by Native Americans (U.S. General Accounting Office 1993d, 1–13).

Additional Issues

The Indian Health Service is woefully underfunded, but even if it were fully funded only a fraction of the Native Americans in the United States would be eligible to use it. Approximately 1.1 million Native Americans are eligible to use the IHS because they are members of federally recognized tribes. In the 1990 census about 2 million people identified themselves as Indians, and millions more identified themselves as having some Indian blood. Becoming federally recognized is a long, expensive, bureaucratic process. As a result, many Native Americans who should be receiving IHS benefits are not. In addition, IHS Service Areas exercise a great deal of latitude in determining who is eligible for their services, leaving many Native Americans in a precarious position over access to health care. On the other hand, the federal government could unilaterally terminate the delivery of health services to Native Americans at any time.

The issue of eligibility in the future may become even more precarious due to the effect of IHS financing regulations on health care for those in mixed marriages. The 1990 census indicated that American Indians, both women and men, are marrying non-Indians at rates exceeding 50 percent. As early as 1970 approximately one-third of all American Indian marriages involved a non-Indian spouse. In the absence of vastly improved IHS funding, this trend may result in services being restricted to fewer Native Americans and their families. If the IHS resorts to using blood quantum criteria for IHS eligibility, the membership of a large number of tribes could be split on this basis, and many Native Americans and their families may be deprived of services altogether.

Medicare

Medicare is a federal health insurance program for people sixty-five years of age or older and for certain disabled persons. The program is administered by the HCFA of the Department of Health and Human Services. The

Medicare program is a huge, important public service, and it is growing rapidly. Between 1975 and 1991 the number of Medicare beneficiaries grew from 25 million to more than 35 million. During the same period, however, claims volume grew by 450 percent. In 1991 the program processed 600 million claims and paid over $110 billion in benefits. This amounted to about 15 percent of the entire national health care bill, making Medicare the nation's single largest payer of health care benefits (U.S. General Accounting Office 1992a, 6). Medicare is divided into two major parts. Part A helps pay for inpatient hospital care and skilled nursing home care, hospice care, and home health care. Part B helps pay for physician and hospital outpatient services, durable medical equipment, and a variety of other medical services and supplies.

The contemporary Medicare program arose out of political struggle for national health insurance going as far back as the second decade of this century (Marmor 1973; Starr 1982). During the 1950s and early 1960s, as the social struggle resulting in Medicare took shape, organized labor provided most of the political muscle and influence to achieve the legislation. The AMA, the AHA, and the insurance industry engaged in a bitter, vitriolic battle to keep government out of health care. These interests perceived government involvement as a threat to the realization of maximum profit and to professional autonomy. However, during this period there was unprecedented popular support for national health insurance. The medical needs of the elderly in particular were repeatedly exposed in the media and widely supported by the public: "Health surveys reported that persons 65 and over were twice as likely as those under 65 to be chronically ill, and were hospitalized twice as long. . . . [O]nly 38 percent of the aged no longer working had any insurance at all. . . . Of those insured aged, a survey of hospital patients reported, only 1/14 of their total costs of illness were met through insurance" (Marmor 1973, 18).

The AMA and the AHA led political interests that successfully obstructed a true national health insurance program for all residents of the United States. Medicare as we know it today, enacted in the mid-1960s, was the compromise. Initially the AMA and the AHA won major concessions even within this compromise. They successfully fought off legislated control over reimbursement for their services under Medicare. These poorly controlled reimbursements for physician and hospital services have been a principal cause of the dramatic escalation in health care costs that began just after passage of Medicare and that persists to this day. The AMA and the AHA also won a victory over the Blue Cross and Blue Shield insurance organizations. Blue Cross insurance was started in the 1930s by the hospitals themselves to ensure payment for services. Blue Shield was established and controlled by physicians at about the same time for the same reason (Law 1976). Politically compromised Medicare legislation allowed Blue Cross and Blue Shield to be fiscal intermediaries between Medicare recipients and the federal government. This needless layer of bureaucracy was and is a huge waste of money and resulted in federal regulators losing direct control over Medicare expenditures.

Medicare Waste, Fraud, Abuse, and Mismanagement

The political compromise resulting in a program burdened with go-between insurance companies has proven to be quite lucrative for the insurance industry, but it has also been a chronic source of waste, fraud, and other serious problems for Medicare. In 1990 the GAO developed a special program to "identify [federal programs] that were especially vulnerable to waste, fraud, abuse, and mismanagement" (U.S. General Accounting Office 1992a, 1). One of the seventeen federal programs identified as high-risk was Medicare. Some of the major problems the GAO found with Medicare include:

- Weak Payment Safeguards.The thirty-five contracted intermediaries and carriers (that is, insurance companies) typically ignored or mishandled beneficiary complaints about provider fraud and abuse because the contractors had no financial incentive to do otherwise. As a result, billings and payments occurred for services not rendered, overpayments were not recovered, and penalties to fraudulent or recalcitrant physicians, hospitals, and other providers were not assessed.
- Flawed Medicare Payment Policies. Medicare payment policies for laboratory services are excessive, providing a profit margin for laboratory work far higher than the national average. About $150 million annually is wasted due to profit gouging of Medicare by medical labs. The proliferation of HMOs qualifying for Medicare payments has posed special problems for the program. HMOs have been plagued by a chronic history of underprovision of medical services, unjustified denial of claims, and unfair marketing practices, and these problems have put Medicare patients at risk in a number of these facilities.
- Weak Billing Controls. Contractors exercise very little control over the issuance and security of identification numbers necessary to bill Medicare for services. This has facilitated the activities nationwide of fraudulent health care providers and medical-equipment vendors.

Seniors Pay More and Get Less

There is no question that Medicare has made an extraordinarily important contribution to the health of America's seniors. As the years have gone by, however, this contribution has been steadily shrinking. Fraud and profit gouging in the private sector have diverted Medicare funds from the important mission of providing health care to seniors. Those interests still opposed to Medicare have turned the looting of Medicare funds by external sources into a critique of the Medicare program itself. Nevertheless, the facts of the situation among the elderly speak just as loudly for public health care assistance today as they did nearly thirty years ago at the birth of Medicare: In the early 1960s, prior to Medicare, senior citizens spent an average of one-tenth of their income annually on health care. In 1991, despite the protections of Medicare, seniors spent an average of *one-sixth* of their income on health care (Wolfe 1992a).

Part of this apparent paradox of the rising proportion of seniors' income going for health care since the advent of Medicare results from the fact that for at least two decades health care costs have been rising at a rate exceeding the general rate of inflation. During the 1980s, for example, the rate of inflation for health care costs was more than twice that of the consumer price index–an increase that hits older people on fixed incomes especially hard. Inflation in the cost of drugs and long-term care–health care items not covered by Medicare–has been particularly difficult for senior citizens. In addition, Medicare premiums, deductibles, and copayments have increased, as has the cost of the private "medigap" insurance currently purchased by 70 percent of all seniors.

Medigap insurance is widely obtained in order to cover a portion of the steadily increasing "gaps" in health care costs not covered by Medicare. In 1990, 22 million seniors over sixty-five years of age paid a total of $16 billion to purchase medigap insurance from private companies (Freudenheim 1990). This monumental expense contributes grandly to the paradox of seniors' increasing health care costs since the advent of Medicare. Unfortunately, a large share of this expense also is wasted year after year in fraudulent scams and vastly overpriced policies. In 1988 the late Congressman Claude Pepper, who had been involved for many years in health care issues affecting the elderly, estimated that more than $3 billion was wasted annually on fraudulent or overpriced medigap policies (U.S. Congress 1988, 10). Repeated congressional findings since the inception of Medicare have demonstrated a pattern of fraud, misrepresentation, and exploitation of the elderly by a sizable segment of commercial medigap insurers.

DRG Does Not Mean "Da Revenue's Gone"

September 30, 1993, was the tenth anniversary of Medicare's diagnosis related groups (DRGs). DRGs are a form of prospective payment system that was to supersede the fee-for-service payment system. Medicare developed DRGs to save money. The idea was to give hospitals a fixed amount for each of more than six hundred specific diagnoses. If the costs of patient hospitalization exceeded the DRG amount paid for that patient's particular medical problem or problems, the hospital absorbed the overrun. If, on the other hand, the DRG payment was in excess of what it cost the hospital to care for the patient, the hospital kept the excess as profit. The theory was that DRGs forced hospitals to cuts costs in order to make a profit. The fee-for-service form of payment replaced by Medicare's prospective payment system has just the opposite effect: A hospital maximizes profits by providing long stays and offering all sorts of diagnostic tests and medical procedures whether or not they are necessary. DRGs were implemented with little research or knowledge about their social or medical consequences. The idea of saving money was the primary, if not exclusive, driving force behind them. Many of the unanticipated consequences were found to be self-defeating or dangerous.

The hospital industry was not dealt the lethal blow by government DRG reimbursements predicted by corporate pundits. The AHA claims that hospital profits based exclusively on DRG payments dropped steadily from 14.5 percent in 1984 to –9.9 percent by 1993. However, *total* profit margins of hospitals dipped from 6.2 percent in 1984 to a low of 4.7 percent in 1987 but shot up to 6.8 percent by 1993. The corporate creation of hospital chains to centralize profits continued, hospitals learned to maximize DRG payments, and they learned to shift costs internally to other profit centers. During the first three years of DRGs the average cost per Medicare case rocketed 28.4 percent, while the index of hospital costs rose just 11 percent (Burda 1993; Bradley and Kominski 1992, 151).

The new mantra of hospital administrators has become the ungainly phrase "DRG optimization." This involves finding just the right selection and mix of DRG categories to assign to each hospitalized Medicare patient in order to maximize reimbursement. All of a sudden faceless coding clerks entombed in hospital basements surrounded by tons of patient records became central to DRG optimization. Hospital administrators bought sophisticated computer programs to help coding clerks find the most profitable DRGs to assign to each patient. Legions of "groupers, encoders, clinical editors, and maximizers" were hired to augment lowly records clerks. A mini-industry of consultants and peer-review organizations blossomed to provide independent assessments of the DRG codes assigned by the hospital staff. In summary, the public-sector scheme to save money resulted in the proliferation of a new, expensive private-sector bureaucracy aiming to outwit the cost-containment effort (Burda 1993).

Hospitals scrambled to reorganize in order to maintain profits after the implementation of DRGs. For example, hospitals offering open heart surgery increased from 10.5 percent to 1983 to 15.2 percent in 1991 because the DRG reimbursements were particularly generous for that procedure. Average patient stays plummeted as hospitals attempted to maximize DRG profits by releasing patients "quicker but sicker." Reimbursement for outpatient care was not regulated by DRGs, so hospitals without outpatient departments quickly jumped into that lucrative arena of health care. The percentage of hospitals with outpatient-care departments grew from 50 percent in 1983 to 87 percent by 1991. Hospital revenues from outpatient-care departments nearly doubled, reaching 25 percent of total revenues between 1983 and 1992. Many hospitals diversified into activities that were unrelated to DRGs, and even unrelated to health care, in search of new profits. These new activities ranged from health clubs and commercial laundry facilities to rehabilitation services and home health care. In 1983, for example, 15 percent of all hospitals offered home health care services, but by 1992 the percentage had more than doubled (Burda 1993).

Some studies have indicated that there have been serious medical consequences for patients released "quicker but sicker" under pressure from the DRG payment system. A major study that reviewed over 14,000 medical records from nearly three hundred randomly chosen hospitals in five states found that "the number of patients who were discharged to home in a medically unstable condition increased from one in 10 to one in six following the implementation of DRGs" (Brook, Kahn, and Kosecoff 1992, 132). In addition the researchers found "that patients aged 65 years and above who are discharged to home in an unstable condition are twice as likely to die within 30 days after hospitalization compared with those discharged in a stable condition (5.9% vs 3.0%)" (Brook, Kahn, and Kosecoff 1992, 132).

Public Health Enforcement I: Environmental Protection Agency

The EPA is one of the principal guardians of public health in the United States. Its purview covers the quality of drinking water, air and water pollution, hazardous waste, radioactive materials, pesticides, and more. The EPA is a large and rapidly growing organization with a $6-billion annual budget and a staff of 17,400 as of 1992. Since its inception in 1970 its budget has increased by a factor of fifteen, and its share as a percentage of all federal expenditures has more than doubled.

Despite the fact that the responsibilities of the EPA and its total budget have expanded greatly in the last two decades, in constant dollars (in other words, taking inflation into account) the EPA's operating budget in 1993 is no larger than it was in 1979. Currently, the United States spends about $115 billion annually to control and regulate pollution. This comes to about 2 percent of the gross domestic product (Hinchman 1993; Wright 1993, 117). The work of the EPA is so extensive and increasingly so important that many environmentalists, members of Congress, and the GAO itself advocate that the agency be raised to Cabinet level and be renamed the Department of Environmental Protection. In hearings in front of subcommittees of the House Committee on Government Operations, James F. Hinchman, general counsel of the GAO, noted that

> as our awareness of environmental problems has increased and EPA's role has expanded, environmental policy has increasingly shaped other domestic and foreign policies. The 1990 Clean Air Act Amendments, for example, which called for switching to cleaner fuels and cleaner coal-burning technologies, are directly linked to the nation's energy policies. The United States' participation in the international agreement to phase out the production of chlorofluorocarbons (CFCs) illustrates the integration of our environmental policies with our trade and foreign policies. As we begin to address global climate change, we will have to examine interrelationships among policies in many areas, including energy, agriculture, overseas assistance, foreign trade, and national security, among others. (Hinchman 1993, 4)

Drinking Water

Protecting Groundwater.   More than half the population of the United States relies on groundwater for its principal source of drinking water. Groundwater flows underground in vast aquifers and is typically accessed by wells punched in the ground by individuals or communities. Until the early 1970s it was thought by most experts that the very fact that groundwater was underground naturally protected it from contaminants that could adversely affect human health. It is now widely understood that aboveground pollution can readily find its way into groundwater, and from there into the homes of communities dependent upon that water. Common sources of groundwater pollution include airborne sulphur and nitrogen compounds from industrial smokestacks, pesticides and fertilizers, leaking septic tanks and a variety of underground storage tanks holding gasoline or other petroleum products, landfills, the runoff from urban areas, and other sources. Once groundwater is contaminated, it is often impossible to decontaminate or, if possible, extremely expensive. As a result, the EPA and most public health officials agree that the best way to protect groundwater is to prevent contamination from all sources in the wellhead area, defined as "the surface and subsurface area surrounding a water well or wellfield, supplying a public water system, through which contaminants are reasonably likely to move toward and reach such water well or wellfield." If the wellhead area is not protected, the human price can be increased illness and death, and the cost in dollars for cleanup can be astronomical (U.S. General Accounting Office 1993a, 8–9).

Under 1986 amendments to the EPA's 1974 Safe Drinking Water Act, the Wellhead Protection (WHP) Program was established to prevent contamination in wellhead areas under state's jurisdiction. WHP legislation requires each state to develop and implement a comprehensive program to protect wellhead areas from contaminants that may adversely affect human health. This program is unique for the EPA because it is preventive rather than after the fact and because it addresses not just a limited number of specific contaminants but, rather, all those that can damage human health. The EPA can approve or disapprove a state WHP plan. The carrot dangled in front of the state is that if their plan is approved, the state is then eligible to apply for federal funds to help implement the program. Unfortunately, Congress did not authorize a stick. The EPA has no authority to design and implement a WHP plan for recalcitrant states that do not submit a plan or that do not get their plan approved. Nor can the EPA impose any sanctions against a state that scoffs at the law.

June 1989 was the statutory deadline for all states to submit WHP programs to the EPA. As of three years after the deadline, and six years after the law was passed, nearly half the states did not have approved WHP programs. Most claimed to be working on them, but Alaska, California, and Virginia politely told the EPA to shove off–they had no intention of developing WHP plans. Of the twenty-six states and one territory that have had WHP programs approved by the EPA, not one of them had actually completed all the key elements that are supposed to be in a WHP program according to the legislation. A GAO investigation of the obstacles to the development of WHP programs by the states found that a principal obstacle was political:

> Some of the EPA and state officials interviewed for this report told us that states do not exert their authority to enact land-use controls because such controls are very controversial issues, which should be addressed by local governments. Furthermore, some of the EPA and state officials interviewed told us that trying to control the uses of land oftentimes creates resentment and bad feelings among landowners, facility owners and operators, and state and local officials, particularly if these groups have not been convinced that their drinking water is contaminated or at risk from potential sources of contamination. (U.S. General Accounting Office 1993a, 18)

Pesticides

Pesticide regulation by the federal government began early in the twentieth century. Congress passed the Insecticide Act in 1910, which had the relatively narrow goal of preventing mislabeling and adulteration of insecticides and fungicides. The Insecticide Act was replaced in 1947 with the more comprehensive Federal Insecticide, Fungicide, and Rodenticide Act (FIFRA). FIFRA originally focused on ensuring product performance as well as protecting those who used the substances from acute health hazards. In the early 1960s pesticide registration with the federal government required that the FDA determine an acceptable pesticide residue tolerance for each product indicating the amount of pesticide that could remain on or in an agricultural product and that the United States Department of Agriculture approve the pesticide container label. In 1970 jurisdiction over pesticide regulation was handed to the brand new EPA. Just a couple of years later FIFRA was extensively amended to require that manufacturers demonstrate that the substance would have no "unreasonable" negative health effects on humans or adverse effects on the environment (U.S. General Accounting Office 1993g, 42).

With the improvement of technology and with growing concern over long-term health effects of exposure to pesticides, the field of health effects testing has moved over the years from a focus on acute (short-term) health effects to mid- and long-term consequences, such as birth defects, cancer, and neurological damage. A rapidly emerging area of concern involves the impact of pesticides on the environment, for example, on nontarget insects, mammals, birds, and fish. Currently the EPA's Office of Pesticides Programs employs about eight hundred persons, of whom three hundred are engaged in the evaluation of test data. In FY 1991 nearly 19,100 food items (but not meat and poultry, which are the responsibility of the U.S. Department of Agriculture) were analyzed for pesticide residues by the Office of Pesticides Programs. Of these, nearly 45 percent were domestic products and the rest were imports.

The EPA reports that 98 percent of the imported foods and 99 percent of the domestic foods contained "no violative residues" (U.S. General Accounting Office 1993g, 84). This does not necessarily mean that these foods were residue free, and it does not necessarily mean that these foods were safe for everyone to eat. It simply means that the foods were within the compromise standards set by the EPA in the heated political environment of public hearings and political influence by corporations with vested interests, and by consumer and public health groups. Moreover, many of the foods found by the EPA to exceed the legal residues wind up in American stores anyway because importers deliver only part of the contaminated shipment to Customs for destruction and spirit the rest away for sale through regular channels (U.S. General Accounting Office 1992b). Additionally, FIFRA amendments in recent years require EPA to reevaluate and reregister about six hundred pesticide ingredients of existing pesticides currently in use. These pesticides were formerly registered under much weaker standards of evaluation and must be reevaluated using modern criteria and technology. Due in part to limited EPA resources and due in large part to industry stalling strategies, it is not anticipated that this project will be completed until at least the year 2006 (U.S. General Accounting Office 1993h, 4).

Under FIFRA the EPA has the responsibility to protect agricultural workers and others who may come in contact with pesticides. However, the EPA *also* has the conflicting responsibility to "balance" their assessment of the health risks by considering economic issues such as the profitability of a regulated industry. In other words, protective standards used by the EPA may not be the highest achievable standard in order to protect human health; instead, they may be a standard heavily compromised by the alleged costs to industry incessantly discussed at EPA public hearings, advisory board meetings, and with legislators by industry lobbyists. The problem with compromised health standards is exacerbated by a very poor system of data collection about the health impacts of pesticide exposure, particularly the long-term consequences. EPA relies on informal, often fundamentally flawed, voluntary reports from state and community sources and on a few scattered databases such as the American Association of Poison Control Centers.

Lawn Care Pesticides.　Homeowners apply about 32 million pounds of pesticides annually to their lawns, while 38 million pounds of pesticides are applied to turf by commercial applicators or are applied to commercial sites such as golf courses. Fully 40 percent of the nation's private lawns are doused with pesticides. Wholesale sales of lawn care pesticides grew from $700 million in 1988 to $900 million in 1992–a growth rate of about 5 percent per year. Only eighteen pesticides account for more than 90 percent of all the pesticides spread on the acres of lawn treated with pesticides. Most of these are not special pesticides developed for home lawn care. All but four of these popular lawn care pesticides are used in high-volume commercial agricultural applications, and all but three have widespread use in home gardens (U.S. General Accounting Office 1993e, 10–11).

Until recently the EPA was almost entirely unconcerned with possible risks to humans after lawn care pesticides were applied because it was felt that human exposure was minimal after the initial application. The EPA focus was on the commercial applicators, who were believed to receive much higher exposure to pesticides and therefore to be at higher risk. Only after being pushed by congressional inquiries and public concerns about environmental exposures and potential harm to children did the EPA begin to reevaluate the adverse consequences of lawn care pesticides after application. Even now the EPA is primarily concerned about adverse health effects, such as neurotoxicity, from occasional short-term exposures, despite the fact that mounting evidence shows exposure to these pesticides has been associated with cancer, birth defects, and chronic poisoning. The amount of lawn care pesticide applied to the nation's lawns is so great and its use is so widespread that the risk to humans is only part of the total picture of adverse consequences. Wildlife and household pets are also at risk of being poisoned, and many of these pesticides are increasingly found in the nation's groundwater, contaminating the source of half our drinking water.

Since the EPA relies on manufacturers to supply all the research necessary for reregistration, manufacturers have every incentive to stretch the process out as far as possible by using tactics such as submitting shoddy research to the EPA in order to be asked to redo it, perhaps adding years to the reregistration process. One cancer study, for example, can last four years and may result in several thousand pages of reports. The full reregistration process may require a manufacturer to submit eighty to one hundred such reports, each of which takes a team of EPA scientists weeks to analyze. Manufacturers also use "independent" laboratories to help them analyze their pesticides to get them through the reregistration process. A number of these labs have been implicated in very shady deals making sure that their pesticide manufacturer client appears to have a safe and effective product.

The chairman of the Subcommittee on Toxic Substances, Environmental Oversight, Research, and Development of the Senate Committee on Environment and Public Works asked the GAO to investigate the progress of EPA reregistration of the top eighteen lawn care pesticides in 1990 and again in 1991. Both times GAO researchers were forced to reply that "EPA had not made substantial progress in reregistering these pesticides." Asked once again the same question by the Subcommittee, in 1993 the GAO had a very similar response: "EPA continues to fall behind its schedule to reregister the 18 major lawn care pesticides. In the meantime, the pesticides continue to be applied in large amounts without complete knowledge of their safety. Since March 1991, EPA's scheduled study completion dates for many of the 18 major lawn care pesticides have slipped significantly, some by as much as 4 years" (U.S. General Accounting Office 1993e, 15).

Buying and Selling Air Pollution

EPA regulations for pollutants have typically employed either performance standards that regulate the amount of pollution that can be discharged by a particular source, or technology standards that regulate industrial practices and pollution abatement technology. These types of regulatory activities are commonly referred to as "command-and-control" regulations. Reviewing the twenty-some years of EPA regulatory history, it is generally thought that command-and-control regulation has worked particularly well for pollution from large, stationary sources such as factories, power plants, and sewage treatment facilities:

> Despite substantial economic and population growth, emissions of several significant air pollutants have fallen. According to EPA's estimates, between 1970 and 1988, emissions of particulate matter, carbon monoxide, volatile organic compounds, sulfur dioxide, and nitrogen oxides were 30, 43, 58, and 72 percent, respectively, of what they would have been if controls had not been established. EPA also points out that discharges of water pollutants from municipal

and industrial sources have declined, as the levels of total suspended solids in and the biological oxygen demand of industrial discharges–two traditional indicators of water pollution–declined by 96 and 93 percent, respectively, between 1973 and the period between 1982 and 1987. (U.S. General Accounting Office 1993b, 9)

Given the proven success of command-and-control regulations for large facilities, it is curious (or perhaps politically suspect) that the 1990 amendments to the Clean Air Act initiated an entirely new type of regulatory system for huge utility power plants. The new "emission trading" program for sulfur dioxide emissions, associated with acid rain, applies almost exclusively to huge public utility power plants. The emission trading program, also known as a "marketable permits system," begins with the EPA determining an overall goal of sulfur dioxide emissions. The agency then hands out permits to all the major polluters, in this case 110 coal-fired electricity-generating facilities, which allow them to produce a certain amount of pollution. Those companies that generate less than their allotment of pollution can sell their pollution credits to highly polluting facilities. Every few years the pollution allowance under the annual permits will be reduced, with the goal of reducing the overall amount of pollution nationwide.

Industry loves this because they are not required to do anything other than sell or buy permits. Even if a power plant is a heavy polluter and relatively inexpensive technology is available to minimize pollution, the plant only needs to spend a couple hundred thousand dollars a year to purchase surplus pollution allotments from another plant. As a result, the EPA entirely loses control over the level of pollution in specific communities, pollution that, under the command-and-control type of regulation, it had been able to control. In fact, it was just on this basis that the attorney general of New York in conjunction with state environmental officials sued the EPA in 1993. They were afraid that power plants in the Great Lakes region would purchase excess pollution permits from other plants and contribute to the acid rain problem damaging New York's Adirondack region (Taylor and Kansas 1993, C14).

Superfund

The EPA's Superfund program was created by the 1980 passage of the Comprehensive Environmental Response, Compensation, and Liability Act (CERCLA) by Congress. CERCLA originally provided the EPA with a $1.6 billion "Superfund" trust fund with which to clean up the highest-priority hazardous waste sites across the nation. Superfund comes complete with a legal stick that can be used to force perpetrators to clean up their own mess or to force them to repay the government if it has to clean up the mess for them. Originally Superfund was thought of as a short-lived program because the scope of America's hazardous waste problems was not fully understood at the time. Since then Superfund has been reauthorized by Congress twice, pumping the fund up to $15.2 billion. The original 1980 Superfund National Priorities List (NPL) grew from about four hundred dangerous hazardous waste sites in the early 1980s to 1,275 sites by mid-1992, and it is expected to top 2,000 sites by the beginning of the new millennium (Hembra 1993).

While $15.2 billion sounds like a great deal of money in the pot, it is a only little over half of what the EPA estimates will be needed as the government's share to clean up sites already listed–and the GAO thinks the EPA estimate is extremely low. The number of Superfund sites could climb to 3,000 in the foreseeable future, in which case it is estimated that public and private costs for cleanup would be about $150 billion in 1990 dollars over a period of thirty years. The scope of many of these cleanups is almost unimaginable. For example, nearly a century of wood treating, mining, milling, and smelting has left a 50,000-acre swath of seriously contaminated lands along 140 miles of the Clark Fork River and its tributaries in Washington. Four Superfund sites are scattered throughout this region and will involve massive resources to clean up. In addition the Superfund has a backlog of more than 7,000 hazardous waste sites awaiting final evaluation for possible inclusion on the NPL and another 130,000 sites that may ultimately have to be assessed for possible inclusion on the list.

The pace of Superfund cleanups has been agonizingly slow. From 1980 to 1992 only forty sites had been entirely cleaned up and removed from the list of 1,275 Superfund sites. Another 109 sites were involved in long-term cleanup efforts, such as groundwater pumping and decontamination, or were wending their way through bureaucratic procedures to remove them from the NPL. Cleanup work had begun or was underway at another 374 sites, leaving 752 sites with little more accomplished than the initial assessment that resulted in their inclusion on the NPL. Even though Congress may not give the EPA enough money to do its job, several studies by the GAO indicate that Superfund wastes a great deal of the money it does receive:

> Our work has disclosed weaknesses in EPA's contracting policy and administration that have exposed Superfund to excessive costs. Many of these problems involved breakdowns in the controls over contractor costs. For example, with cost-reimbursable contracts, EPA should carefully review contractors' spending plans before approving them, check bills for allowable charges before paying them, and verify charges later by auditing contractors' records. However, we have reported that EPA has not adequately used these controls. (Hembra 1993, 7–8)

While the GAO believes that the EPA is now taking steps to improve contract management in order to reduce excessive costs, at the same time it points out that the EPA has been remiss in collecting money owed it. As of fall of 1992 the EPA had determined that it could recover $5.7 billion in cleanup costs from polluters, but it had in fact recovered only about 10 percent of that. The reasons for this low recovery rate range from inadequate records and understaffing to statutory limitations and an unwillingness to aggressively pursue costs from polluters. Finally, the GAO believes there are "serious questions" about how effectively the EPA cleans up a site even when the money is spent efficiently and properly (Hembra 1993, 11).

Public Health Enforcement II: Occupational Safety and Health Administration

Each year about 10,500 workers are killed on the job across the United States, and another nearly 7 million are seriously injured or made ill. Annually, approximately 1.7 million of these suffer disabling on-the-job injuries. Each year nearly 400,000 new cases of occupationally related diseases are reported, and 100,000 workers die as a result of occupational diseases (U.S. General Accounting Office 1993f, 1). These are not elderly people dying of chronic diseases but, rather, young people in the prime of their lives. The National Institute of Occupational Safety and Health (NIOSH) reports that during the years 1980–1988, 105,500 working people died as a result of workplace injuries or illnesses (but illnesses are vastly undercounted in these figures). Moreover, some states are far more dangerous to workers than are others. During this same period the average annual fatality rate per 100,000 workers was only 1.9 in Connecticut but 33.1 in Alaska. The chances of a worker dying on the job in Alaska were nearly seventeen and a half times as great in Alaska as in Connecticut (Wolfe 1992b). To some extent the disparities can be accounted for by workforce age differences and job mix, but the high degree of variability in state health and safety enforcement probably plays a prominent role.

Joseph Dear, OSHA director in the Clinton administration, estimated that this carnage in the workplace cost American industry $115 billion in 1992, yet OSHA and state governments together allocate a piddling $380 million per year to occupational safety and health. This comes out to less than $4 per worker per year. Compare this figure with $6 billion annually spent to protect the environment, $1.1 billion to protect fish and wildlife, or $441 million to protect the safety of food. The National Safe Workplace Institute was not far off when it charged that there were more park rangers than OSHA inspectors. Estimates in the early 1990s indicated that there were so few inspectors that it would take federal OSHA eighty-four years to inspect, only once, each of the 6 million workplaces for which it is responsible. It would take those states that have contracted with federal OSHA to be responsible for their own programs between 11 and 167 years to inspect their workplaces only once, depending upon the state (Noble 1994; Wolfe 1992b; McNeely 1992, 20).

Prior to 1970 regulations concerning occupational health and safety were left entirely up to each state. Decade after decade of excessive deaths and maiming in the nation's workplaces proved that local corporate influence typically overwhelmed political will to establish truly effective state-run occupational safety and health programs. Following several major industrial tragedies, and pushed strongly by organized labor at the national level, particularly by the AFL-CIO, federal OSHA was finally established via the 1970 Occupational Safety and Health Act as a joint federal-state program. Initially, the OSHA Act abolished all state programs and fanned out across the nation to directly enforce job safety and health in every state. The act provided, however, that once a state was brought up to certain federal OSHA standards, the state could contract with federal OSHA to operate its own OSHA program with minimal federal supervision. In addition, federal OSHA would contribute a considerable sum of money to help the state run its own program.

As of the end of 1993, federal OSHA directly covered private sector places of employment in twenty-nine states, but two of these had state-run programs exclusively for state and local employees. Federal OSHA is prohibited by law from protecting federal, state, or local government workers, leaving about 7.3 million public-sector workers in twenty-seven states largely unprotected. State-run OSHA programs in twenty-one states cover all private-sector and public-sector employees. Federal OSHA has a long history of weak oversight of state-run programs (Crawford 1993, 4).

The Politics of OSHA

Prior to the 1970 act establishing federal OSHA, the multitude of state programs were political rallying points for corporate antipathy to government interference in the way business was conducted, for management control over labor, and for management control over the allocation of resources. Once the federal government took over, the influence of smaller local businesses decreased, but the influence of larger national and multinational corporations increased. During the first year of OSHA's existence, over one hundred bills flooded Congress seeking to modify or eliminate the agency. Until the 1993 election of President Clinton, four of the five presidents governing since the enactment of federal OSHA were unequivocally pro-business conservatives, particularly Presidents Reagan and Bush, in the 1980s and early 1990s. Easily yielding to corporate pressures, OSHA budgets were minimized, and the appointed OSHA leadership often consisted of political hacks whose nationally publicized incompetence or compromised ethics were occasionally an embarrassment even to the Republicans who had appointed them. During the Reagan and Bush administrations, OSHA had ten different directors. Constantly under attack by the Office of Management and Budget under both Reagan and Bush, underfunded, beset by revolving-door staff and administrators, and decentralized back to the states, which allows maximum corporate influence, the critical public health task of occupational health and safety was a victim of intense political lobbying and power plays.

In 1976 Congress stripped OSHA of its regulatory authority over farms with fewer than eleven employees, despite the fact that American farms are among the most dangerous workplaces in the nation. A 1979 proposal by the Senate would have exempted nearly 40 percent of the nation's workplaces from OSHA oversight, but this was defeated through a monumental lobbying effort by organized labor, which has always been a strong proponent of an effective OSHA. During the 1980s the Reagan administration required that all proposed OSHA standards had to be submitted to the Office of Management and Budget (OMB) for a cost/benefit analysis. Despite the fact that the courts have prohibited cost/benefit analysis as grounds for rejecting OSHA standards, OMB review slowed down the process and seriously weakened several OSHA regulations. Under the subsequent Bush administration, the preferred institutional form of obstruction was Vice President Dan Quayle's Council on Competitiveness, which was directly influenced by private industry. On the other hand, the courts have been used by industry to challenge nearly every major health standard. This tactic has had the desired effect of delaying implementation of the regulations and sometimes of weakening them or rejecting them altogether (McNeely 1992, 19). Antiregulatory forces made sure that OSHA's ability to make new rules and regulations is as byzantine as possible in order to delay new rules and in order to provide maximum opportunity to weaken them prior to promulgation (McNeely 1992, 19).

The Future of OSHA

In 1992 organized labor and public health professionals, among others, pushed hard to get the first comprehensive reform of OSHA through Congress, but it died for lack of Republican support. As of early 1994 a similar bill, sponsored by Democrats Senator Edward Kennedy and Representative William Ford, had the support of the Clinton administration. In short:

It requires all companies to set up safety and health programs. . . .
It extends OSHA coverage to public employees now excluded. . . .
It increases the criminal penalties under OSHA. . . .
It updates the exposure limits on toxic substances. . . .

It . . . requires contractors on multi-employer sites to coordinate safety plans, and requires contractors in general to draw up health and safety plans for particular projects. (Noble 1994)

Important as this proposed legislation is, it lacks some critical features. For example, under this new legislation OSHA will still not have the right to close down an imminently hazardous workplace without the long and cumbersome process of first getting a court order. Contrast this with the Mine Safety and Health Administration (MSHA), which can instantly close down particularly dangerous equipment, or even entire mining operations. This kind of authority saves lives. Waiting on court orders can lose lives. And this legislation has not yet made its way through Congress, where it will undoubtedly be made even weaker or perhaps killed altogether.

Public Health Enforcement III: Food and Drug Administration

The FDA is a critical piece of the national public health effort and a sizable bureaucracy within the Public Health Service in the Department of Health and Human Services. The FDA oversees the labeling, quality, and effectiveness of America's food, prescription and over-the-counter drugs, cosmetics, medical devices, radiation-emitting products like microwave ovens and X-ray equipment, and food and drugs for animals. The administration has approximately 7,000 employees, who monitor nearly $600 billion worth of goods annually. About 1,100 FDA investigators and inspectors regulate 90,000 businesses across America. These inspectors take 70,000 samples a year for examination by 2,100 scientists in forty laboratories located throughout the country. The FDA detains over 20,000 import shipments at ports of entry for closer inspection, and seizes or orders withdrawn from the market about 3,000 domestic and imported products every year (Food and Drug Administration 1991).

Regulating New Food Technologies.   Hungry? How about a nice big genetically engineered potato! It is presumed to be safe to eat because it has been tested for glycoalkaloid solanine, a toxic substance sometimes found at high levels in new potato varieties. But anyone who is allergic to wheat gluten had better not try it, because it was genetically engineered to have elements of wheat gluten in it. Not too enticing? Then how about heating up a nice package of frozen vegetables that have been genetically engineered with DNA and bits of protein from Lampyridae luciferase, an insect, to make the vegetables more appealing after having been frozen. These are genetically engineered foods, on the frontiers of food technology, based on the discoveries in biotechnology since the 1970s that permit direct modification of genetic materials of plants, animals, and microorganisms in ways that are largely foreign to Mother Nature. According to an article published in the Journal of the American Medical Society by Dr. Henry Miller from the FDA's Office of Biotechnology, the FDA has no problem regulating foods engineered by the new biotechnology:

> The FDA's science-based approach to foods produced with the newer genetic techniques . . . focuses safety evaluations on the characteristics of the food: substances newly introduced into the food supply; increased concentrations of toxicants beyond the range known to be safe; alterations of important nutrients that may occur as a result of the genetic modification; and possible transfer of allergenicity (Miller 1993, 912).

Unfortunately, a major study of FDA's ability to regulate new food technologies conducted by the GAO paints a far less rosy picture of FDA's abilities. A GAO list of bioengineered food safety concerns that the FDA may have difficulties dealing with include

- the production of unexpected effects, including multiple effects resulting from a single genetic change . . . , of potential health significance;
- an increase in levels of naturally occurring toxins and allergens or the activation of dormant toxins or allergens;
- the introduction of known or new substances that may be toxins, allergens, or antinutrients;
- an adverse change in the composition, absorption, or metabolism of important nutrients;
- a reduction in the effectiveness of some antibiotics through the use of antibiotic-resistant marker genes . . . ;
- the production of adverse environmental consequences, including harmful effects on wildlife and ecosystems;
- an adverse change in the quality and nutritional sufficiency of animal feed or an increase in the level of toxins in plant byproducts fed to animals. (U.S. General Accounting Office 1993c, 35)

Apart from a couple of minor exceptions, the FDA does not require food producers and manufacturers to register with the FDA or notify them that they are in business. As a result, frequently the FDA does not even know these businesses exist and learns about them only after a food safety problem has occurred. This is of particular concern in the arena of genetically engineered foods. In addition, even when the FDA suspects a problem, it does not have the authorization to inspect a food manufacturer's processing and distribution records. Industry lobbyists struggle mightily to protect this corporate prerogative and kill or weaken most bills to expand FDA regulatory powers. Finally, chronic funding problems plague the FDA's future abilities to regulate food technology advances. In an internal assessment looking at resources needed to pursue its mission through 1997, the FDA concluded that

> it needed to strengthen its science base to regulate food products produced by new technologies, such as new biotechnology. [It was] estimated that over 2,000 staff years and over $215 million above current levels will be needed for expected food safety regulatory activity between 1993 and 1997, including 50 additional staff years to process food petitions related to biotechnology. (U.S. General Accounting Office 1993c, 90–91)

The Political Failure to Regulate Medical Technology

The ultra-conservative Reagan presidency of the 1980s gutted federal regulatory agencies under the ideological slogans of reducing paperwork and encouraging free enterprise. Budgets were slashed, programs were dismantled, top administrators were replaced with political ideologues, and employees were demoralized. Effective regulation of industry to promote and preserve public health was severely undermined. Nowhere was the assault on public health felt more severely than in the FDA's failing oversight of medical devices. During the entire 1980s the leadership of the FDA's Center for Devices, in direct opposition to the law, saw their job primarily as facilitating the marketing of new medical devices and encouraging growth of the $35-billion industry. John Villforth, the director of the center for most of the 1980s, described himself as a regulatory "pussycat" who did not believe in mandatory standards and who stonewalled Congress by blaming the lack of medical device regulatory progress on staff shortages rather than ideology. His deputy and successor in 1990, James Benson, said outright "enforcement isn't the mission of the agency" (both quoted in Ingersoll 1992). The price paid in public health because a regulatory agency became a friend of industry is devastating:

> The upshot: of 60,000 devices on the market today, from breast implants to lasers, the vast majority received the same cursory review as the innocuous tongue depressor, according to government auditors. . . .
> A 1989 congressional audit found that of 53,000 reports on adverse incidents filed with the FDA by device manufacturers, 55% involved serious injuries to patients and others; 3% involved deaths. Malfunctioning devices were to blame for 42% of the cases. Alarm failures on infant breathing monitors resulted in the deaths of four babies. One device alone–the fracture-prone Bjork-Shiley heart valve–is blamed for more than 300 deaths. FDA officials are looking into at least 15 fatal cases of anaphylactic shock apparently triggered by latex tips on enema devices. (Ingersoll 1992, A1)

In 1976 special legislation was passed requiring that the FDA do certain things to ensure the safety and effectiveness of medical devices. Entire sections of that legislation were routinely ignored by top FDA administrators for at least fifteen years after its enactment. For example, the legislation required that the FDA set mandatory safety standards for 830 "medium-risk" categories of medical devices, such as surgical saws and resuscitators. A decade and a half later, not one standard had been set. The legislation mandated that the agency review 140 categories of "high-risk" medical devices, such as those implanted in the human body. A decade and a half later it had accomplished less than 2 percent of that mandate. On the other hand, the FDA has allowed a 1976 medical devices grandfather clause to be drastically misused to permit an avalanche of new medical devices to skip through a cursory FDA review before being marketed and used nationally. According to James Benson, then head of the FDA's Center for Devices, "If we didn't do it, we'd be slowing up products coming to market"(Ingersoll 1992, A6). Unable to force an ideologically driven government bureaucracy to follow the law after about fifteen years of trying, Congress simply passed another, even less effective law:

> Two years ago, members of Congress who oversee the FDA gave up trying to prod the agency into writing performance standards and thoroughly reviewing product safety. For one thing, neither the Bush administration nor Congress was willing, given the budget deficit, to underwrite the cost. For another, the mind-set of senior device regulators was still decidedly deregulatory. So lawmakers voted to de-emphasize pre-market review in favor of much stronger post-market surveillance.
>
> The 1990 law requires hospitals, nursing homes and outpatient clinics–and eventually device distributors–to report deaths and serious injuries and illnesses involving medical devices, just as manufacturers have had to do since 1984. The new requirements, by all accounts, will double the number of these reports to 50,000 a year–far more than the agency can evaluate. (Ingersoll 1992, A6)

The irony is that postmarket surveillance responds to dead and injured bodies; premarket mandated performance standards are designed to prevent deaths and injuries. Not only will the Center for Devices be overwhelmed with 50,000 incident reports per year, but it is likely that the system itself will be plagued by rampant underreporting. A study by the nonprofit government watchdog Public Citizen Health Research Group of thirty-five medical device manufacturers found that they did not report hundreds of malfunctions to the FDA, some of which had caused death and serious injury. One manufacturer of insulin-infusion pumps, for example, received 1,500 complaints from users in the field but only reported 15 to the FDA.

In 1990 Dr. David Kessler was appointed commissioner of the FDA. He rapidly established himself as an aggressive enforcer, in stark contrast to previous commissioners. Medical device manufacturers fret about his "policeman's mentality" and bemoan the days when the FDA and the medical device corporations "cooperated" to the virtual exclusion of FDA's mandate to protect the public health. Under Kessler the FDA seized sixty-seven defective products in FY 1991, up over 100 percent from the previous year. Also in FY 1991 approval of new products fell by 43 percent compared to the previous year, presumably because of closer scrutiny. However, no matter how aggressive, effective, and concerned Kessler may be as an individual, he heads the same bureaucracy that stonewalled Congress for over a decade and a half. His charismatic leadership can penetrate the bureaucracy only so far during his tenure as commissioner.

The Politics of Regulating Drugs: Where Science Fears to Tread

The third major area of consumer products regulated by the FDA involves prescription and over-the-counter drugs. Despite the complex and expensive FDA-mandated scientific testing and monitoring new drugs are supposed to pass through prior to and even after being marketed in the United States, scientific findings may ultimately play a small role in a drug's social fate. Politics, the corporate quest for profit, even religious beliefs can dominate judgments about research, investment, development, FDA approval, and marketing–relegating the findings of scientific evaluation to distant corners of the social universe in which the whole drama plays out. For example:

- FDA advisory boards are very influential in the determination of a drug's progress through FDA testing requirements, but many of the scientists on these advisory boards have clear conflicts of interest because of their financial entanglements with drug companies (FDA Sets New Rules 1992, 26). The potential for decisions based on self-interest rather than scientific evaluation is great.
- The "revolving door" problem affects the integrity of all regulatory agencies. FDA administrators and inspectors, for example, may have the prospect of a better paid position with drug manufacturers if they "cooperate" during their career with the FDA.
- Corporations heavily lobby Congress to manipulate the FDA, and may even bribe FDA officials directly to speed up approval of their drugs ("Mylan Settles Suits over Bribes" 1993).

Summary and Discussion

Two of the principal areas of health care in which the federal government is involved are medical care and public health (primarily preventive services). Each of these areas of involvement is fundamentally split between the direct provision of services either by the federal government or by another level of the public sector via federal grants, and the funding of services in the private sector. For example, the Military Health Services System provides medical care directly to those in the military and under certain circumstances to their dependents. CHAMPUS provides health insurance coverage to enable military dependents and retirees to use health care services in the private sector. The Indian Health Service provides direct health care services to Native Americans via IHS facilities operated by the government or Native American entities, and under certain circumstances it provides payment for medical care provided by the private sector. Medicare is strictly a health insurance scheme funneling money to the private sector. In the arena of public health, the EPA, for example, provides some services directly or through partially funded state programs and subcontracts out hundreds of millions of dollars of work to the private sector every year. It converts air pollution into a commodity that can be bought and sold in private markets.

Private-sector corporate interests exert massive influence over every aspect of the federal government's involvement in health care. Corporate resources vastly outweigh those of private, nonprofit consumer advocacy groups or environmental activists. Frequently, corporate influence diverts vast resources and distorts the nominal mission of government health care efforts. Virtually every aspect of federal involvement in health care is influenced through Congress by an army of tens of thousands of well-financed lobbyists, scores of millions of dollars in PAC money and individual contributions, bribes, and a host of illegal or unethical emoluments. Public health laws and regulations are weakened and destroyed before they are promulgated and are challenged continuously afterward. Nationwide public relations campaigns and fabricated "grassroots" movements cultivate corporate-condoned beliefs among the public and exert significant pressure on Congress. The revolving door phenomenon continuously replenishes top government positions with administrators linked to private-sector interests while siphoning off public-sector scientists, lawyers, administrators, and enforcement officials and high-ranking military officers. The oversight role of government employees is too often immobilized by the ever present potential for a lucrative private-sector job, while highly placed government administrators "on loan" from the private sector frequently have a not-too-hidden agenda to weaken and paralyze government regulatory functions.

Weak government oversight and revenue-maximizing strategies in the private sector combined with tens of billions of dollars in cost-plus contracts and federally funded health insurance promote widespread fraud, waste, and overbilling. Billions of dollars are diverted from medical care for those who need it the most, and billions of dollars are diverted from public health programs designed to prevent unnecessary injury and death. Meanwhile, in the public sector massive bureaucracies tend to insulate program administrators from influence by commissioners and secretaries, by Congress, and by the private sector, particularly the weaker nonprofit elements. Financial ties by high-level public-sector bureaucrats to corporate or other private-sector institutions may exert considerable influence over bureaucrats who are not adequately held accountable in their relatively protected positions.

Nearly all of these structural relationships tend to maximize profit in the private sector and tend to maximize private influence over the public sector, with the final result that the most vulnerable populations are deprived of public health and medical care. The corporate onslaught on the EPA to reduce funding and weaken enforcement disproportionately affects low-income and minority communities because hazardous waste sites are far more likely to be located in those communities. Corporate interests that want to slash Medicare funding and AMA and AHA interests that want to raise reimbursements have the same effect on Medicare recipients: less money to provide health care for those who need it. Congressional and DoD budget slashers who want to cut CHAMPUS funds do not achieve their cost-containment goals by contracting out to huge private-sector managed care bureaucracies. At the same time, those who are dependent on CHAMPUS medical care experiments may be subject to inferior care. An FDA numbed by a decade and a half of corporate dominance has a history of stonewalling Congress and appears to have a primary mission of safeguarding private sector profits. Meanwhile, tens of thousands of people die, are seriously injured, or become ill because of lax or nonexistent enforcement.

The federal government does not exist in a social vacuum. It is a type of government that has evolved in the context of a mature capitalist society in which culture, economics, and politics are dominated by the interests of the ruling class. Health-related laws, regulations, policies, and programs in the federal government are largely the result of political contests among different elements of the capitalist class, and organized efforts among working-class minorities, organized labor, grassroots environmentalists, consumer advocates, and others. In any political contest, those with the greatest resources tend to wield the most political power. In this case the multibillion dollar assets of multinational corporations wield far more influence directly on Congress and directly on the shaping of culture and beliefs of most people than do grassroots organizations of working people or organized labor. On the other hand, the daily struggle against poverty, discrimination, sexism, poor health care, unsafe jobs, modern epidemics, and an increasingly hazardous environment continually re-create the conditions around which people organize for resistance and fundamental change.

References

Ambler, Marjane. 1994. "Taking Care of Our Own: Training Indians to Heal Indians." *Tribal College* 5(3):10–16.

Bradley, Thomas B., and Gerald F. Kominski. 1992. "Contributions of Case Mix and Intensity Change to Hospital Cost Increases." *Health Care Financing Review* 14(2):151–63.

Brook, Robert H., Katherine L. Kahn, and Jacqueline Kosecoff. 1992. "Assessing Clinical Instability at Discharge." *Journal of the American Medical Association* 268(10):1321–22.

Burda, David. 1993. "What We've Learned from DRG's." *Modern Healthcare* (October 4):42–44.

Crawford, Clarence C. 1993. "Occupational Safety and Health: Changes Needed in the Combined Federal-State Approach." Testimony before the Subcommittee on Labor Standards, Occupational Health and Safety, Committee on Education and Labor House of Representatives. U.S. General Accounting Office. October 20.

Cunningham, Peter J. 1993. "Access to Care in the Indian Health Service." *Health Affairs* 12(3):224–33.

"FDA Sets New Rules to 'Fast-Track' Drugs." 1992. *Chemical Marketing Reporter* (December 14):5, 26.

Food and Drug Administration. 1991. "The Food and Drug Administration: An Overview." *FDA Backgrounder* (pamphlet). February.

Freudenheim, Milt. 1990. "Pressure Builds to Curb Medigap." *New York Times* (April 24):D2.

Hembra, Richard L. 1993. "Superfund: Progress, Problems, and Reauthorization Issues." Testimony before the Subcommittee on Transportation and Hazardous Materials, Committee on Energy and Commerce, House of Representatives. U.S. General Accounting Office. April 21.

Hinchman, James F. 1993. "Creation of a Department of Environmental Protection." Testimony before the Subcommittee on Legislation and National Security and the Subcommittee on Environment, Energy, and Natural Resources, Committee on Government Operations, House of Representatives. U.S. General Accounting Office. May 6.

Ingersoll, Bruce. 1992. "Health Risk: Amid Lax Regulation, Medical Devices Flood a Vulnerable Market." *Wall Street Journal* (March 24):A1, A6(W).

Kenkel, Paul J. 1990a. "CHAMPUS' Budget Billions Draw Crowd of Vested Interests." *Modern Healthcare* (June 4):32.

——— 1990b. "Navy Shoves Off for Cost-Control Waters." *Modern Healthcare* (June 4):32–33.

Lanier, Jack O., and Charles Boone. 1993. "Restructuring Military Health Care: The Winds of Change Blow Stronger." *Hospital and Health Services Administration* 38(1):121–32.

Law, Sylvia A. 1976. *Blue Cross: What Went Wrong?* 2nd ed. New Haven: Yale University Press.

Marmor, Theodore R. 1973. *The Politics of Medicare*. Chicago: Aldine.

McNeely, Eileen. 1992. "Tracking the Future of OSHA." *AAOHN Journal* 40(1):17–23.

Miller, Henry I. 1993. "Foods of the Future: The New Biotechnology and FDA Regulation." *Journal of the American Medical Association* 269(7):910–12.

"Mylan Settles Suits over Bribes to FDA with Two Companies." 1993. *Wall Street Journal* (November 30):C4(N).

Noble, Barbara P. 1994. "Breathing New Life into OSHA." *New York Times* (January 23):F25(L).

Palmer, Elizabeth A. 1993. "Base Closings May Add Weight to Health-Care Burden." *Congressional Quarterly Weekly Report* (February 27):473–76.

Potter, Max. 1990. "Military Dependent Medical Care During World War II." *Military Medicine* 155(2):45–47.

Starr, Barbara. 1993. "U.S. Military Enters the Managed Care Battle." *Business and Health* (April):74–80.

Starr, Paul. 1982. *The Social Transformation of American Medicine.* New York: Basic Books.

Taylor, Jeffrey, and Dave Kansas. 1993. "Environmentalists Vie for Right to Pollute." *Wall Street Journal* (March 26):C1, C14(W).

U.S. Congress.1988. House Committee on Energy and Commerce. Hearing before the Subcommittee on Commerce, Consumer Protection, and Competitiveness. *Private Health Insurance for the Elderly.* 100th Cong., 1st. sess.

U.S. General Accounting Office. 1992a. *Medicare Claims.* Washington, D.C. December.

———. 1992b. *Pesticides: Adulterated Imported Foods Are Reaching U.S. Grocery Shelves.* Washington, D.C. September.

———. 1993a. *Drinking Water: Stronger Efforts Needed to Protect Areas Around Public Wells from Contamination.* Washington, D.C. April.

———. 1993b. *Environmental Protection: Implications of Using Pollution Taxes to Supplement Regulation.* Washington, D.C. February.

———. 1993c. *Food Safety and Quality: Innovative Strategies May Be Needed to Regulate New Food Technologies.* Washington, D.C. July.

———. 1993d. *Indian Health Service: Basic Services Mostly Available; Substance Abuse Problems Need Attention.* Washington, D.C. April.

———. 1993e. *Lawn Care Pesticides: Reregistration Falls Further Behind and Exposure Effects Are Uncertain.* Washington, D.C. April.

———. 1993f. *Occupational Safety and Health: Differences Between Program in the United States and Canada.* Washington, D.C. December.

———. 1993g. *Pesticides: A Comparative Study of Industrialized Nations' Regulatory Systems.* Washington, D.C. July.

———. 1993h. *Pesticides on Farms: Limited Capability Exists to Monitor Occupational Illnesses and Injuries.* Washington, D.C. December.

Weissenstein, Eric. 1993. "Managed-Care Project Studies May Stall Growth." *Modern Healthcare* (March 15):8.

Wolfe, Sidney M., ed. 1992a. "Senior Citizens Pay Twice as Much on Health Costs Today as They Did Before Medicare Began; New Study Reveals Damaging Effects." *Health Letter* 8(4):10.

———. 1992b. "Work-Related Injuries Reached Record Level Last Year." *Health Letter* (December):1–3, 9.

Wright, John W., ed. 1993. *The Universal Almanac.* New York: Andrews and McMeel.

11

Medicaid and the States

In terms of various medical care and public health programs, the federal government and the states have a variety of relationships. In the case of Medicaid the federal government provides the majority of money and mandates minimal standards for Medicaid, but the states actually run the massive medical care program with a great deal of autonomy. At least one analyst has quipped that Medicaid is not a single federal program but, rather, fifty different state programs. This chapter will focus on the importance of Medicaid to providing medical services for low-income families. In addition to the role of local politics will be explored as they relate to the tremendous variation among states in terms of Medicaid eligibility criteria. Physician boycotts of Medicaid patients, fraud, and obstacles to qualifying for Medicaid are some of the other issues discussed in this chapter.

Medicaid

Medicaid is a federal-state program that provides long-term-care insurance and health insurance or health services through HMOs for more than 28 million people–one of every ten Americans:

> The Medicaid program is in effect three distinct health care programs, each with a different beneficiary group and different proportional uses of funds. The percentage of total spending devoted to each of these efforts varies greatly from state to state, because state officials may exercise considerable discretion about which of these three programs to encourage. The three groups are as follows. (1) Low-income elderly people represent 13 percent of Medicaid beneficiaries, but their use of services accounts for 32 percent of all Medicaid expenditures. This aspect of the program provides primarily long-term care. Most of these senior citizens were not poor when they retired, but their incomes have been eroded by inflation, loss of spousal income, or other factors. As they age, one fifth of the elderly find themselves alone in nursing homes, forced to look to

Medicaid for support that is not provided by Medicare. (2) The severely mentally retarded, the blind, and the physically disabled represent 15 percent of Medicaid beneficiaries and generate 36 percent of all Medicaid expenditures. Medicaid provides medical care and nursing home services for persons with severe, permanent disabilities and higher-than-average needs for medical care. This group includes an increasing number of people with acquired immunodeficiency syndrome (AIDS). (3) Low-income children from single-parent families and their parents comprise 72 percent of beneficiaries; their care represents only 32 percent of all Medicaid expenditures. This group accounted for nearly half of new Medicaid enrollees during 1988–1991. (Blendon et al. 1993, 133–34)

Medicaid is now the primary insurer for patients with AIDS, paying 40 percent of all AIDS-related expenditures. Between 1989 and 1993 all Medicaid expenditures have more than doubled, to $140 billion, totaling 16.5 percent of all health care expenditures in the United States. In 1991 over 28 percent of all Medicaid payments reimbursed inpatient hospital care, and about 27 percent reimbursed long-term care (for example, nursing homes). Drugs accounted for about 7 percent of the Medicaid bill, physicians' services for about 5.3 percent, and a variety of other medical and related services for the balance. The federal government provides cash grants to the states and the District of Columbia based on a formula determined by need, and it has established certain guidelines for the states to follow. Beyond that, each state has a great deal of latitude to determine who will be covered for which services and at what reimbursement rate. This has resulted in a wide range of program variability among the states (Iglehart 1993, 896–97, 900):

> Less than half of all Americans whose annual incomes fell below the federal definition of poverty in 1992 ($7,141 for a single person and $14,343 for a family of four) are eligible to receive Medicaid benefits. . . . Most people achieve eligibility by falling within a federally defined category (i.e., they are aged, blind, disabled, or a member of a single-parent family with dependent children) and meeting stringent requirements regarding income and assets that vary widely according to state. Furthermore, people may be discouraged from applying by the complicated enrollment process, even if they meet the qualifications. . . .
> . . . Among the states, the income threshold for eligibility ranged from a low of $1,788 for a three-person family in Alabama up to $11,076 in Alaska. (Iglehart 1993, 897)

Medicaid spending per beneficiary also varies tremendously state by state. In Mississippi the 1991 average amount spent per beneficiary was barely over $1,600, and in California it was well under $1,900. However, in Connecticut it was nearly $6,000, and in New York it was nearly $5,600. Medicaid coverage is nominally fairly comprehensive. In order to receive federal matching payments, states must provide physician and hospital services, lab and diagnostic imaging services, long-term care and nursing home care, and a range of prenatal and preventive services. States may offer services beyond these and commonly cover, for example, prescription drugs, intermediate institutional care for the mentally retarded, eye care, and other services.

Medicaid eligibility has steadily expanded since its inception, but not without struggle and political ingenuity. In the 1980s both the Bush and Reagan administrations were adamantly opposed to the expansion of Medicaid as well as other social services programs because these Cold War presidents were busy shoveling funds from social services to the military and were deficit-spending for the same purpose. During the 1980s, however, the large number of low-birth-weight babies born in the United States and the high infant mortality rates, particularly among minorities, required action on the part of those in Congress who were concerned with the fate of the nation's babies from low-income families. Representative Henry Waxman buried a proposal deep in the huge annual omnibus budget-reconciliation bills enacted by Congress, which expanded Medicaid to address this problem. Using this strategy, the bill sneaked past the cold warriors and state governors who did not want to be saddled with more underfunded federal mandates. Federal law now requires states "to cover pregnant women for pregnancy-related services and all children under the age of six in families with incomes up to 133 percent of the federal poverty level" (Iglehart 1993, 897). Federal law also expands coverage for pregnancy-related services to those whose incomes are within 185 percent of the poverty level for states that opt for it (fewer than half at this time) and raises Medicaid coverage for children in low-income families up to the age of eighteen.

Federal and state legislators have been unnerved in recent years by the rapid growth of Medicaid, which seems to be almost uncontrollable. Every state receives at least 50 percent matching funds from the federal government, and some receive as much as 83 percent, based upon a formula setting federal grants at a rate inversely related to average state per capita income. During most of the 1980s Medicaid expenditures grew about 10 percent per year, but between 1988 and 1992 total Medicaid expenditures grew at a compound rate of 21.6 percent per year. In 1992 the federal share amounted to $65.9 billion and the state share was a tad under $50 billion. A variety of factors are generally thought to have contributed to the astonishing growth of Medicaid payments. The working poor are increasingly losing health insurance as it becomes priced out of range for their employers, and many of these families fall back on Medicaid. In addition overall annual inflation in the cost of medical services and products has added to Medicaid costs, congressional mandates have added new eligible populations to the Medicaid roles, and court decisions have required states to increase reimbursement rates (Iglehart 1993, 897–99). During the 1980s and early

1990s states tried to limit Medicaid eligibility by severely limiting income eligibility for Aid to Families with Dependent Children (AFDC), required as a prerequisite for Medicaid eligibility.

An extremely detailed study of the recent growth in Medicaid funding by Holahan and colleagues (1993) illuminated an area too often obscured by ideology or ignorance. One myth often heard is that the big increase in costs from 1988 to 1992 was primarily the result of recent legislation extending Medicaid coverage to an additional 3.4 million children and pregnant women and an additional 2.7 million enrollees from low-income families during this period. The research shows that only 14.6 percent of the total growth of Medicaid expenses during this period resulted from these added enrollees. Compare this figure to the contribution of the general inflation of medical prices, which accounted for 26 percent of the growth of Medicaid costs during the 1988–1992 period. The growth of hospital inpatient use accounted for an additional 21.5 percent of the period's increased Medicaid costs. In a reversal of recent trends, government projections revised in early 1994 indicated that between the years 1995 and 2000 the federal government will save about $25 billion in Medicaid expenditures over previous projections, implying that the states will save roughly $20 billion in matching funds. "Officials attribute the savings largely to state efforts to rein in Medicaid costs, and also to a leveling of Medicaid enrollment due to a pickup in the economy" (Stout and Wessel 1994, A1).

The use of medical services by those insured by Medicaid has approximately paralleled the rate of use by the general population since the late 1970s. One major difference, however, is that Medicaid users are far more likely to use an emergency room or a hospital outpatient department than to go to a physician's office. Although the media tends to engage in victim-blaming by discussing ways to reduce the "inappropriate use of emergency rooms" by Medicaid recipients, there is another important side to this story: Emergency rooms and hospital clinics are not convenient to use. Medicaid recipients tend to travel further for their medical care and are more likely to wait longer to be seen than are privately insured patients. Nevertheless, the working poor often cannot take time off from work to seek medical care and are dependent on after-hours facilities, such as emergency rooms.

The Politics of Medicaid Inequities

Inequities in Medicaid funding do not happen by accident or random distribution but, rather, are largely influenced by social power, that is, politics. To some extent the players at the federal and state levels are the same. Business interests–typically a well-organized lobby–generally want to discredit Medicaid and cut benefits in order to reduce their tax burden. A host of ideologies, myths, and "facts" are invoked to support these positions, frequently generated by corporate-sponsored private foundations and "think tanks." Hospitals and providers, also with well-organized lobbies, are interested in maximizing Medicaid income through high reimbursements on the one hand but want to weaken federal and state oversight as much as possible on the other. Medicaid beneficiaries–low-income persons, female-headed single parent families, disproportionately minority, elderly, or disabled–are among those with the least political power to influence Medicaid inequities. Legislators commonly want to pass laws that appear to benefit the poor, elderly and disabled but that objectively meet the needs of the business community and providers.

As part of a most interesting study, researcher Colleen M. Grogan reviewed the literature pertaining to the politics of Medicaid at the state level. Among her major findings was that provider interests have more political clout than beneficiary interests. For example, states with below-average spending per Medicaid beneficiary tend to have comparatively generous reimbursement for providers. A related finding was that states with politically stronger constituents supporting higher reimbursements, such as hospitals, nursing homes, physicians, and senior citizens, do indeed tend to have higher reimbursements (Grogan 1993). A number of studies have come to the conclusion that among Medicaid recipients, the elderly and disabled, covered by Medicaid because they are eligible for the Supplemental Security Income (SSI) program of Social Security, have more political clout than do the single-female heads of households who qualify for Medicaid under the AFDC program, that is, "welfare." Increasingly, white, middle-income elderly constituents use Medicaid to pay for long-term care, and they are a far better organized lobby than are single-female heads of households, who are often members of a minority group and who are often morally stigmatized by critics of welfare and Medicaid. The conclusions of unequal political power are based in large part on the basis of the unequal budgets, established via a political process:

> AFDC recipients represent 66% of Medicaid's case load but constitute only 25% of expenditures. In contrast, the aged and disabled represent only 29% of Medicaid cases but account for about 72% of total Medicaid expenditures. . . . Although total Medicaid spending has increased for all groups, spending for aged and disabled recipients has increased more than twice as fast as spending for AFDC families. (Grogan 1993, 752)

Physicians Who Boycott Medicaid Patients

Low-income neighborhoods are typically underserved by medical facilities, greatly limiting choices. In addition, a very large number of physicians refuse to see Medicaid patients or severely limit the number they will see. In 1989 nearly one-quarter of all pediatricians would not see Medicaid patients, and an additional 30 percent limited the number they would see. In the state of New York in 1990, less than a quarter of the 43,000 practicing physicians would see Medicaid patients. Physicians typically cite low reimbursement rates, higher risk of malpractice suits, and excessive paperwork as the reasons they refuse to see or limit Medicaid patients. States have tried to encourage physicians to take Medicaid patients by substantially raising Medicaid rates, but with generally poor results (Iglehart 1993, 899; Unger 1991, 30). However, since the geographic areas with large Medicaid populations are usually precisely those areas that are seriously underserved by physicians and medical facilities, increasing the reimbursements for all physicians cannot be expected to have much of an impact.

In order to justify the boycott against Medicaid beneficiaries, physicians frequently invoke the stereotype of Medicaid patients who are overly eager to sue for medical malpractice and of juries who are overly sympathetic to the plaintiff and see the physician as having conveniently deep pockets. Although this stereotype makes effective propaganda and feels morally righteous, it is completely false. In the larger picture only two of every hundred victims of medical malpractice resulting in serious adverse medical consequences ever institute legal action, and only one of those two victims of medical malpractice wins the suit (Saks 1993, 9). According to a comprehensive study by the GAO, compensation for fatal or injurious malpractice is even more unlikely for Medicaid and Medicare patients (U.S. General Accounting Office 1993b, 2–3).

Other Obstacles to Medicaid Enrollment and Use

Complex and Lengthy Application Process.   A GAO study of barriers to Medicaid enrollment in Washington, D.C., found a number of problems that exist to a greater or lesser extent across the country (U.S. General Accounting Office 1992). The application for Medicaid eligibility is ten pages long, complicated, and requires a substantial amount of time-consuming and often difficult to locate additional backup material. The application obstacle is almost insurmountable for people who are illiterate or who have not sufficiently mastered the English language.

Long-Term-Care Ironies.   Medicaid funds pay for a large portion of the nation's long-term care–primarily nursing homes but also institutions for the mentally retarded and home- and community-based noninstitutional care. However, in order to take advantage of this benefit the beneficiary has to be in poverty with virtually no assets. This frequently leads to the bizarre situation in which an elderly person's life savings is "spent down" until the person and his or her spouse are in dire poverty before being eligible for Medicaid-paid long-term care. It is easy to quickly dump one's life savings into long-term care since the annual bill for a nursing home can start at $30,000 and run to two or three times that. An entire industry has evolved of book writers, attorneys, and lecturers who help middle-income elderly hide their assets in largely legal ways in order to become eligible for Medicaid-subsidized long-term care. Some of the classic suggestions to handle this dilemma include divorce, with the nonill spouse taking as much of the assets as possible, trusts, private long-term-care insurance, and asset transfers to friends or family. While the trade group American Association of Homes for the Aged wants to slap liens on the homes of long-term-care users benefiting from Medicaid, the American Association of Retired Persons says there is little evidence that the middle class is muscling in on Medicaid resources for long-term care (Cotton 1993).

Recently the situation may have become a bit better for the elderly. Federal regulations have changed to allow a spouse up to $14,000 annually for living expenses, California now allows married couples to split assets in half, and several states have enacted or are considering a plan that allows people to protect their assets while on Medicaid by purchasing long-term-care insurance (Cotton 1993, 2344).

Over a hundred private insurance companies have leaped into the $60 billion long-term-care market, which has become the fastest growing insurance market in the last few years. In 1992 long-term-care insurance premiums topped $1 billion, and that money is coming only from the 5 percent of the elderly (plus 1 percent of the rest of the population) who had purchased long-term-care insurance to date. Project the market out to tens of millions of elderly who might purchase such insurance, and there are, indeed, some extraordinary profits to be made. Nevertheless, for those who do not own an insurance business, there are also some serious drawbacks to private long-term-care health insurance. To begin with, it can be very expensive, particularly if it is to be a useful policy when it is needed. Even the Health Insurance Association of America admits that "only" 40 percent of elderly Americans cannot afford to buy it. Consumer advocacy groups estimate the percentage of the elderly who cannot afford a reasonably good policy is closer to 97 percent. Some agents drastically misrepresent the benefits in the policies they sell, and some agents are simply fraudulent. Some long-term-care policies have provisions that make them very difficult to use, while others have no inflation clause in them so that when benefits are needed twenty years after purchase they may be next to worthless. Some policies have high copayments or high annual premiums–of up to $7,000 per year–and there is the threat with most policies that premiums may be raised substantially sometime in the future (Randall 1993). Private long-term–care insurance does not appear to be a satisfactory answer to this difficult and growing dilemma.

Adverse Consequences of Cost Containment. Medicaid prescription drug benefits have grown rapidly in the last decade and now cost billions of dollars per year. In an attempt to slow down the enormous ongoing increase in Medicaid expenditures, state legislators and policymakers have often applied various cost-containment measures to drug expenditures without having a very good idea of what the consequences of those actions might be. One of the most popular cost-containment strategies involves cost sharing; that is, Medicaid does not pay the full cost of prescribed drugs. Prescription drug cost sharing may involve patient copayments of a few dollars per prescription or a limit on the number of prescriptions Medicaid will pay for per month. A limit of three covered prescriptions per month is not uncommon. The theory bandied about by budget-slashing legislators is that cost-sharing strategies will force Medicaid patients to limit drugs of marginal utility. The blatant fallacy of the argument is that the burden of choice falls on patients, who typically are poorly informed about the medical aspects of drugs that have been prescribed and who are not at all in a good position to evaluate and eliminate "marginal" drugs. Multiple drug users and the poorest Medicaid recipients are at the greatest risk because cost-containment policies hit them the hardest. Soumerai and colleagues conducted a comprehensive review of all the research relating to the medical and social consequences of Medicaid cost-containment policies; they concluded:

> Medicaid enrollees and other low-income populations appear to be sensitive to copayments as low as 50 cents to one dollar per prescription (or about 10 to 15 percent of average prescription costs). Three studies of similar copayments in three different Medicaid programs all observed declines ranging from 5 to 10 percent in overall drug utilization. . . .
> [A]bsolute restrictions on reimbursement (e.g., three-drug limits) have been found to increase costs and nursing-home admissions significantly among elderly persons with chronic illnesses. . . . Because of these observed adverse effects, it is recommended that state and federal drug benefit programs eliminate the use of arbitrary prescription limits as cost-containment strategies. (Soumerai et al. 1993, 244–45)

Medicaid Fraud

In 1991 prescription drug benefits under Medicaid cost $5.5 billion and accounted for 7 percent of all Medicaid spending. This was more than was spent for physician services. The Medicaid drug bill for 1996 is projected to be around $10 billion. The illegal diversion of prescription drugs is big business nationwide. The Drug Enforcement Agency (DEA) estimates that the annual street value of diverted prescription drugs is about $25 billion. The DEA estimated that 36.5 million Medicaid prescriptions were "abused" in 1989, yielding a street value of $8.7 billion. The profit in diverted prescription drugs is often phenomenal. Seconal, for example, costs the pharmacy 33 cents per pill but reaps a street price of $6, for a profit of over 1,700 percent. A pharmacist buys Dexedrine for 13 cents per pill but the street price is $5, a 3,750 percent profit.

Thus far it has been left primarily up to the individual states to control Medicaid drug fraud, but they have generally not done a very good job of it. Some states do not even have specialized units to investigate and prosecute Medicaid fraud. In fact, the HCFA, the federal parent of Medicaid, does not have a special section, not to mention a national plan, for dealing with Medicaid fraud. Fraud units in states that do have them are often understaffed, demoralized, and overwhelmed by a backlog of cases. Fines and punishments are minimal for those who are eventually convicted, and law enforcement agencies tend to get the local small-time guys while the larger fraudulent drug operation grinds away as if nothing had happened. The problem is bigger than the individual states, and in fact it is increasingly international in scope.

Managed Care

State interest in Medicaid managed care plans arose for two main reasons: The first is the history of the virtually uncontrolled growth in costs associated with Medicaid, and the second is the dwindling number of physicians willing to take Medicaid patients. Managed care has been sold as a panacea for what has ailed Medicaid under the traditional fee-for-service system, but the grand managed care experiment has yet to clearly live up to its promises. Between 1987 and 1992 Medicaid managed care enrollment more than doubled, to 3.6 million beneficiaries in thirty-six states. Those in managed care programs included about 12 percent of the entire Medicaid population, up from just 2 percent in 1982. As of 1993 seventeen of the states had established primary care case management (PCCM) programs, which physicians favor because they are allowed to charge on a fee-for-service basis and are not closely monitored. In addition, they are paid a fee to manage all the patient's health care needs. However, for these same reasons such plans are less likely to be cost effective. In 72 percent of the states with Medicaid managed care programs, the plans are mandatory, meaning that Medicaid enrollees are required to participate in a managed care program. A number of other states are likely to implement Medicaid managed care programs in the coming years, mostly of the PCCM type (U.S. General Accounting Office 1993a, 4, 16, 24; "Managed Care Used in Medicare, Medicaid" 1993, 66).

Some Problems with Medicaid Managed Care

One problem with Medicaid managed care involves continuity of care. It is a premise of successful managed care that a long-term relationship must develop between patients and the primary care gatekeeper physician. Medicaid beneficiaries, however, frequently become ineligible for Medicaid and are forced to drop out of the plan. Others drop out because they become dissatisfied with the quality of service, do not have effective access to health care providers, or cannot negotiate the bureaucratic procedures to obtain care in a managed care system.

Commercial HMOs, which contract with state Medicaid programs to deliver managed care, have a long history of deceptive and even fraudulent marketing techniques, which probably account for dropouts in some states. As early as 1974 the GAO found such fraudulent marketing techniques widespread in California, particularly in door-to-door sales. Although most states now ban this type of direct marketing in order to eliminate related fraudulent practices, some major players, such as New York and Michigan, currently allow door-to-door sales. HMO shills can still frequently be found drumming up business in food stamp outlets and other gathering points for low-income people.

The risk of losing money by underestimating what it will cost to treat patients in a capitated plan is not just an abstract accounting issue at corporate headquarters. A study by Joan Buchanan and colleagues of ten Medicaid managed care programs scattered across the nation found that half of them employed cost-containment measures that could directly affect physician income in the event of a cost overrun (Buchanan et al. 1992). Ronda Kotelchuck underscores the concerns with cost-cutting strategies under managed care:

> Managed care creates a financial incentive to decrease costs, largely through reduced use of expensive services. While this incentive can support a good model of care (for example, reduced utilization through good primary and preventive care), it can far more easily promote the opposite. Plans can reduce utilization in far cheaper, quicker, and more certain ways, both by design and by default. They can rely on screening and control of utilization to deny authorization of care; long waits for appointments or discourteous service to discourage patients from seeking care; and inadequate telephone lines or insufficient numbers of operators to make it impossible for Medicaid enrollees–many without telephones in their home–to gain access to the system. (Kotelchuck 1992, 9)

The principal selling point of managed care has always been the promise that it will save money. Ironically, GAO researchers report that research findings on this question are the most ambiguous (U.S. General Accounting Office 1993a, 38). One very important reason that Medicaid managed care programs fail to clearly contain costs is that the establishment of a managed care HMO or other type of contractor itself creates a very expensive new bureaucracy that does not exist under the traditional fee-for-service system (Buchanan et al. 1992, 80).

States are obligated to safeguard the quality of the managed care programs in which they often force Medicaid recipients to participate. For example, federal regulations require states to conduct annual medical audits of each managed care contractor, to monitor plan enrollment and termination practices, and to evaluate proper operation of plan grievance procedures. In addition, the plans themselves are required to maintain a comprehensive quality assurance system. The problem has been that both the states and the contractors have often been far too lax in implementing these required safeguards. An in-depth investigation during the late 1980s of Chicago-area HMOs with Medicaid contracts found that

> the plans' internal quality assurance programs were seriously deficient. We reported that the plans had not adequately documented the services they provided on patients' medical records, did not systematically collect utilization data, and did not follow up from prior reviews to see if corrective actions were taken. As a result, we reported that Medicaid beneficiaries enrolled in Chicago's HMOs were prone to underservice and inadequate care. (U.S. General Accounting Office 1993a, 44).

Medicaid Reform

In response to political pressure from the governors, early in 1993 the Clinton administration made it much easier for states to introduce new and innovative Medicaid programs by ordering the Department of Health and Human Services to streamline state applications for Medicaid waivers (Friedman 1993). The effect of this was to further weaken federal ability to set minimal Medicaid standards and benefits in each of the fifty states and to create the potential for even greater inequities in health care treatment between the states. The groups most likely to be hurt by increasing control at the state level, meaning increasing local political control, are those who are politically the weakest. Racist and ideologically driven reductions in AFDC income eligibility criteria will further hurt 20 million low-income, disproportionately minority adults and children. Three million politically weak elderly persons, mostly single women, currently assisted in long-term care, may be singled out for diminished benefits of various kinds as may be 4 million disabled persons. Further discretion at the state level will probably result in larger holes in the safety net for many who are barely hanging on.

Summary and Discussion

Medicaid is an immense $140 billion federal-state medical and long-term-care insurance plan covering about one of every ten Americans. Moreover, due in large part to general medical inflation and increasing hospitalization, the annual cost of Medicaid is spiraling up at an alarming rate. Despite Medicaid's origin as a federal program and despite the predominance of federal funding for the program, there is tremendous variation among the states in terms of program eligibility, benefits, and access to providers. For example, in many areas a large number of physicians and other providers entirely boycott or severely limit the number of Medicaid patients they see. In addition there are numerous obstacles to Medicaid enrollment, so that many who are eligible for the program are not enrolled. There appears to be a great deal of fraud associated with Medicaid, primarily by health care providers and medical laboratories, which neither the states nor the federal government are adequately prepared to deal with. Finally, while the use of HMOs in state Medicaid programs is proliferating, there are serious questions about both the cost savings and the quality of care they offer.

References

Blendon, Robert J., Karen Donelan, Craig Hill, Ann Scheck, Woody Carter, Dennis Beatrice, and Drew Altman. 1993. "Medicaid Beneficiaries and Health Reform." *Health Affairs* (Spring):132–43.

Buchanan, Joan L., Phoebe A. Lindsey, Arleen Leibowitz, and Allyson Ross Davies. 1992. "HMOs for Medicaid: The Road to Financial Independence Is Often Poorly Paved." *Journal of Health Politics, Policy and Law* 17(1):71–96.

Cotton, Paul. 1993. "Must Older Americans Save Up to Spend Down?" *Journal of the American Medical Society* 269(18):2342–43.

Friedman, Thomas L. 1993. "President Allows States Flexibility on Medicaid Funds." *New York Times* (February 2):A1(N), A13.

Grogan, Colleen M. 1993. "Federalism and Health Care Reform." *American Behavioral Scientist* 36(6):741–59.

Holahan, John, Diane Rowland, Judith Feder, and David Heslam. 1993. "Explaining the Recent Growth in Medicaid Spending." *Health Affairs* (Fall):177–93.

Iglehart, John K. 1993. "The American Health Care System: Medicaid." *The New England Journal of Medicine* 328(12):896-900.

Kotelchuck, Ronda. 1992. "Medicaid Managed Care: A Mixed Review." *Health/PAC Bulletin* 22(3):4–11.

"Managed Care Used in Medicare, Medicaid." 1993. *Employee Benefit Plan Review* (March):66–67.

Randall, Teri. 1993. "Insurance–Private and Public: A Payment Puzzle." *Journal of the American Medical Society* 269(18):2344–45.

Saks, Michael J. 1993. "Malpractice Misconceptions and Other Lessons About the Litigation System." *The Justice System Journal* 16(2):7–19.

Soumerai, Stephen B., Dennis Ross-Degnan, Eric E. Fortess, and Julia Abelson. 1993. "A Critical Analysis of Studies of State Drug Reimbursement Policies: Research in Need of Discipline." *The Milbank Quarterly* 71(2):217–52.

Stout, Hilary, and David Wessel. 1994. "Health Outlays Are Moderating, New Data Show." *Wall Street Journal* (January 14):A1, A12.

Unger, Michael. 1991. "Going Public: Aid Recipients Face Care Restrictions." *New York Newsday* (December 6):17, 30.

U.S. General Accounting Office. 1992. *District of Columbia: Barriers to Medicaid Enrollment Contribute to Hospital Uncompensated Care.* Washington, D.C. December.

———. 1993a. *Medicaid: States Turn to Managed Care to Improve Access and Control Costs.* Washington, D.C. March.

———. 1993b. *Medical Malpractice: Medicare/Medicaid Beneficiaries Account for a Relatively Small Percentage of Malpractice Losses.* Washington, D.C. August.

12

Conclusion

The planning function of public health was an early casualty of the development of capitalist relations in health care. Public health, with few commodities to sell, was sidelined early in the drama and relegated to a largely irrelevant public-sector presence. As a result there are no health care planning bodies at the federal or state levels that in any fundamental sense control or direct the development of the health care industry. Planning bodies exist, but they have few carrots or sticks with which to exert real influence. There are, in addition, regulatory agencies that intercede in narrow areas of the health care industry, but neither the planning bodies nor the regulatory agencies have the mission or the capability to rebuild a health care system to meet a rational model of human need.

Huge corporations are the driving force of health care in the United States. They act in their own best interests by squeezing maximum profits out of illness and injury and by devoting massive resources to influencing government to allow the private sector to continue to maximize profits. However, the overall social consequences of "free enterprise" in health care are the tendency toward monopoly control on the one hand and, on the other, the restriction of access to health care for tens of millions of "unprofitable" Americans who are either shunted onto public-sector programs or simply excluded altogether.

Currently in the United States, institutions involved in health and health care are beset by fundamental and growing social and political-economic contradictions. For example, whereas the wealthy and the well-insured are often overmedicated and overtreated by fee-for-service physicians, those with inadequate private insurance or with no health insurance tend to receive inferior health care. Those with poorly reimbursing public health insurance or with none at all are often boycotted by the same physicians striving to court well-insured patients. Self-referring private physicians profit from their tendency to charge excessively and to order unnecessary procedures, while low-income patients using public facilities are subjected to long waits, understaffed facilities, obsolete equipment, and frequently inadequate care. Hospitals construct facilities in communities where they are least needed in order to win market share in areas glutted with well-insured patients. Meanwhile, public-sector hospitals and clinics in underserved neighborhoods suffer successive years of cutbacks and closures. Few in these communities even dream of building needed health care facilities. Although minority health care providers are more likely to practice in underserved communities, a history of racism and institutional discrimination has resulted in a scarcity of minorities in the higher-paid health professions. At the same time, the lowest-paid health occupations are overrepresented by minority workers.

Profit gouging, excessive and deceptive advertising, and the development and production of useless "me too" drugs characterize the prescription drug industry. At the same time, however, low-income people desperately in need of adequate health care and useful drugs for serious ailments ponder over-the-counter preparations and search local flea markets for false remedies, outdated prescription drugs, and dangerous potions and elixirs of questionable origin. The system of private health insurance prevents tens of millions of poor or "high-risk" Americans from obtaining adequate health insurance while wasting tens of billions of dollars annually that could provide such Americans with all the health care they need. Extremely expensive high-tech medical equipment is rapidly marketed across the United States to physicians and hospitals eager to install new "profit centers." Although top quality medical care is often associated with the availability of such equipment and related procedures, high-tech medicine is often used unnecessarily—contributing to the excessive cost of health care and creating avoidable injury and death.

As the private health care industry focuses ever more intently on the wealthy or well-insured sector of the population, the number of Americans who are inadequately or entirely uninsured continues to escalate dramatically. As federal, state, and local programs are forced to assume responsibility for more and more of those disenfranchised by the private health care sector, well-financed industry coalitions struggle mightily to convince legislators and the public that effective health care reform is "government interference" that should be prevented. As the health care crisis looms more and more menacingly, political and class forces arrayed to protect the status quo grow increasingly stronger–but so do the forces for fundamental social change. The political-economic stage is set for social struggle over the question of whether we will have tinkering health care reform or fundamental health care reform, perhaps revolutionary changes in terms of who owns and controls the institutions of health care. Questions that remain include "How can proposals for health care reform be evaluated?" and "What social forces are struggling for fundamental health care reform against vested corporate, professional, and political interests?"

The American Public Health Association

The American Public Health Association (APHA) is the largest professional public health association in the United States, with about 50,000 members in affiliates nationwide. In 1976 the president of APHA somberly announced in his regular column in the association's monthly newspaper that "as a result of a resolution passed by the Governing Council, APHA is now on record as endorsing a National Health Service (NHS) rather than National Health Insurance (NHI)" (Pickett 1976). The APHA has never withdrawn this endorsement. A national health service has neither public nor private health insurance; instead, it provides health care directly through publicly salaried providers in public facilities. Congressman Ron Dellums's United States Health Service Act (discussed below) is such a plan. In the summer of 1989 the APHA Executive Board distributed a Sense of Congress resolution outlining the organization's thirteen principles for a national health program. The principles advocate:

- Health care coverage for everyone in the U.S.
- Comprehensive benefits ("Including health maintenance, preventive, diagnostic, therapeutic, rehabilitative services for all types of illness and all health conditions" ["APHA Compares Eight Health Reform Bills" 1992, 10]).
- Elimination of financial barriers to care.
- Financing based on ability to pay.
- Publicly accountable administration with a major role for governmental health agencies ("Organization and administration through publicly accountable mechanisms to assure maximum responsiveness to public needs, with a major role for federal, state and local government health agencies" ["APHA Compares Eight Health Reform Bills" 1992, 11]).
- Quality and efficiency assurances ("Incentives and safeguards to assure effective and efficient organization of services and high quality care" ["APHA Compares Eight Health Reform Bills" 1992, 11]).
- Fair payment to providers that encourages appropriate treatment by providers and appropriate utilization by consumers.
- Ongoing evaluation and planning with consumer and provider participation.
- Disease prevention and health promotion programs.
- Education, training, and affirmative action for health workers ("Support of education and training programs for health workers. . . . Affirmative action in training, employment, and promotion of health workers" ["APHA Compares Eight Health Reform Bills" 1992, 11]; note that this statement combines two of the thirteen principles).

- Nondiscrimination in the delivery of health services.
- Education of consumers about their health rights and responsibilities (*A National Health Program* 1988)

It was the Executive Board's hope that Congress would adopt these principles to guide the formation of a national health program, although since their inception Congress has largely ignored the principles. In February 1992 APHA's monthly publication, *Nation's Health,* published a two-page table entitled "Eight National Health Proposals Compared to APHA Principles for National health Care." Representative Dellums's United States Health Service Act received twenty-four "pluses," or points in the APHA rankings, fully 70 percent more points than the next two leading contenders, which were tied at fourteen points each.

Congressman Dellums, of California, has repeatedly introduced this bill into Congress since the mid-1970s. This act would establish a national health service replacing all current federal health insurance and health care programs and replacing nearly all private health insurance, private health care providers, and private health care facilities with a community controlled, federally financed system. All health services would be available to all residents free of charge. Nearly all providers would be civil servants, providing care as a service rather than as a way of generating wealth. The private health insurance industry would have no significant role whatsoever. The national health service would be financed by funds currently paid into federal health programs and by shifting current employer payments for private health insurance to payments for the national health service. Additional sources of income, such as corporate and steeply progressive individual income taxes, would be implemented. Cost containment would be effectively achieved by permanently eliminating hundreds of billions of dollars of medically unnecessary costs in the insurance and medical industries such as profit, commissions, excessive administrative salaries and perks, overutilization of expensive high-tech medical equipment, and fee-for-service practice leading to excessive medical procedures (U.S. Congress 1989).

Few people have heard of Dellums's United States Health Service Act despite the fact that the APHA–the largest public health association in the United States–gave this proposal top billing in terms of the association's principles for national health care. Since the act proposes a "nationalized" health care system similar to England's, it has simply not been taken seriously by most legislators and nearly all national media. Even the APHA has decided to ease out of its long-standing commitment to a national health service, slowly coming to prefer a Canadian-style single-payer system–apparently deemed politically more feasible. The APHA Executive Board discontinued active support of the Dellums proposal by 1992 if not earlier on the grounds that despite the proposal's superior ranking in the APHA's own evaluation, support of health care reform efforts must take into account other factors, such as current "political support and momentum." About the same time the Executive Board passed a number of guidelines for their own lobbyists, including one clearly stating that "preference is for a single-payer system" (quoted in "APHA Compares Eight Health Reform Bills" 1992, 9).

It is quite true that the concept of a national health service currently has little "political support" or "momentum," but why? Dellums's bill establishing a national health service would terminate financial exploitation of health care services by most vested financial and political interests. Entrepreneurial fee-for-service physicians would become salaried employees (as so many of them already have in the Public Health Service and in private HMOs). All the corporations, investors, and physician-entrepreneurs with investments in hospitals, clinics, labs, MRIs, and all other medical facilities would be bought out by the federal national health service. All the facilities would be operated by health care providers on wages, and no private investors would be involved at all. Since health care would be provided free to all residents, the private health insurance industry would play no part. Implementation of the Dellums proposal would knock out hundreds of billions of dollars of profit-making holdings by medical industry corporations. This would literally be a revolution in health care rather than merely health care reform. As a result, this proposal has been politically buried for well over two decades by legislators and the media–which is why most people have not heard of it before.

Looking North for Inspiration:
The Canadian Health Care System

On the other hand, most people probably have heard of the Canadian single-payer health care system, although until the late 1980s and particularly the 1990s the Canadian system was also a well-kept secret from the U.S. public. There have been a number of national and state-level proposals over the years based on this model. For example, the highly ranked Russo bill, introduced as H.R. 1300 Universal Health Care Act, 1991, by Representative Marty Russo (D–Ill.), was one of these ("APHA Compares Eight Health Reform Bills" 1992). These proposed systems would eliminate the private insurance industry and negotiate physician's fees and global budgets with hospitals to contain costs. Physician-entrepreneurs and all the investors in hospitals, HMOs, drug companies, and medical equipment would feel the pinch of serious cost containment directly or indirectly because there would be a single government buyer for most health care services and products. This has created a very formidable corporate political obstacle against the idea of a Canadian single-payer system in the United States. On the other

hand, the well-known superiority of the Canadian system in several important areas compared to our current system has created a groundswell of
media attention and political organization advocating a single-payer system
for the United States. Let us take a closer look at the Canadian health care
system upon which U.S. proposals are based.

But Not Perfect

There are problems with the Canadian system. It is still a system dominated
by hospitals and physicians. Public health continues to be a minor league
player. Hospitals play a particularly strong political role in the medical system, with the result that it is nearly impossible to close down an unneeded
facility. Physicians continue to charge on a fee-for-service basis, which both
encourages and allows them to partially circumvent provincial cost-containment strategies. The cost of health care in Canada continues to rise at a rate
slightly exceeding the rate of growth of the gross domestic product (GDP).
There is sporadically an excessive amount of "queuing" (that is, waiting for
appointments) in some cases. There is a chronic nursing shortage in Canada,
due in part to aggressive recruiting by U.S. hospitals. The sum total of these
problems, however, next to the sum total of problems with the current U.S.
health care edifice, appear rather minor and fleeting.

However . . .

Contrary to unceasing AMA and insurance industry accusations of "socialized medicine" in Canada, the Canadian health care system looks more like
that of the United States than does the health care system of any other industrialized nation. Fully 95 percent of Canadian physicians work for themselves rather than for the government, and most of them earn their income
by charging on a fee-for-service basis. Moreover, 90 percent of all hospitals
are private, nonprofit corporations (U.S. General Accounting Office 1991,
12). The financing of health care in Canada, however, is quite different than
it is in the United States. Each of Canada's ten provinces and two territories
has a single public health insurance plan that is required to meet certain minimal federal standards. These standards include:

universal coverage for all legal residents,
comprehensive coverage of all medically required services,
reasonable access to insured services with no deductibles, copayments,
   or extra billing [i.e. providers may not bill patients],
portability between jobs and residences, and
public administration on a nonprofit basis. (U.S. General Accounting
   Office 1991, 20)

The comprehensive core of hospital and physician health benefits are quite similar across provinces, although some provinces offer additional benefits, such as routine dental care for children and outpatient prescription drugs for the elderly and poor. In Canada every legal resident is covered by comprehensive health insurance. No Canadian residents are ever excluded from coverage on the basis of income or health status. In addition, Canadian health insurance is portable, meaning that it is not limited or tied to a particular job, province, or provider. It is effective in every province and territory in Canada, and to some extent it is even effective when a Canadian travels outside the country. Canadians are free to see any physician they choose.

For the most part, private health insurance companies are not allowed to operate in Canada. Each province plans and operates its own public health insurance plan and reimburses providers directly. The federal government reimburses each province for about 40 percent of its health care expenditures, and both the provinces and the federal government finance the single-payer health insurance system via some combination of general revenues, premiums, and taxes. Altogether the provincial health insurance systems pay for about three-quarters of the nation's health care services. Since the provincial governments are almost the sole source of payment for physicians and hospitals, the provinces are in a very good position to negotiate cost-saving reimbursement rates with physician's organizations and annual (so-called global) budgets with hospitals. This single-payer system also drastically reduces the administrative overhead of physicians and hospitals since they deal with only one insurer, have minimal paperwork, and have no bad debts to collect. As a result Canada spends about 23 percent less per capita on health care than does the United States (U.S. General Accounting Office 1991, 28–29).

The growth of hospital costs in Canada has been effectively curtailed by the use of global budgets. In negotiations with provincial authorities, each hospital receives a fixed sum for the year, adjusted for past real and future projected needs. By controlling capital expenditures and operating funds, provincial health authorities can effectively regulate the growth of hospital expenditures and the acquisition of expensive, high-tech equipment by hospitals. The result of this process has been that real expenditures per capita for hospital care in Canada has grown at about half the rate of such growth in the United States. Despite more admissions and longer stays compared to U.S. hospitals, Canadian hospital per capita expenditures were 18 percent lower than those in the United States in the late 1980s. The savings in Canadian hospital costs have contributed about a third of the difference between Canadian and U.S. per capita health care spending (U.S. General Accounting Office 1991, 43).

As a consequence of the careful scrutiny of hospital expenditures on high-tech equipment and procedures, Canada has fewer "units" per million persons compared to the United States. For example, in the late 1980s the

United States had 150 percent more open-heart surgery units, 600 percent more MRI units, and about 560 percent more radiation therapy units per million persons than Canada. More, however, is not necessarily better: "It is not clear from these data, however, whether the United States has an over-abundance of equipment, Canada a scarcity, or both" (U.S. General Accounting Office 1991, 49). The Canadians like to point out that their high-tech services and equipment tend to be used more efficiently than comparable U.S. units, which often sit idle waiting for patients. Moreover, the average open-heart surgery unit in Canada is bigger than the comparable average U.S. unit and may be safer for patients, since more frequently used open-heart surgery units tend to have better survival rates.

Access in the Province of Ontario

In terms of access to health care, Ontario is reasonably representative of the situation throughout the provinces. Primary care is available to all Ontario residents without queues and without lengthy waiting periods for appointments. Nearly all expectant mothers, for example, receive adequate prenatal care in Ontario, whereas in the United States about a quarter of expectant mothers received no prenatal care in the first trimester, and 6 percent receive it only in the third trimester or receive none whatsoever. The situation is different, however, for expensive surgical procedures and for the use of high-tech equipment:

> Waiting lines, or "queues," have developed primarily for selected expensive surgical procedures and diagnostic equipment that emerged in the 1970s and 1980s, such as MRIs, cardiac bypass surgery, lithotripsy, lens implants, and hip replacements. For these services, physicians must ration care on the basis of medical need rather than providing it to all who may benefit. Ontario health care providers contend that queuing is the result of the provincial government's attempts to control health expenditures. The Ministry believes that queues are a natural result of the "rationalization" of health care–"getting the right patient to the right service at the right time." (U.S. General Accounting Office 1991, 52)

According to GAO researchers, there is surprisingly little systematic information about queuing in Ontario or the other provinces. As a result, late in 1990 GAO researchers interviewed the directors of eight specialty care programs at Ontario's twenty-six teaching hospitals, where such services are concentrated. The programs included "CT scanners, MRIs, lithotripsy; cardiovascular, ophthalmologic, and orthopedic surgery; specialized physical rehabilitation, and autologous bone marrow transplants" (U.S. General Accounting Office 1991, 53).

Physicians in Canada generally categorize the medical needs of patients for services with queues as "emergent," "urgent," and "elective," in order of how critical the need for the procedure is. All together there were forty-eight programs of the kinds listed above that categorized patients in this manner (not including physical rehabilitation and autologous bone marrow transplants). Only a single lithotripsy program had a waiting period for emergent patients, ranging from one to 90 days. About the time GAO researchers were doing their study, the Ontario Ministry of Health approved the establishment of a second lithotripsy unit in response to excessive queues. Fewer than half the programs reported queues for "urgent" cases, but all programs reported queues for "elective" cases, ranging from six months to more than two years (U.S. General Accounting Office 1991, 55).

The AMA and the U.S. health insurance industry love to point to the alleged hordes of Canadians streaming to the United States for high-tech health care unavailable under Canadian "socialized medicine." While this makes for great political theater, it is an allegation not borne out by the facts. Despite the aggressive marketing in Canada of U.S. health care facilities along the border, few Canadians seek care in the United States. A survey of nine major U.S. border hospitals by none other than the AMA concluded that less than 1 percent of all admissions to eight of those hospitals were Canadians. The ninth hospital, Buffalo General Hospital, experienced about 3 percent Canadian admissions (U.S. General Accounting Office 1991, 58–61).

Saving Money and Insuring Everyone Canadian-Style

GAO researchers took the major features of the Canadian single-payer system and estimated what the impact of such features would have been on U.S. health care costs for 1991. Here's what they found:

> We expect that both the savings and the added costs would be concentrated in the insurance, physician, and hospital sectors. Savings achieved from reductions in administrative expenses could more than offset the added costs of increased utilization. . . . [I]ntroducing universal coverage and eliminating cost-sharing payments could increase expenditures by about $64 billion. However, nearly $67 billion in estimated savings in administrative expenses could offset the added costs. The net impact, after transition and for the first full year of full implementation, would be to reduce national health spending by about $3 billion, or roughly 0.4 percent of the 1991 health expenditures projected for the United States. (U.S. General Accounting Office 1991, 63)

In other words, GAO researchers found that if the United States replaced the wasteful, inefficient private-sector health insurance industry with a single public health insurance scheme, so much money would be saved in currently wasted administrative costs that the tens of millions of uninsured people could be fully insured, that all deductibles and copayments for everyone could be eliminated, and that the new, vastly expanded, eminently humane health care system would cost less than the current one!

Summary and Discussion

For over twenty years the APHA has been on record as supporting a national health service over national health insurance. A national health service would remove all profit motive from providers and hospitals, and under the Dellums proposal would be democratically run by elected boards, rather as school districts are managed by elected boards. In the 1990s, apparently for reasons of political expediency, the APHA Executive Board dropped their advocacy of a national health service in favor of advocacy of a single-payer system, despite the results of their own evaluation, which appeared to rate a national health service proposal superior to a single-payer proposal. The Canadian system, while avoiding many of the problems of the U.S. private-insurance-dominated system, nevertheless still suffers from serious drawbacks, primarily resulting from the fact that the delivery of health care remains in the hands of private fee-for-service providers. Despite Canadian government attempts at cost containment, the fee-for-service basis of health care delivery promotes profit maximization by providers, resulting in a tendency to undermine cost containment.

Finally, today in the United States the health insurance industry is rapidly transforming itself into a health care services financing empire—accumulating multibillion dollar hospital chains and HMOs, then forging them into regional and national health care monopolies. In today's environment a single-payer system would simply shovel our medical dollars into the same corporate hands that are currently wasting those dollars. When a single-payer system was created in Canada, no such corporate monster waited to suck up the public financing. In the United States, the time for a single-payer system has come and gone.

The fundamental split in the political struggle over health care reform in the United States appears to be between those who advocate a public single-payer system similar to Canada's and the advocates of most other proposals, which preserve domination of the private health insurance industry. During the late 1980s and early 1990s hundreds of grassroots organizations, some important professional physicians' associations, several major unions, and important leaders of major corporations have coalesced to leverage political influence on behalf of a single-payer system. To the extent that by 1994 nearly one hundred congressional representatives cosponsored a single-payer bill, the movement has been successful. At the same time vested corporate and provider interests have fought back with all the ideological influence and political favors that tens if not hundreds of millions of dollars a year can buy. As of mid-1996, the result has been political stalemate.

The emerging political struggle for health care reform has been fought at both the federal level and in state legislatures across the country. Thus far, I believe, we have seen skirmishes. The fatally compromised health care reform bills likely to pass in the next few years will probably cause as many new problems as they were promoted to cure. The struggle for a high-quality, democratically controlled, affordable health care system equally accessible to all will probably be prolonged–perhaps in the U.S. tradition of great national social movements such as the struggles for abolition, the right of women to vote, the eight-hour working day, and civil rights. The massive political-economic forces lined up to preserve the status quo cannot be underestimated. On the other hand, the popular forces of a truly mass movement appear to be organizing across the United States. The stage is set for years, perhaps decades, of social struggle to define who the winners and losers will be in the new institutions of public health and medical care.

References

"APHA Compares Eight Health Reform Bills to Association's Policies." 1992. *The Nation's Health* (February):9–11.

A National Health Program For All of Us. 1988. American Public Health Association pamphlet.

Pickett, George. 1976. "President's Column." *The Nation's Health* (December):2.

U.S. Congress. 1989. House. H.R. 2500. *U.S. Health Service Act.* Introduced by Representative Ron Dellums (D–Calif.). 101st Cong., 1st sess.

U.S. General Accounting Office. 1991. *Canadian Health Insurance: Lessons for the United States.* Washington, D.C. June.

Glossary

AIDS. Acquired immune deficiency syndrome. This disease is caused by the human immunodeficiency virus (HIV).

Allied health professions. A range of health professions other than physician and nurse, including, for example, medical assistants, laboratory technologists, occupational therapists, and so on.

Allopathic medicine. A term commonly used for the most common form of the practice of Western medicine to distinguish it from homeopathic medicine.

Blue Cross/Blue Shield. A network of private health insurance companies that were originally founded in the 1930s by hospital administrators and physicians, respectively.

The Blues. See Blue Cross/Blue Shield.

Capitalism. A political-economic system based on the private ownership of productive resources by the capitalist class (those who own capital) and their exploitation of the working class (those who have only their labor to sell to capitalists for wages) in order to maximize profits.

Capitation. A set amount of reimbursement based on the number of patients a physician sees. The amount is not related to the quantity or type of medical procedures. Under a pure capitation form of payment, additional income for the physician is dependent solely on his or her seeing more patients. The purpose is to influence physician behavior to keep expensive medical procedures down and, in the private sector, corporate profits up.

Chiropractic. A type of medicine founded on the belief that the body had to be mechanically in the proper relationship in order to have structural and functional balance. Osteopathy was founded about the same time in the late 1800s on similar principles.

Computerized axial tomography (CAT). A diagnostic method that uses a type of X-ray equipment to take images of an organ or tissue at a specific depth and that then enhances the images by computer.

Copayment. The portion of a medical bill that an insured patient is responsible for according to his or her health insurance policy. For example, many policies pay 80 percent of a medical bill and require the insured person to pay the remaining copayment of 20 percent.

Deductible. A certain amount of money a person with health insurance has to pay for medical care before the insurance benefits kick in. Under some policies, for example, an insured family has to spend $250 for medical care before their policy will pay for a portion of their medical bills.

Diagnostic related group (DRG). DRGs involve the setting of fixed Medicare reimbursement sums for specific diagnoses and procedures regardless of what the actual cost is for the hospital. The reimbursement system was devised as a way of curbing hospital costs.

Domestic health care. Until approximately the last decade of the 1800s women in the household ministered to most of the births and health and medical needs of their families. In this system of domestic health care, they were typically not paid for their services. They performed these services not for profit but strictly for their "use value," that is, principally because all concerned believed that the health care provided was beneficial.

Drug misadventuring. The unexpected consequences of taking a prescription drug. Such consequences can result in a range of effects from mild discomfort to fatality.

Dumping. An illegal practice occurring when a physician refuses to see or treat a patient in an emergency room because the patient has no insurance, has AIDS, is perceived to be likely to file a malpractice claim, or for some other reason. Typically the patient is then referred to the local public hospital, which takes all comers.

Eclectics. Practitioners of medicine in the latter half of the nineteenth century who were similar to the "regular" physicians but who shunned the bleeding and harsh drugging characteristic of the regulars.

Experience rating. A procedure used by commercial insurers in order to determine the conditions of group coverage. The prior claims experience of the company as a whole (that is, the cost of benefits paid out by the insurer) is used as the basis to set premiums for the next period, usually a year.

Fee-for-service. A method of physician reimbursement for services whereby the patient is charged for each medical procedure.

Fee splitting. An arrangement in which a physician pays money for a referral from another physician. Typically illegal or unethical.

Generic drugs. Typically prescription drugs that have lost their patent protection so that they may be sold by any manufacturer as long as the original brand name is not used.

Gross domestic product (GDP). Total value of a country's output of goods and services produced in one year.

Health maintenance organization (HMO). A prepaid health care program typically featuring comprehensive health care provided by a specific group practice network.

Homeopathic medicine. A theory and practice of medical care based on the belief that diseases can be cured by the application of very small doses of drugs that in large doses produce symptoms of the disease.

Horizontal growth. An economics term relating to a corporate growth strategy in which a company acquires or builds more units of the kind it already has.

Ideology. Shared beliefs about the world. Ideologies may be specifically constructed and disseminated by organizations or individuals who want to influence people to believe in a certain way.

Joint ventures. In the health care industry this term refers to medical or related facilities such as free-standing radiation labs fully or partially owned by physician-investors or hospital-investors.

Magnetic resonance imaging (MRI). A high-tech imaging technique using a strong magnetic field in order to see images of the heart, large blood vessels, brain, and other soft tissues.

Managed care. A system to limit which providers a patient sees and what kinds of medical procedures he or she may receive. Typically such a system is implemented by a health insurer or a health maintenance organization (HMO) to limit costs.

Managed competition. An untried theory of health care reform involving the organization of health care services by huge, "competing" regional networks of private health care providers.

Medicaid. A federal-state program that provides long-term-care insurance and health insurance or health services through HMOs for over 28 million people.

Medi-Cal. California's Medicare program.

Medical underwriting. The procedure used by health insurers to determine under what conditions individual coverage (in contrast to group coverage) might be approved or denied.

Monopoly capital. Found in a mature form of capitalism in which key sectors of the economy are controlled by one or a few huge corporations, effectively crushing competition and destroying market processes that in a competitive economy would tend to keep prices down.

Osteopathy. A type of medicine founded on the belief that the body had to be mechanically in the proper relationship in order to have structural and functional balance. Chiropractic was founded about the same time in the late 1800s on similar principles.

Over-the-counter drugs. Medications that may legally be sold without a prescription.

Patent medicine. Commercially manufactured and sold medicines that are available "over-the-counter," that is, without a prescription.

Political Action Committee (PAC). An entity that pools money–presumably from many contributors–to funnel it toward legislators in order to influence their actions.

Positron Emission Tomography (PET). A high-tech diagnostic imaging device that tracks the internal distribution of radionuclides to produce transverse sectional images of the body.

Preferred Provider Organization (PPO). An organization that contracts with a number of physicians to provide health care at a discounted price. PPO patients receive better insurance coverage if they use physicians and facilities on the PPO list, but they may use any provider or facility if they are willing to pay more out-of-pocket.

Premiums. The payment made for commercial health insurance.

Proprietary hospitals. Privately owned hospitals.

Public health. The science of preventing disease and promoting health through organized community efforts.

Race. A scientifically debunked concept referring to groups of people socially defined on the basis of a common genetic heritage. Furthermore, there is often the erroneous presumption that intelligence or other behavioral attributes correspond with certain physical attributes such as skin color.

Racism. Domination and discrimination by one group over another based on presumed "racial" characteristics such as skin color, national origin, and so on.

Regular physicians. See Allopathic medicine.

Resource-Based Relative Value Scale (RBRVS). A system in which the medical management and evaluation activities that primary care physicians tend to do are reimbursed at a higher rate and the medical procedures that specialists tend to do are reimbursed at a lower rate than prior reimbursement system used by Medicare.

Self-referral. A situation in which a physician who owns an interest in a laboratory, a rehabilitation facility, an X-ray unit, or some other medical service or facility refers his or her patients to these facilities, often without informing the patient of the financial conflict of interest.

Single-Payer. In the context of health care reform, a medical care reimbursement system in which there is one purchaser for all health care (that is, a "single payer" of all medical bills). An example of a single-payer system is Canada's, in which each provincial government directly provides health insurance as a single payer.

State guarantee funds. Programs established in most states to pay insurance claims left by insolvent insurers. Typically the money is provided by an assessment on surviving insurers in the state.

Tailgate medicine. The name informally given to the illegal sale of prescription, banned, or unapproved drugs.

Third-party payer. A payer of health care who is neither the patient (the first party) nor the health care provider (the second party). The third-party payer is usually a health insurer.

Underwriting. The process of selecting which groups will be most profitable to insure and which groups will not. See Medical underwriting.

Utilization review. An evaluation procedure instituted by insurance companies to limit claims or the cost of claims. Presumably the cost, quality, efficiency, or effectiveness of a physician, procedure, or hospital is evaluated–with the result that a patient is denied or allowed benefits or advised to pursue another course of action.

Vertical integration. Corporate expansion in which a company acquires its suppliers or customers.

Women, Infants, and Children (WIC). A federally funded program for low-income women and children that encourages prenatal health education and provides vouchers to buy food.

About the Book and Author

During the twentieth century, the issue of health care burst out of the private confines of the physician's office to become a monumental contentious social issue. Giant multinational corporations scooped up proprietary hospitals and nursing homes and assembled them into vast chains crisscrossing America. The incomes of entrepreneurial fee-for-service physicians grew several times faster than the rate of inflation year after year; at the same time, the cost of health care swelled to consume 14 percent of the gross domestic product, and it continues to climb. The government gingerly applied cost-containment strategies while hospitals expanded capacity and filled multiple "profit centers" with expensive high-tech equipment. Health care administration emerged as the fastest growing segment of all health-related occupations.

Meanwhile, infant mortality in the United States is increasingly excessive compared to that of other industrialized countries, and the gulf of health status disparities between white and minority Americans yawns ever wider. Tens of thousands of Americans each year die from complications due to unnecessary but profitable surgeries, while millions suffer from medical neglect because they cannot pay for health care. The cost of malpractice insurance skyrockets while the fraternity of physicians pretend to discipline one another.

Health care is a nationwide problem, and the social devastation in its wake is a tragedy of national scope. Existing assumptions, power structures, political and economic interests, and social organizations have contributed to the crisis. In *Private Medicine and Public Health*, Lawrence Weiss dispassionately questions and analyzes the many issues of the health care crisis in search of much-needed solutions.

Lawrence D. Weiss is an associate professor in the Department of Sociology at the University of Alaska at Anchorage.

Index